In 2006, Craig McDonald published *Art in the Blood,* a collection of probing, long-form interviews with twenty major crime writers that was immediately hailed as a definitive text in the study of modern crime and mystery fiction.

Now McDonald—"a genuine expert on the history of crime fiction" (Eddie Muller, *San Francisco Chronicle)*—returns with *Rogue Males,* a collection of no-holds-barred interviews with 16 authors who have shaped and defined narrative fiction and songwriting.

Rogue Males includes conversations with crime fiction legends Elmore Leonard and James Crumley (in one of his last interviews); premier stylists James Sallis and Daniel Woodrell; noir kingpins James Ellroy and Ken Bruen, and top thriller writers Lee Child and Randy Wayne White.

Stephen J. Cannell and Max Allan Collins hold forth on the intersection of crime novels and the silver screen while Andrew Vachss, Pete Dexter, Craig Holden, Alistair MacLeod, Tom Russell and Kinky Friedman round-out this one-of-a kind collection on the craft of writing—an array of "mavericks, trailblazers and the gadflies. Men of conscience, entrepreneurs and magnificent bastards," as McDonald puts it in his introduction.

Also by Craig McDonald

Art in the Blood

Head Games

Toros & Torsos

Rogue Males

Rogue Males

Conversations & Confrontations About the Writing Life

By Craig McDonald

BLEAK
HOUSE
BOOKS

Published by
BLEAK HOUSE BOOKS
a division of Big Earth Publishing
923 Williamson St.
Madison, WI 53703
www.bleakhousebooks.com

Printed in the United States of America
12 11 10 09   1 2 3 4 5 6 7 8 9 10

978-1-60648-036-6 (hardcover)
978-1-932557-45-9 (paperback)

Dedicated to the memory of

JAMES CRUMLEY:

You showed the way and set the bar high.

"Writers may be disreputable,

incorrigible, early to decay or late to bloom,

but they dare to go it alone."

—JOHN UPDIKE

CONTENTS

Introduction 1

PART I **The Legends** 5
   JAMES CRUMLEY: The Right Madness. 7
   ELMORE LEONARD: Ten Rules 21

PART II **Kith & Kin** 33
   DANIEL WOODRELL: Crime in the Ozarks. 35
   ALISTAIR MACLEOD: The Tuning of Perfection. 53

PART III **Dark History** 67
   ANDREW VACHSS: Two Trains Running. 69
   JAMES ELLROY: To Live and Die in L.A. 89

PART IV **Page To Screen and Back** 109
   MAX ALLAN COLLINS: On the Road. 111
   STEPHEN J. CANNELL: Hollywood Tough. 125

PART V **Duty & Honor** 145
   CRAIG HOLDEN: Love & Death 147
   PETE DEXTER: The Poetry of Violence 157

PART VI **Thriller** 167
   RANDY WAYNE WHITE: Perfect Law 169
   LEE CHILD: One Shot. 179

PART VII **Troubadours** 199
   TOM RUSSELL: Tough Company. 201
   KINKY FRIEDMAN: Independence Day. 217

PART VIII **The Desert Dialogues** 229
   JAMES SALLIS. 237
   KEN BRUEN. 267

Appendix 293

INTRODUCTION

Joseph Campbell asserted it is the obligation of every journalist to be educated in public.

For the past several years, it's been my privilege to have my lessons regarding the craft of writing fiction conducted on the record. I have engaged in dozens of thirty- to forty-five-minute recitations with the best and most compelling fiction writers working today.

We've discussed writing, the strategies of self-promotion, the rigors of book tours and the double-edged sword of reviewing and interviewing.

I've prodded authors for admissions about what their craft has cost them, and about the sometimes potentially lethal loneliness resulting from the solitary pursuit of writing. In a couple of cases, I've been afforded glimpses of the potential pitfalls associated with what has come to be called (often with scorn) "the writing life."

Hemingway, the über Rogue Male, American writer—the *template*—wrote, "Writing, at its best, is a lonely life."

Too many of our finest writers have fallen prey to addiction and alcoholism. A number have ended up in therapy, or, like Hemingway, they've killed themselves.

Even the writers who don't crack-up or flame out question the ineffable compulsion to spend so much time in the act of solitary creation.

As Kinky Friedman observes elsewhere in this volume, a shelf of one's own books can sometimes seem a harrowing "index of an empty life. That's all it can mean."

Other authors beg to differ: they freely admit that the central allure of writing fiction is leaving behind a shelf of books that might outlive them.

Ken Bruen endeavors to keep his ego in check with a quote of Somerset Maugham's that he has posted above his writing space. "I regard it as the curse of Somerset Maugham," Bruen says. "He didn't intend it as such, but to me it is: 'The compulsion to write and no talent.' That keeps me humble."

· · · · ·

My college years were spent studying journalism and English for what proved to be a dubious dual major. The two tracks made sense to me, but the professors in my school's journalism and English departments were wary of my interest in the other's curriculum.

It was the early-1980s, and Derrida and deconstruction were just finding their sorry way to Midwest campuses. I chose sides early and impulsively: I fell in love with Hemingway for a number of valid reasons, but also because the Ohio Derrida partisans just couldn't get their de(con)structive arms around Papa. They instead endeavored to marginalize him. They fawned over Faulkner, whose novels I still find unreadable.

Tony Hillerman once observed that contemporary "literature" is about not much happening to people that nobody can care about. My English professors seemed hell bent on impelling their students to write precisely the kinds of books I can't stand to read.

So I found crime fiction. Max Allan Collins was my gateway drug. James Ellroy made me an addict.

The best of 1980s U.S. crime fiction was continuing the narrative traditions and unflinching, unsentimental treatment of the American experience in the manner that the stories and novels of Hemingway, Steinbeck, O'Connor and Algren had in previous decades.

After reading all there was of Ellroy, I found James Sallis and then Daniel Woodrell. Just as I ran out of all there was of Woodrell, I discovered the short stories of Alistair MacLeod … the novels of Ken Bruen and the songs of Tom Russell.

But I was no longer content just to read their fiction, or to listen to their songs.

Hemingway again: "As you get older, it is harder to have heroes, but it is sort of necessary."

This collection of interviews includes discussions with several of my personal hero authors, "The Three Jims"—Crumley, Ellroy and Sallis. Rounding out my personal pantheon in this volume are Daniel Woodrell and Ken Bruen.

"It is a dangerous thing to know a writer," Papa cautioned.

But I've chased down and tried my best to corner the writers whom I most revere. I've pressed my heroes for *answers*.

The writers I've spoken with over the past five or six years have by turns been funny, warm, truculent, insightful and sometimes brusque. Some have been extremely thoughtful, and some have been flip or prickly.

The interviews have been cordial and charged.

They've rarely been less than provocative.

In the following interviews, you will encounter mavericks, trailblazers and the gadflies. Men of conscience, entrepreneurs and magnificent bastards.

They are variously crusaders and reformers ... exhibitionists and isolates. These are writers who have lost parents and wives and children, sometimes through tragedy, sometimes for pursuing their art, and sometimes as a result of their own head-shaking bad behavior. When it comes to their excesses, most of these men are their own harshest and best/worst critics.

Through it all, to a man, they have remained stubbornly creative, working alone, writing novels and stories through all manners of turmoil and adversity.

These writers embody Papa's admonition and they "use the pain" to inform their best compositions—the works that are likely to be the ones that will endure and influence the next crop of rogue males who are, for better or worse, just testing the fences.

Echoing James Ellroy, "Here's to them."

—CRAIG MCDONALD
September 2006

PART I

The Legends

JAMES CRUMLEY

The Right Madness

(May 3, 2005)

"You might come here Sunday on a whim.
Say your life broke down. The last good kiss
you had was years ago."
—RICHARD HUGO,
"Degrees of Gray in Philipsburg"

James Crumley's opening lines of 1978's *The Last Good Kiss* are now arguably the most famous and fondly held in hardboiled crime fiction:

"When I finally caught up with Abraham Trahearne, he was drinking beer with an alcoholic bulldog named Fireball Roberts in a ramshackle joint just outside of Sonora, California, drinking the heart right out of a fine spring afternoon."

The worthy crime fiction cognoscenti have committed that paragraph to memory.

In Crumley's watershed book, private investigator/professional pourer C.W. Sughrue is recruited to find "missing" writer and drunk Abraham Trahearne. Abe is a synthesis of Ernest Hemingway and poet/Crumley friend Richard Hugo. Sughrue's investigation becomes an accidental road trip and pursuit race through the bars and taverns of the American West.

As Dennis Lehane confided to me in April 2003, speaking for himself and fellow crime authors George Pelecanos and Michael Connelly, "I think it's funny we all hold the same book in a certain high regard, which is James Crumley's *Last Good Kiss*.

I think that's the thing we're swinging for—'there's the benchmark, let's go after that.' That's a book that stands head and shoulders above any concept of genre fiction."

Indeed, Crumley started out down a different apparent writing path: he came out of the hyper-literary Iowa Writers' Workshop. His first book was the Vietnam novel *One to Count Cadence*.

The Texas-born author struggled for a follow-up to that book but couldn't find anything that felt right. About that same time, Richard Hugo introduced Crumley to the crime novels of Raymond Chandler shortly after Crumley moved to Missoula, Montana, where he made his home.

Crumley's second novel was the Chandler-inspired *The Wrong Case*, a crime novel that introduced readers to the character of Milo Milodragovitch.

He followed that book with *The Last Good Kiss*. With those two novels, Crumley, butressed by fellow writers George V. Higgins and Elmore Leonard, changed the terrain of contemporary crime fiction. Plot was subordinated to character and language came front and center. For the first time, a poet's sensibility and style were brought to bear on the mystery novel.

In 1996, Crumley wrote *Bordersnakes*, a novel set along the West Texas and Mexico border. That novel unites C.W. Sughrue and Milo Milodragovitch, who switch off narrative duties.

C.W. Sughrue returned in 2005 in *The Right Madness*, investigating a series of deaths tied to the practice of a psychiatrist friend. The novel takes its title from another Richard Hugo poem.

The Right Madness is also striking for its unusual dedication note to "the people who stepped up to the mark when things went badly for me," who "organized a benefit for me that kept us up and running during the time I couldn't even write my name."

James Crumley died on September 17, 2008 at the age of sixty-eight.

• • • • •

The Right Madness opens with a pretty attention-getting author's note. What happened to you?

They never found out. I just suddenly filled up with fluid—my lungs and the heart-sack, or muscle, or whatever it is. My wife was out of town and I was actually sort of staying home behaving myself very well. When she got back I went out to the airport to get her and realized that something was wrong. I was in the ICU for eleven days and I was on a ventilator, which was not pleasant. The nurse in charge at the ER said she had to put me on a ventilator. By that time, my carbon dioxide level was so high that I was fairly incoherent, but I said, "What if I don't want to be on a ventilator?" She looked at her watch and said, "Well, two or three hours, you'll get into a coma … two or three days, you'll be dead." [*Laughing*] She was straight and matter-of-fact. So I said, "Okay. Let's get one. Let's do it."

How are you doing now?

I seem to be doing fine. I got out in October, when I was sixty-three. I'm sixty-five now, so it's been almost two years. No recurrence. This is actually the third time that something strange like this has happened to me. And they never found out what happened then, either. You know how doctors are: patients don't know anything. I told the doctor on the case about the others, but it took him a while. They took the last of the fluid out of my left lung and it came back absolutely clear. No TB … no cancer, no viruses, no bacteria. He said, "Well, I guess you knew what you were talking about."

It was quite an exciting time. I think the hardest part was recovering from the paralytics that they give you to keep you still there on the litter. I had an enormous number of hallucinations while I was away, but they all seemed to be connected to what was going on around me. My internist is an old friend of mine. He said, "I thought your ancient, 'lizard-tail brain,'" as he says, "was still flickering away." It took a while to adjust and I was right in the middle of the book when it happened.

It's been four years since *The Final Country*. Tell me a little about the catalyst for *The Right Madness*. Something you've been thinking about for a while?

Yeah, thirty-some-odd years. I didn't know what to do after the opening. I mean, it was so long ago that I was still playing flag-football … that was what the game was at one time.

So this was something you started and went back to?

I often do that. With *The Last Good Kiss*, that's the eighteenth draft of the first chapter. I never knew exactly what happened next until I got it right and then I *knew*. That tends to be the way I work. I run around in circles until I know what happens next.

I read a piece John Harvey did about you a while back that indicated there are a number of books started, stopped … sometimes picked back up again. So that is your process?

Yeah. And some of the stuff never gets picked up again.

Are there whole books of yours we haven't seen yet?

There's an eight-hundred-page manuscript that went into a fireplace at one time.

You actually burned it?

I thought that maybe it would put the burden away.

Did it?

[*Laughing*] No. No. I've been working on it off and on since, jeez, since I finished my first novel … '69? 1968? Somewhere in there. It's a Texas novel. It's very difficult for me to write about Texas. I have had numerous attempts. That was the second time I'd burned all the pages … not *all* the pages … not eight hundred pages in a line, but it was a lot of work. The unfortunate thing is I remember every *goddamn* word. I *hate* that.

I've heard of that book. I've read allusions made to it over the years. It's not in any danger of turning up anytime soon, then?

I don't think so. God, I hope not [*laughing*].

Do you get back to Texas often?

Not too often. My mother is still alive down there. I've got old friends in Austin I sometimes go see. But I go long periods of time without going back.

How about El Paso? Get back there much?

Not as often as I'd like. I sort of like that part of Texas more than the part where I grew up, which was outside of Corpus Christi.

There's a songwriter who lives in El Paso who I like a lot, guy named Tom Russell, and he has written about how the sprawl is starting to affect even El Paso.

That's funny—he just sent me a CD the other day. I just remembered that. I get things in the mail and they get on my desk and my desk looks like my garage and my garage looks like the dump. I'd completely forgot about it.

Tell me a little bit about your writing process. How many times do you go over a draft, typically?

It doesn't seem to take me as long as it used to. I used to say I get one page out of ten. I think now I get one page out of three or four. Something like that. You know, I've been doing it for forty years, so I should learn something. But every time you start another book, it's like, "I don't know how I did the last one." That sort of thing. I've always had trouble with openings.

The opening of *The Last Good Kiss* has become an icon within the crime world. You have people who have actually committed those opening lines to memory. They are revered by so many writers: Dennis Lehane and George Pelecanos cite that book as the novel that really kick-started them. Do you have a sense of what that book means to other writers within the genre?

I have some idea. But I don't take myself too seriously. It's really nice when writers like Connelly and George Pelecanos—who is a friend of mine—meet you and like what you've done. Writers who like writers are good. But sort of the strangest person that ever mentioned it was a woman who was a librarian on NPR. It was a piece about best first lines. I'm not up in the mornings much, so I didn't hear it myself, but somebody sent it to me on the e-mail. It was very nice. Pete Dexter, in Seattle, recently said something at a reading about that line. So that part's good. It's just a lot of pressure: they want you to do the same thing over and over again. It would be like keeping my characters the same age over and over again. Those guys have gotten old and it shows on them.

Yes, their bodies are starting to betray them and they can't bounce back from those beatings like they once did. Is there an upward limit on how far you would go in portraying them? Is there an age you draw the line at in terms of trying to depict them?

No, not really. I've never written anything set since 9/11. I'm trying to do that now, but it's really hard to do something without acknowledging the effect that 9/11 had. Some things are just simply too traumatic to write about. So, we'll see. I haven't killed 'em off yet. At one time—maybe *Final Country* or somewhere—I was trying to move to a third-person voice and kill Milo, but my wife talked me out of it.

That's what they're there for—to save us from ourselves.

Right. She was right. Plus, I've never written a third-person novel and I've never written a first-person short story, as far as I know. If I knew how this stuff worked, I wouldn't be doing it, I guess.

Do you have a preference between your two guys—Milo and C.W.?

Not really. They're older than some of my children—I've got two sons in their twenties—but they've been in my head for years. One of the reasons I wrote *Bordersnakes* was because of those people who were always telling me all the books were in the same voice. I didn't get here by being smart, I got here by being crazy: there's nothing that works better than telling me not to do something.

Have any of your children shown an interest in following you into writing?

I've got daughters who are artists and readers. My one son is a twenty-three-year-old who just finished art school and he's

fiddling around with film. My younger son, if he could be whatever he wanted to be, he'd be a basketball player [*laughing*].

He'd need to be about six-seven or six-eight …

Yeah, it really broke his heart when he didn't get tall. But then, I
know how that feels. I was telling somebody the other day that I
knew I had to get old, but I didn't know I'd have to get shorter
—that seems really unfair.

**I think Elmore Leonard has said the same thing—the fact that he was
afraid he was just going to vanish.**

He's a great guy. I sure like him. A lot of the guys of that generation are really great gentlemen. Wonderful writers.

**I've been reading a lot of your short fiction recently and really enjoy-
ing it. You had a remarkable football story in the Otto Penzler collection, *The Mighty Johns*. I enjoyed another one in a recent Penzler
Best-of-Year anthology. Were these stories you wrote on request, or
do you write short fiction and then try to place it?**

There's no way to tell. Sometimes I just sit down and a story
starts. It's pretty much impossible to make myself do something
like that, but every now and then, it works.

**A number of crime writers I've interviewed have said they would hap-
pily make their living as short story writers if they could make a living
doing it. They much prefer writing those stories to writing a novel. Are
you of that school of thought?**

I'm not a natural short story writer. I have lots of friends who are.
It's just never sort of been my format. I wrote 'em when I first
started because it seemed easier to throw something away that
was short. I think for short stories you really have to think that
way. You've got to arc very quickly. My short stories tend to be
truncated novels or the sort of things where I haven't got any idea
what's going on. Sometimes I will write one on purpose. There's
a story called "Hostages" that was in Dennis McMillan's collection *Measures of Poison* which has suddenly been anthologized
several places. It's a ten-page short story set in the Depression. I

don't know where that one came from, but my wife made me do it again because it was so short: "It's nice, but it's just too short."

I was in Arizona a few weeks ago and I briefly met Dennis McMillan. He was frustrated that your publisher had not allowed him to go ahead with a limited edition of *The Right Madness*.

Yeah, I could not seem to be able to get anybody to do that. For one thing, we went after it a little late. And nobody could seem to understand what he was trying to do. Writers don't have any influence over that kind of thing. I was disappointed, too. Dennis and I are old friends. He does *good* books. The books are artifacts. It doesn't do anything to the sales of the trade copy, so I just never understood what happened. They even made him pay for the disc they sent him.

Music comes up a lot in your books. You were friends with Warren Zevon … you mention Lucinda Williams in the new book. Who do you listen to now?

Oh, I pretty much listen to everybody. I go all the way from Shostakovich to Steve Earle. Warren was a wonderful guy. I told him he was probably the smartest songwriter in America and he told me, "The words are just something I hang the music on."

Have you been pressured to put up a Web site?

I have. I've been using a computer for a long time, but the maintenance of a Web site is not something I want to take on. I don't know if it works or makes a difference. I have enough trouble cleaning out my e-mail. I don't know that *my* fans are interested in sitting down in front of a computer, either. I've often thought most of my fans were in jail, or should be … on the lam or in the slam.

Do you still do film work at this point at all?

[*Laughing*] Not as much as I used to, unfortunately.

Well, the money is certainly there. I tend to dwell on the books screenwriting may have cost us from Faulkner, from Fitzgerald and some others. But you do have to make money …

I had to pay for a fairly expensive divorce, yes. And you know, I like movies. But like every other idiot writer in the world, when I went to Hollywood I thought, "It's easy to do because it's a lot of white space." But you have to learn a new form. I've never not gotten paid for a script, although I have as many good Hollywood horror stories as anybody else.

You've done quite a range of work: from *Judge Dredd* to Ellroy's *The Big Nowhere*.

Yeah, that one was a chore.

Bet it was … that's such a sprawling piece of work. How do you approach something like that by another crime writer?

Well, I just sort of did something else. The producer that owned the option, Tim Hunter, and I had a drink with him the day he picked up the option. I said, "I feel sorry for the poor screenwriter that has to deal with this." A year later, it was me. That was a real chore. The guys who figured *L.A. Confidential* out, I thought were geniuses. I spent a lot of that time working with Robert Towne on *Dancing Bear* and couldn't do anything else at the time. Wrote a couple of books during that time and couldn't get any screenwork.

And I live in Montana and nobody quite knows where it is.

Flyover country.

Worse than that. Some woman from ABC News in the recent past wanted to talk to me about something. I was going to do a soundbyte. I said sure. She said, "How will I find you? Where would I land?" I said, "Well, you could land at the jet airport here in Missoula, Montana." And then maybe she wasn't so interested as she thought she was. Another friend of mine, when he joined The Writer's Guild, they put him in The Writer's Guild East because they thought it was Missouri.

I was guilty of that, too, when I first came to Montana to teach Freshman Comp. When I got out of graduate school, I had all the schools in the west listed to start sending vitas out—except Montana, where I got to by pure wonderful chance. I've never been able to quite successfully leave.

There were a lot of writers living there at one time.

There still is. I knew a guy from Dallas who sold his advertising firm—one of the few people I ever knew who sold a novel over the transom. He moved to Missoula because he didn't think there would be any writers here. But he knew Dorothy Johnson lived here, so he went over and had tea with Dorothy one afternoon. Then he finds out that two novels doesn't buy you anything in Missoula. You can find a cocktail party full of fifteen people who have published four or five novels. So finally he moved away somewhere … back to Texas maybe.

It is easier to live someplace where people understand the problems with writing. I'm mostly not much of a literary guy. It's like when two writers get together, they don't talk much about literature. They talk about contracts … the complicated parts. I've always said that in these writing programs they should teach a course in the business aspect.

I could see that—in terms of the contracts and taxes and investment and budgeting. You get these big checks, then you go fallow for a period until the next check for the next book.

[*Laughing*] *Budgeting?* Excuse me? Yes, but there are lots of things you don't know until it happens to you. I often think that working in Hollywood helped me to understand how to deal with publishers. The business is so *strange* now. I sold my first book in 1967. It still occasionally is like a gentleman's business, but that's almost all gone.

Vietnam—you're very associated with that topic and the war runs as a thread through your books. The Vietnam generation is getting up there; it doesn't loom as a shaping event or a prism through which to view the world for those forty or so and under … is that a good or a bad thing?

Well, it's another piece of traumatic history we would have been better off not to know … not to have ever happened. Must have been summer before last, there was this organization of guys who did what I did in the Army, except they did it in Vietnam. These guys asked me to join them because of *One to Count Cadence*. I went down to their convention in Colorado Springs. I never knew any of these guys before. They were a little bit younger than me and they were some great guys. They were obviously connected in that way and they still are. I haven't been back to another convention, but I'm in touch with them all by e-mail. It's clear that war had a terrific effect on their lives and it doesn't go away. I figured out some years ago that almost all of my old friends are either writers or Vietnam vets. Just one of those sort of accidental things.

Oddly enough, I did all the research for that first book [*Cadence*] and I sort of changed my mind about the war in the middle of it, which was a good thing. I never have been to Vietnam—been to Southeast Asia—but I was concerned I would do something wrong ... *really* stupid ... like have the sun go down in the east. The vets who read it in manuscript said the only thing I got wrong is there is not a tree in Vietnam that two guys can carry, 'cause they're so heavy from being wet.

But it's like Eliot said: "Bad writers imitate, good writers steal." Although he then said that he may have stolen that from a French poet. You build on the people who did the work before.

Speaking of Europe, you take C.W. to Scotland in the new novel. *The Final Country* ends with Milo thinking about maybe moving to Paris, France. Scotland and Paris are a long way from Montana, or El Paso. We're not going to hear of you moving to Europe, are we?

The Scottish part comes from Richard Hugo. When he was living on Skye I went to see him. Then my wife and I went back, shit, seventeen years later. There is something about Scotland—the landscape and the skies—that just felt good and still feels good. It's a very odd place. The first time I went, I was by myself and wearing cowboy boots and a leather jacket and nobody would talk to me. But I couldn't understand them, sometimes, anyway. Over the years, I've become quite fond of France. But I can't live someplace without cable TV and American football.

Do you have a personal favorite among your own books?

That's like choosing among your children [*laughing*]. *The Last Good Kiss* was pretty easy once I got it figured out. It's like one of those books where you do a lot of work and then it drops out of you very nicely. *The Wrong Case*—that was my first attempt and most of which I owe to [Raymond] Chandler. I owe Chandler to Richard Hugo. He came here the year before I did. When he found out I had never read any Chandler, he was like [feigning a smack to the head] *whack* ... "What kind of smart-ass graduate student were *you*?"

That first summer I was in Mexico working on *Cadence*, the Chandler books had come out and were in the grocery store with those wonderful Tom Adams art deco covers. So I read 'em all at once. I thought, after failing at the Texas novel for six years or something, "Maybe I'll write a detective novel"—little knowing that it would be taken more seriously and do better than the first book. It's been an up and down thing. *The Last Good Kiss* only sold forty-four hundred copies in hardback. But it's never been out of print.

It's not a sprint, it's a marathon?

I don't know what it is, anymore. I just know I can't stop doing it.

You've criticized the depiction of the Old West and of American Indians in a number of films. Have you seen *Deadwood*? Any thoughts on that?

I have seen it. Great technical work. Someone in the *New York Times*, I think, said that I have a fine ear for filthy speech. But I think David Milch doesn't quite understand that profanity is about rhythm—it wears me out, just watching it. It is a very interesting show and I think probably as realistic as anything ever done about the West has a chance to be. It has that real grit to it. I tend to watch it every week and I usually watch it twice: the second time is when it starts to make sense again.

Is there anything you'd particularly like to get out about *The Right Madness*?

Well, it was a great feeling to finish ... a great feeling to finish *again*. Not only all that time I lost in the middle there, but a funny thing about the drugs they gave me—I lost all my compound words: steamboat, motorboat, machine gun. If it was a compound word, I didn't have it any more. I've pretty much gotten those back. The other thing I lost was touch-typing. I simply couldn't touch-type anymore. Maybe because of my arthritis, maybe because of my brain. I was always the "touch-type with one hand and hunt-and-peck with the other" sort.

Anything else in the works right now?

Oh, I've *always* got something in the works.

Do you have a strong sense of where you're headed for the next one? Maybe that's the better way to phrase the question.

No, because I don't have a hundred pages. It takes me about a hundred pages to be sure that I'm going to finish a book. I have a notorious inability to write before another book comes out. You'd think I'd be used to this. I was telling somebody Saturday, "Jesus, you'd think I'd know about this by now." But it always makes me antsy and nervous.

I was going to ask you if it is still a thrill for you when a new book comes out, but it sounds like a big anxiety.

The thrill comes when you pick up a finished manuscript. All the rest is kind of fluff. But, you know, if you're going to make a living at it, the fluff is what counts. But, *God* ... I'd just as soon not have to do it again. But I don't have any choices anymore. I guess I never did have any choices.

ELMORE LEONARD

Ten Rules
(October 12, 2007)

Elmore "Dutch" Leonard was born on October 11, 1925 in New Orleans. During World War II, Leonard served in the U.S. Naval Reserve from 1943-46. (Vision problems kept Leonard out of the marines, with whom he'd tried to enlist.)

Following his military service, Leonard studied at the University of Detroit, graduating in 1950 and launching a seventeen-year career in advertising.

Leonard published his first piece of fiction—a Western short story—in Argosy in 1953 (he scored a $1,250 advance for his 1961 Western novel *Hombre*, so he was a long while quitting his day job to write fiction full time).

After a long run writing Western novels and short stories—and faced with the decline of the genre he'd made his name in—Leonard shifted to crime fiction in 1969 with the release of the paperback original *The Big Bounce*. That novel's publication followed a reported eighty-four rejections.

His crime novels drew critical praise for their taught, clean prose and ear-true dialogue, but his audience didn't really begin to grow until the 1980s. Leonard's '83 release, *LaBrava*, earned an Edgar Award. In 1985, *Newsweek* published a cover story on Leonard, declaring him "the best American writer of crime fiction alive."

On his way to that success, Leonard quit drinking in the 1977. He endured the break-up of his long, first marriage to his college sweetheart (the couple wed in 1949) and struggled with a middling screenwriting career (among his screen credits is an ill-advised TV-movie sequel to *High Noon* that starred Lee Majors).

In the late 1970s, "Dutch" (the nickname is a nod to a Washington Senators' pitcher) began to hit his stride with Detroit- and Miami-based crime novels such as *Stick*, *Swag* and *The Switch*.

Leonard's 1985 novel, *Glitz*, hit the bestseller lists and sat there for sixteen weeks—Leonard's breakout book had finally arrived after thirty-two years as a published author.

Elmore Leonard was interviewed in conjunction with the publication of a slim little book entitled, *Elmore Leonard's 10 Rules of Writing*. The interview was conducted the day after Leonard celebrated his eighty-second birthday.

• • • • •

Let me start off by wishing you a happy birthday.

Oh, thanks, that was yesterday. I got a lot of calls, too.

Did you do anything grand for the day?

I tried to work, but I don't think I wrote anything down. Maybe a line. The phone would ring. So then my family—we all went out to dinner last night and that was it.

Are you one of these writers who feels a driven need to write every day?

No, I don't feel driven, but when I'm writing a book I definitely want to write every day, because if you miss a day, you forget. You've got to keep it with you. You've got to keep it going all the time in your head.

There are writers who claim they get knocked off stride for a week or so, and then the book dies on them.

Oh *yeah*. If you are away from it for a week it will take more than a week to get back to it.

Do you practice the Hemingway technique of rereading what you've written every day to kick-start the writing process?

Yeah, or in the morning, before I'll start out, I'll read from an older book. One that I like. I like 'em all, but I'll read something just to get the sound back that I want. The attitude. Then I'm off. Once I start to write, then I'm into it. I get lost and the time just flies by. That's the beauty of this work. I look at the clock and it's three o'clock in the afternoon and I say, "Good, I've got three more hours." You know—after *fifty years*.

Is there still an excitement for you when a book comes out? You've had this extraordinary run. Not to say you'd be jaded about it, but ...

My last two or three books, I've gone back into the 1930s or 1940s, beginning with the serial in the *New York Times*. That was a different pace. I was experiencing different things then in the research. Memories. I was in the service at that time—in the forties. So many things came back to me, like food rationing ... gas rationing. That kind of stuff. That was interesting. I'm glad to get back to the contemporary. I like to keep my books fresh—references to what's going on today.

I interviewed a lot of crime writers immediately after September 11, 2001 and the terrorist attacks. They all said they were having a hard time writing anything contemporary or relevant in the wake of those events. It swamped their ability to write and seemed to shrink the importance of what they were writing. Several subsequently began to write books set in pre-9/11 eras. Was any of that sentiment factoring into your decision for your own writing trips back into the 1930s or '40s?

No, no I hadn't thought of that. There are writers of course who have used it—working it [the attacks] into a plot.

The novel you're writing now is going to bring back Foley from *Out of Sight?*

Yeah. In fact, I'm bringing back three characters from three different books. Right away, I thought well, "Foley, definitely. I'm going to do Foley because George Clooney likes Foley."

That's a compelling reason to do it ...

And Foley is easy to write for me because I know him pretty well, now. So then I brought another character in, Dawn Navarro, who is a psychic. I brought her in out of *Riding the Rap*. And then Cundo Rey. Cundo Rey is a character in *LaBrava*. He was a very smalltime hustler and a Go-Go dancer. He was just a hip little guy. I was hoping that he was still alive. I didn't remember.

So you had to go back and revisit your own book?

Yes, I had to look it up. He got shot, three times, in the chest. And I thought, "Oh my God." But Joe LaBrava shot him and then immediately left. He knows he's dead. But he *wasn't*.

You had some wiggle room ...

Yes, the emergency guys picked him up and see, "My God, he's bleeding, he's bleeding." He's still alive. So they rush him to the hospital and he's in a coma. He extends the coma—pretends to be in a coma longer than he is—to find out where he is and what's going on. Then he has one of the guys working in the hospital who was also Cuban, also in the boatlift—the Mariel boatlift—sneak him out. Then he goes to L.A. and gets into dealing drugs to people in the movie business. He makes a lot of money, but then he's arrested but they're not sure they can convict him in California. So they send him back to Florida where there's a detainer on him on a homicide. He gets a very good lawyer and he's out in seven and a half years.

Now Foley, he's back in prison, so he's talking to Cundo Rey. Foley is facing thirty years. He doesn't think he's going to make it —this is terrible. Cundo Rey says, "Hey, I'll get you my lawyer," who is a young woman—very very savvy ... knows what she's doing. She gets Foley's conviction reduced from thirty years to thirty months. And so they both get out about the same time and go out to Venice, California where the story then will take place.

And that will be an '08 release. Let's talk about the book coming out now—*Elmore Leonard's 10 Rules of Writing*. The rules have been around for a while. What was the catalyst to put them out in book form now?

My researcher is the one who kept pushing me.

Greg Sutter?

Greg Sutter. Yeah. He's been getting stuff for me for, say, twenty-five years. He said, "It's time to have these rules published because people are using them all the time … referring to them.

They are all over the Internet …

Yeah. We proposed it my editor at HarperCollins and she thought it was a great idea so we did it. We have it illustrated [by Joe Ciardiello].

It's a slim little book. Were you under pressure to throw in another ten rules?

[*Laughing*] No, we got ninety-five pages out of ten rules.

That's impressive …

That's not bad at all. You see, this started in the year 2000. I was guest of honor at Bouchercon. That afternoon in the hotel in Denver, I wrote up these ten rules. They're in much different form. Then, when I came down off the stage, a guy approached me and said, "Can I have those?" These two pieces of yellow paper … I said, "Sure, here," and handed them to him.

Hell of a collectible …

Well then, a few years later, the *New York Times* asked me if I would do something for their column *Writers on Writing*. I made up the ten rules again and put them in an order that I thought was right. I also made reference to different writers who wouldn't need my rules. For example the rule about don't describe your characters in detail. I said, "Hell, Margaret Atwood can do it all she wants because she's good at it."

It's funny, because the two sheets of paper all of the sudden appeared for sale at a bookstore on the Internet. My researcher who was just looking around happened to see them the day that they were offered. A friend of his was a lawyer in L.A. and he told him about it and bought them immediately. Then Greg said to the lawyer, "*I* was going to get them." The lawyer said, "We'll *both* put in to buy them." They got this page and a half, at most, for six-hundred bucks. If the guy had waited until the rules book came out ...

He'd have had a five-figure collectible ...

I know! My researcher has for years been trying to get me to save all my papers because I write everything in longhand.

I would think universities would be all over you to donate those manuscripts.

I tried saving the longhand sheets but it's not a perfect sheet. It's mostly just crossed out. There's more crossed out than is there. That's why I started doing it longhand because it's so hard to x-out things on a typewriter.

This might be too precious a question, but I'm wondering if the rules and your instinctive commitment to them—even if you hadn't formalized them or written them down—shape you as a writer? I'm trying to chicken and egg it a little ...

When I started out, I thought they're kind of tongue-in-cheek. But then the more I looked at them I realized, no, they're not.

A lot of people certainly don't read them that way.

The way I wrote the rules seven years ago, I say, "Forty-nine years ago last month, I sold my first story. Since then I've come up with ten rules for success and happiness in writing fiction. One: try to leave out the passages that readers tend to skip. It's the ones you spend the most time on. Number two: Never open a book with weather." That is number one, now.

You mention exclamation points and that you only get to use two for about every one hundred thousand words. I think it's a great rule.

Two or three.

Two or three. I was at a book conference recently and I picked up the paperback *Three-Ten to Yuma and Other Stories*. I started reading the very first story, "Calvary Boots." By my count, you've got about eleven exclamation points in that story, which can't be more than four or five thousand words long.

Don't tell anybody! When those stories came out again, ones that I wrote in the 1950s, I hadn't read them in more than fifty years.

I wondered if you have a real strong temptation to go through and kind of massage 'em.

No. No, I had to leave them alone because this is what they sounded like.

I also wondered if editors had inserted some of those exclamation points.

Maybe. I had adverbs in there, too … "ly"adverbs. That's the worst sin of all.

You praise some contemporary writers in the book, but also, obviously, Steinbeck and Hemingway are prominently mentioned. Are there writers working today whom you admire for having tight, clean economical prose?

There was one I learned a lot from in the '50s and that was Richard Bissell. He's probably very hard to find right now, but I loved his books set on the Mississippi River. He was a pilot. "7 1/2 Cents" became *The Pajama Game*. Then he wrote a book, *Say Darling*, about the making of the play. I learned more from him than I did from Hemingway. Because Hemingway I learned a lot from, I know, but he didn't have a sense of humor.

I've seen you remark on that before, and I've heard a lot of people say that. I see some humor in some of the early stories and novels. *A Moveable Feast* is funny in places, though it's a nasty kind of funny … very mean humor in that one.

I was giving a talk and someone said, "What do you mean he doesn't have a sense of humor?" I said, "What are you going to tell me about? Sordo's stand on the hill [in *For Whom the Bell Tolls*]?" Because that's very ironic what he's yelling at and so on.

Which of Hemingway's works do you admire? In terms of the novels I'd guess *For Whom the Bell Tolls*.

Yeah. And of course I couldn't wait to read *The Old Man and the Sea* when that came out. I was working at an ad agency and I remember getting the issue of *Life Magazine* at the cigar store downstairs in the General Motors Building and running back up to my office and starting to read it right then. I was really in love with his prose at that time. I still have his *Forty-Nine Short Stories* on my desk. And I can look at those at any time. Some of those are really terrific.

I notice there are no Faulkner references in the *10 Rules of Writing*.

No, I've never been able to read him.

Hemingway remarked, "Writing is architecture, not interior design." That sounds like something you would subscribe to as an axiom. You say in the *Rules* that if something reads like "writing" you have to strike it. It sounds from your description of your hand-written drafts that's still something you do quite a lot of.

Oh yeah. If it sounds like writing, rewrite it. Someone will ask me, "What do you mean by that?" And I say, "Upon entering the room …"

There you go. Knocks you right out to the story.

That's it. It's the way we were taught to write in school, with the dependent clause first.

I guess what you're saying is a key to good writing is unlearning formal writing, first.

Yes.

You wrote an introduction to George V. Higgins *The Friends of Eddie Coyle* a few years back. In that introduction, you quote Higgins as saying "Writing can't be taught." Do you subscribe to that notion? Is it an innate skill?

My son just got a two-book deal at St. Martin's. He started writing fiction two or three years ago, maybe. He started out writing screenplays because he figured that would be the fast buck. I said, "You're crazy—you've got to be out there if you're going to be a screenwriter. You should be out there because all of the people who went to film school, that the screenwriter went to film school with, they're studio executives and they're buying the stuff." Then he started to write a book. All of his friends and his sons loved it. They told him, "This is great. This is bound to sell."

Then I read it, and I said, "Who's the main character?" He said, so-and-so is. The woman. I said, "Well, she doesn't come off as the main character to me." So he sent it to my agent in New York, Wylie, and they gave it to eight different publishers and they all said the same thing: Who's the main character? So now he listens to me. He's really into it. He's older—he's in his fifties. I said, "Why didn't you start earlier?" He said, "I didn't want to."

Is he going to publish under the name "Leonard?"

Oh yeah, Peter Leonard. Sure. They just made a deal for him in England with Faber. He's really into it now. He's got his own company—an ad agency. He's got two partners and he's just trying to write his way out of it the same way I did back in '61.

There's much said now of the death of midlist authors, and the death of book reviewing, and the computer monitoring of sales and the effect of that on writers who don't sell great numbers of books. What would your advice be to someone just going out into the market as a beginning author? I mean, you're above and outside much of this because of your level of prominence and your readership ...

But I don't sell *nearly* as many books as ...

... As I would think?

[*Laughing*] Yeah. If I sell one hundred thousand hardcover, that's good.

That is a hell of a lot, still.

It is, it is, but there are people who their first printing is eight hundred thousand copies or two million.

That guy, James Patterson, he'll have three books sometimes on the list. But you know that the other guy whose name is printed much smaller on the cover than his [Patterson's] is doing all the work.

Patterson has more or less become his own corporate brand now.

And his chapters are never more than three pages.

If that. Do you still regard *The Friends of Eddie Coyle* as the best crime novel ever written?

Definitely.

You've had this extraordinarily long career ... do you think a career like yours can be replicated in today's market?

I think the reason that I'm still going is that I didn't really hit the big time until the mid-'80s. But I started in the 1950s.

You more than paid your dues.

Yes. By the time I got on the *Times* list, boy, I had a backlist, you know? And that was great. Then the backlist gets bought by whomever is publishing me.

You finally get your money back on those early works?

That's right—everything ... *everything.* Even the short stories that I got two cents a word for. Like *Three-Ten to Yuma* I got ninety bucks. I sold the screen rights for four thousand dollars. The publisher of *Dime Western* could take 25 percent of a film sale and he did, because the pulps were starting to go out of business then.

All the magazines ... there were so many magazines that would publish short stories in the 1950s. You'd aim for the *Saturay Evening Post* and *Colliers.* Then you'd come down through *Argosy*, and then the pulps. There were a couple of dozen pulps, at least.

What'd you think of the new *Yuma* film?

I liked it. It looked good. The ending made no sense at all ... But on the whole, the reviews have been good.

Ever get the itch to write another Western novel?

If they were to pay as much as crime novels do, yeah, I could do one.

I was Googling you earlier today and I came across an item that for the first time in years, Halloween costume rentals of Western outfits are up. They attribute the spike to the new *Yuma* film.

There's another use of Yuma in Cuba, where they call America "La Yuma." And individuals from the United States are referred to as "Yuma." And this is because of that movie that was released in the 1970s in Havana, because Castro wouldn't allow the picture to show originally.

Did you find yourself watching *Deadwood* on HBO?

No, I never got into that. The language amazed me.

You've often cited movies as an early influence on your writing. Do you still find films you can enjoy? So many seem to be put together by committee and test-audience …

As many as I've sold and have been made from my work, there have only been a few good films. I think it's mostly luck that good movies are made because there seem to be so many people in the business, studio people, who are just trying to wreck things. There's that joke about the two agents who are out in the desert. They're dying of thirst. Finally, they come to this well. "Oh, here's water we can drink." And the one says, "Wait, let's piss in it, first."

Are you comfortable with gauging or trying to characterize your own influence on crime writing?

I really don't know what that is. I hear good things from George Pelecanos and some others. My editor will tell me more and more books are sounding like mine and that I've opened the door for a certain type of writers. It's funny though, because when I'm sent a manuscript by the publishers, there'll be a reference to the fact that this guy supposedly sounds like me. I don't see it at all.

PART II

Kith & Kin

DANIEL WOODRELL

Crime In The Ozarks

(June 21, 2006)

Daniel Woodrell grew up in the Ozarks, far from any literary scene. The high school dropout lived a kind of gypsy existence for many years, drifting around the country and settling here and there for a year or two before moving on again.

At age seventeen, Woodrell (pronounced Wood-*RELL*) enlisted in the Marine Corps during the height of the Vietnam War. The Marines helped Daniel further his educational studies and put him on a path to an eventual college degree.

Fortunately, Woodrell was bounced out of the service before having to serve "in country," and eventually found his way, like James Crumley before him, to the Iowa Writers' Workshop.

Woodrell is hard-pressed to point to any great rewards from that Iowa experience, apart from having met his wife, novelist Katie Estill.

He made the literary scene in 1986 with the publication of *Under the Bright Lights*, the first novel that he, to use his word, "completed."

Despite affection for that book, if he had it to do over again, Woodrell indicates he might do it differently.

Under the Bright Lights was immediately tagged a crime fiction novel and shelved in the mystery sections of bookstores everywhere. That designation yoked the author to a stubbornly enduring, misapplied genre collar you sense he'd dearly love to shake.

As Woodrell laments through the vessel of novelist-narrator Doyle Redmond in *Give Us A Kiss*: "I always get called a crime writer, though to me they are slice-of-life dramas."

Under the Bright Lights introduced Detective Rene Shade, an ex-boxer-turned-cop ... a man "about sixty stitches past good-looking." He polices in a town where "girls acquired insurmountable local reputations" and where fuck-up prone, working-class criminals fret, "I hope to god the FBI ain't buggin' this house, Emil. They'll ridicule us in court."

The first book was a while finding a publisher, so while he waited, Woodrell ran in a distinctly different direction, penning his Civil War-era novel *Woe to Live On* (1987). Woe is a coming-of-age tale centered on sixteen-year-old Jake Roedel. Woodrell's second novel drew favorable comparisons to Pete Dexter's *Dead-wood* and Cormac McCarthy's *Blood Meridian*.

When his first novel with Rene Shade finally sold, Woodrell was impelled to course-correct again and secured his genre designation by writing the first of two successive Shade sequels.

Muscle for the Wing (1988) followed loosely in its predecessor's path—just enough there to assuage publishers pushing for a mystery series, but already showing the traits of Woodrell's late-1990s-vintage standalones.

And in *Wing*, Woodrell's inimitable narrative voice is already firming:

"Beaurain measured five foot seven standing on your neck." Or, as an elderly matriarch with ankle-length hair observes, "He's been mean ever since pantyhose ruined finger fuckin'."

The novel opens with a bang: "Wishing to avoid any hint of a snub at the Hushed Hill Country Club, the first thing Emil Jadick shoved through the door was double-barreled and loaded."

In 1992, Woodrell rounded off the Shade cycle with *The Ones You Do*, a book focused on Rene's pool-hustling old man, John X. Shade. Though touted as part of a series, the novel is closer in spirit to Woodrell's more recent works and Rene is shunted into a supporting role.

With four under-selling books to his name, Woodrell was at a crossroads. Through Doyle Redmond he confided, "My life's work to this point being four published novels nobody much had read, let alone bought or reviewed prominently."

Four years passed before *Give Us A Kiss* (1996), Woodrell's startling novel about a struggling "crime" novelist who returns to his Ozarks home to become tangled up with his brother in a marijuana-growing scheme and murder that pits them against the infamous Dolly clan.

Woodrell's follow-up was *Tomato Red* (1998), a well-received and enthusiastically reviewed novel that finds a couple of West Table, Missouri, siblings, Jamalee and Jason Merridew, tangling fortunes with Sammy Barlach. With *Tomato Red*, Woodrell finally thought he was hitting his stride. He told another author, "It is really from *Tomato Red* on that I really feel like I'm *really* starting to have a sense of what we're doing and what I want to do."

Woodrell followed that novel with the remarkable *Death of Sweet Mister* (2001), a wrenching coming-of-age tale narrated by pudgy thirteen-year-old Shuggie Akins. Shug lives with his drunken mother in a shack by a cemetery the two are entrusted to maintain. In and out of their lives drifts the feral "Red"—a nasty, self-centered no-account who uses mother Glenda for sex and a punching bag and who forces Shug to commit petty crimes such as breaking-and-enterings and shaking down the area elderly and terminally ill for pills.

Woodrell's evocation of Shug's unknowingly knowing voice —and the boy's unhealthy but inevitable and mounting interest in his own mother—is staggeringly well-realized.

Dennis Lehane said of *The Death of Sweet Mister*, "I thought it was hands-down the best coming-of-age story that I had come across in twenty years. And just one of the most vicious, brilliant noirs."

After *Sweet Mister*, Woodrell struggled with a long-envisioned Marine Corps novel. He completed a draft of that book, but wasn't satisfied with it. So he turned to a second coming-of-age tale, this one entitled *Winter's Bone* (2006).

The heroine of that book is Ree Dolly, a sixteen-year-old girl who is the most mature and the oldest soul in her family. She is mother to her two brothers and mother to her own, ailing mother.

Ree accessorizes her dresses with combat boots and dreams of a hitch in the military as an escape hatch from a life lost in her Ozarks ancestral home.

Winter's Bone finds Ree wandering through the Ozarks' snow and ice in search of her wastrel father who has jeopardized their lives by putting their home up for collateral against a bond.

Daniel Woodrell spoke with me in mid-June 2006 from his home in the Ozarks along the Arkansas border. He was anticipating the arrival of a Sundance-awarded director who had optioned *Winter's Bone* and was coming to town to get a feel for the region that provides the novel's setting.

Woodrell was also close to inking a deal to write a script for a film adaptation of *Give Us A Kiss*, and he was anticipating a possible film deal for *The Death of Sweet Mister*.

• • • • •

I'm told you'll have a film crew tracking you in July. I see several newspaper critics have, as I have myself, written summer reading previews singling out your novel as a must-read. Do you have a sense that *Winter's Bone* might be—that dreadful term—your "breakout book"?

Oh, I'm almost afraid to use it, being you know, highly superstitious. I know that I have not had so much attention in advance on a book before. It's already coming out in England right now—I've never had that happen this way before, either.

It is a little strange—you're such an American writer and voice—that Europeans are getting the book two months ahead of us in the States.

I do think Americans maybe think they already know all the regions of America or have heard all they need to hear sometimes, and are less intrigued. But it does seem that the UK is paying attention, especially this time.

It's been five years since *The Death of Sweet Mister*, which was another well-received novel. I remember seeing a title floated somewhere, for a work called *Paradise Moves*. Were there starts on other novels since *The Death of Sweet Mister*, or has Ree Dolly's story been the one you've been shaping these past few years?

I spent a little over two years on a Marine Corps novel that wasn't mature. Something just wasn't coming. Even though it looked like we could publish it, I decided I don't want to. I'll save it and hope it gels.

Winter's Bone—that's about two years of your writing time, then. Is that a story that's been speaking to you for a while?

I had the opening paragraph, kind of. It was just one of those things: It came to you. I wrote it down. It was like a non sequitur. It didn't have anything to do with what I was working on at the time and I put it up on the wall and kept looking at it. I started to write it once and she was an adult with several children and everything and that didn't seem right. I put it away and about six months later I really started getting it the way it is now. This isn't unusual for me to have to circle around on something like this.

It's interesting that The Death of Sweet Mister and Winter's Bone both are centered by young characters—flip sides of the coming-of-age tale, perhaps. I wondered if this was deliberate planning on your part, or—

No, no. I'd *like* to have deliberate moves.

You've been a while away from the third-person point of view (POV). How'd you come to tell Ree's tale from the outside-in, so to speak?

Well, one is, as you say, I'd done a number of first-person things and I really sort of consciously didn't want to do another first-person thing unless it absolutely had to be first person and was better in first person. And this one, it didn't seem to me, was either of those things. It seemed like it was meant to be written this way. And it had been a while and I thought, "Well, I'll see if I can even get it goin' that way."

In terms of third-person POV, it's been since 1992 and The Ones You Do ...

That was a little different too, because in those books [the Shade novels] I didn't just follow one person—I dipped all over. So I wasn't sure it would start rolling this way. Once it did, I was hooked all the way and in fact I'm probably going to go fifty-fifty from now on, I guess.

You've always salted your novels with formidable, or at times even elemental women ... particularly mothers, which Ree, in most respects, is to her younger brothers. And she is mother to her own ailing mother. As her creator, how does Ree stack up against some of these other women you've written? I assume there are certain characters you have more affection for than others.

She is definitely one of my all-time ... well, when I was done with it, I remember telling either my agent or my editor that it's kind of hard to move on. Because she's also got more qualities that are admired by wider elements of the world than many of the people I write about. And I found myself responding to some of those—pluck and drive and whatnot, just like anybody else would.

Someone who wrote one of those previews of *Winter's Bone* decided, at least in their own head, that there is an inevitable sequel. Is Ree a character you might return to?

No. There isn't going to be a sequel. There will be other works about members of the extended family, but I would doubt that Ree would even be mentioned.

Ree is sixteen and charting a military career as a means of escape from her home. You enlisted at seventeen and I've noticed almost all, if not all, of your jacket blurbs mention your military service.

Yeah, they do. I guess they think that's defining, or something.

I've seen indications that for you, the military was also a tactic of escape ... just a way to get the hell away from where you were at the time.

Basically. I didn't like where we'd ended up living. In fact, there's a bit in *Give Us A Kiss* where [Doyle Redmond] talks about why he joined the Marines. He'd read this Jack London book and Jack was already living as an oyster pirate with a prostitute when he was fifteen. [Doyle] was sixteen and he says, "Hey, life just passed me right by." There was some of that, too. It suddenly dawned on me I was old enough to leave and here was a way to go. I was trying to join the Navy, but they had a long waiting list in the middle of the [Vietnam] war like that. I stepped outside and the

Marine guy was standing there. He said, "What'd they tell ya?" I said, "They told me they've got a long waiting list for high school drop-outs, especially." He said, "Well, we don't. I'll have you there today."

Let me ask you about that: You dropped out of high school and you got a college degree I think in your late twenties … twenty-seven? How'd you go from one to the other? Most colleges, that can be a real hurdle—getting in without the high school diploma.

Well, I got a GED when I was on Guam. Me and two sergeants. I went to a ju-co for a while, then I went to another college in western Kansas. When I got the junior college degree, KU—the University of Kansas—I think they had to let you in, at least as a trial, and I did okay. Although it took me a while—I didn't go consecutively.

Does military enlistment remain the chief escape hatch from poverty in your region?

Yeah, I think so.

Has the current war affected that in ways you detect?

We've had a few from the general area get hurt. Where I do my outdoor exercise is a track, and I see 'em over there—I guess you have to do a certain speed for a mile or something to get in. I see 'em over there with fresh ones, all the time.

Family has been a central theme in all of your novels. We've had the Shades, the Redmonds, the Dollys. Do you presently live in a setting that boasts a lot of kin?

There once were many, but now it's down to me … my mom, and me. My mom's remarried. I'm the last Woodrell left here, or the last I know of. There may be some hidden around. Both my parents' families are from around here. Fifty or sixty years ago, there'd have been a ton. It's hard to make a living here and my dad got a taste of the world in World War II, as did his brother, and neither of them ever wanted to live here again until they were retired—because you can't make a living here.

What brought you back?

I was tired of kicking around and feeling like I didn't really belong any of the places I was living. They were interesting. I liked 'em. I liked Lawrence, Kansas. I liked Iowa. I liked a lot of places. I liked San Francisco, but I felt like I was never going to get any roots there.

I'm from Ohio: I noticed you omitted your time spent in Cleveland.

We liked Cleveland, too. My wife is from Cleveland and we lived there for two years. Well, I say Cleveland; she's from right outside of Cleveland. That's were I learned the East Side-West Side dichotomy.

Here: This was always the center of home even if I didn't grow up here day-by-day. All the family lore and legends, it all came back to *here*. We lived in the Arkansas Ozarks for a while. I thought, "That's nice, but it's not the same." I live two blocks from a cemetery that's just full of dead relatives. It ended up, much to my surprise, meaning something to me after we came here and settled. We only intended to be here a year or so, and we're still here.

The Dolly clan hovers on the fringes of your earlier work [*Give Us A Kiss*], but they've finally come front and center with *Winter's Bone*. You once spoke of a Dolly short story cycle. Still the plan?

Sort of. That's kind of what I'm fiddlin' with now. It could end up being a pure novel, but it also could end up … well, I can't tell yet. It's in that neighborhood, though.

Woe to Live On was a short story first and then you expanded it into a novel. Does that happen to you often with other books?

After one more novel, I promised my wife I'm going to take, like, two years or three years and just write short stories. I really like it when I do find an occasion to do one. But I respect the form enough to realize to really get any good at it you're going to have to focus on it consistently for a little while. I've written a couple for anthologies lately, like a Jason Starr one that's coming out. *Murdaland*, this new magazine coming out, they asked for something. And I really had fun doin' it. But *Woe to Live On* is the only novel that started as a short story.

So there is not enough back there yet for a collection?
No. In fact, really in the last twenty or thirty years, I've only written three or four stories.

The Jason Starr anthology is conceived around horse racing. Is that something you find you can do: someone can throw a theme at you and you can write a story to that theme?
That time it happened I could. *Murdaland* just wanted somethin' dark. I actually sort of liked the notion: "All it has to do is have somethin' to do with horse racing." *Okay.* Well, that was sort of fun for me. Part of it is I don't put the same level of expectation on myself with short stories so I relax and they might could be just as good. But I'm not pressuring myself. Whereas with novels, I really feel required—I'm one of these types, I'd hate to publish one that I thought wasn't in the league with the one before, that's all.

That's a perfect segue to my next question: There are tremendous pressures placed on authors to whip out a book a year. *Winter's Bone* makes eight books in twenty years. How have you resisted this pressure?
I tried at one point to do it, and I didn't like the stuff. I wrote a complete novel for Holt at one point. They said it's publishable, but I kept saying, "It's not as good." It was me trying to make sure I had one done on time. So I said, "I'm not going to do that anymore." If it's five years, it's five years. If it's two years, it's two years.

Your first three books came bang-bang-bang in '86, '87 and '88. Was your output that fast at the time, or more an effect of stockpiling, so to speak?
The first one had been done for a couple of years before it sold. And I had assumed it wouldn't sell, and I had assumed I wouldn't be doing any more of those, so I started writing *Woe to Live On*. I was about in the middle of that when I found out the first one had sold. But it was a two-book deal and so forth.

Under the Bright Lights **was your first published novel. Was it also the first you wrote?**

No—no *completed* ones before that. That was one of the reasons I was so glad to have tried that book. I did complete it and I thought it was good enough at the time and that was an important psychological thing.

Thirty-three is an evocative age at which to publish your first novel. Can you remember your reaction at the time?

Oh yeah: I was thrilled. I didn't know writers or anything growing up. I'm not from a writerly milieu. So the idea that somebody from New York's gonna pay you money and print it, hey, I had no second questions about that. At the time, I was just jumpin'.

Not to say you might be jaded, but is there a vast difference between your anticipation of a book's release then and now?

There are certain experiences you've already had now. I remember once, a long time ago, Elmore Leonard saying he didn't want just another book, he wanted a book that did what he wanted it to do, or something to that effect. That's more of what I'm feeling now. I'm excited about publishing books that I think are going to give me the opportunity to publish more ... more that maybe range more widely afield than this one. I'll never be very far from dramatic criminal things, probably. But there are so many ways of getting at it, that's what's exciting about this world—call it crime writing or whatever you want to call it. I just call it dramatic writing now, because, who knows? I don't ever seem to come up with an idea that doesn't at some point have a crime in it.

You've said that in college you tried to write plays. Any nuggets or elements of your current work in those plays?

Actually they were all about winos and stuff, standing around talking absurdist non sequiturs about the state of the world.

Okay, so *that's* how you ended up in Iowa. Do you ever look back at your Iowa Writers' Workshop writing efforts? Reactions?

A couple of the short stories I like. You know one thing that was good for me at Iowa was I did write a lot while I was there and you got exposed to a lot of other kinds of writers—and young writers who really admired things that for one reason or another you'd never taken a good look at. That opened me up to take a look at things, so that was good for me. The last time I pulled out my cream of the Iowa years I looked at it and I said, "Yeah, it's all got somethin' and it's all flawed." It was a good experience, but it's not like there's a neglected masterpiece in there.

Let's jump ahead a little bit to *Give Us A Kiss* where you really take on that whole experience. You also take some dead-on and devastating swings at the Iowa Writers' Workshop-style writing culture and those peopling it. Ever hear back from your Iowa confreres about that book?

There's a famous translator who has ties to the region here and she passed word to me that she and her friends *loved* it. They particularly loved that part. And then I did have a review where a great guy, a great writer himself, said he didn't care for that Iowa part much. But most of my friends who were there with me thought I wasn't even unfair.

Give Us A Kiss is probably the single book in your body of work that almost invites the reader to confuse character and creator. A deliberate tactic on your part?

Well, I was kind of thinking of it as a fake memoir. I was a little premature on the fake memoir craze. When I started it, I was even toying with calling it a "Memoir in Fiction" or something. So I was deliberately blurring those lines. It seemed like fun to me to do it that way. I didn't realize I'd be getting asked at readings for years if I had robbed gas stations to put myself through college.

Your picaresque life?

Right!

I'm going to guess you probably wouldn't write about a writer again.

No, I don't think so. I saw the pluses and the minuses there.

You have a thinly disguised Elmore Leonard type in "Elrod Chucky" and a Dominic Dunne sort in "Nickolai Noonan."

I knew somebody would be gettin' that. I'm not sure Elmore liked it.

I'm almost certain he probably wouldn't have.

[*Laughing*] Well, I don't care to be honest with you. I don't care what Elmore thinks.

Doyle realizes his wife is composing a poem about him as she is casting him off. Being around so many writers, and being married to one, is that something you've experienced, or sensed others experiencing in your presence?

Yeah! That was like the standard joke at Iowa. Every time something painful would happen, somebody would say, "Hey, maybe I can use that!" Or if somebody did something extravagantly stupid we'd say, "There they go, building their personal legend."

The career! The career!

Right, it was kind of in that nature. But yeah, I think if you're involved with a writer, you have to know you're runnin' the risk of ending up between the pages.

That book was described as a "country noir." Noir as a term has become almost valueless as it is so liberally applied by those who don't have a good working definition. I've read you have a pretty strict definition of the term in your own mind, and it is focused on what noir requires for an ending. Could you illuminate that?

It has to end tragically, that's all. It just has to end tragically to be actual noir. That's why *Winter's Bone*—the "country noir" term is still getting used here and there—it's not actually a noir. It doesn't really fit the requirements by my standards. Although some other people use noir in a way where I guess it would fit. But to me, I like the stricter definition because it thereby makes it discrete from all the other forms of dark fiction. I do see the term on books that would not be in the least noir by my standards.

You wrote three books that are often linked as a trilogy or identified as a kind of series, about Rene Shade, and the last is about his father. Were you following your own impulses, or were there pressures on you as a misidentified genre writer to produce a series?

I was under pressure to do it and at the time we were broke and

I was not in a position to say "no" to it. Everything I've published, it was the best I could do at the time I published it. I tried hard at all of them, and I like all of them in their own way. But I wouldn't do it again. If I was asked by a young writer about that, I'd say, "If you're okay with the brand it'll put on you, then go ahead. But if you have other ideas you're better off to skip it. Because once it's on you, it's just there and it's not coming off." I really had not been sophisticated enough to appreciate that.

The Ones You Do struck me, even though it is nominally the third and closer of the Shade trilogy, as a transitional book. Was that deliberate on your part?

Yeah, I think so. And I was under some encouragement to write another one or two after that and I didn't want to. That book: To me, yeah, okay, it has a number of the elements of crime fiction. But the core of it really isn't. That's my favorite of those books and I don't know that it's the public's or critics' favorite.

It'd be mine. It seems more of a piece with your later work in many ways.

Yeah. It's not anything to do with opposition to crime fiction. I remember a long, long time ago when I was reading Higgins the first time around. It was the quotidian details of these gangsters' lives that opened up a new door for me. Eddie Coyle's got to take out the garbage before he can go sell those hot pistols. There's tuna in the fridge 'cause the wife's working nightshift at the hospital, or whatever it was. It took a long time for that to bleed into my writing I suppose, but I remember reading that and thinking, "The human-scale of these criminals' lives is what I'm attracted to."

There's a lot of pool in your works, and none more so than _The Ones You Do_. You play much yourself?

I used to shoot a lot, but I haven't in recent years. This is the first place I've lived where I didn't have access to a table I liked. Iowa was kind of a hotbed of pool, and so was Lawrence.

Woe To Live On **was retitled for release to capitalize on the film adaptation and took the movie's title of** *Ride with the Devil***. Titles are such hard-fought-for things at times …**

Yes. They *are* …

Were you bothered by the switch in title?

I had no say.

The book has kind of almost assumed the title of the film, now.

That's the big thing. When they're listing it inside, I always say, "No, go ahead and put my title." Then they say, "Retitled *Ride with the Devil*" in parentheses. No, I didn't have anything to do with that. And I knew when you sold the rights—I did by then know enough to know—you have to stand out of the way.

I think Ellroy's line is: "My book, your movie."

Right.

Although in this case, they kind of came around and put a placard on your book.

Right. But that was a good experience and I knew they were going to have to do some things.

While we're on the subject of film and Westerns, let's touch on HBO's *Deadwood***. It seems to me to be doing some of the things with language and dialogue and setting that you did first in** *Woe to Live On***. Are you a viewer?**

I haven't seen every episode. I have seen a number. And I've been getting a lot of encouragement to start over from the beginning.

There have been intimations of something to come eventually from you, at least in the vein of *Woe to Live On***. That still a prospect in your mind?**

Yeah, something loosely related to it I hope to get to. It's not ready yet, but it's related to the Civil War in this area. I've been beating it around for a long time.

Tomato Red opens with this great long sentence/paragraph that reminds me of a similar, uncharacteristically long sentence penned by Ernest Hemingway in The Green Hills of Africa about the Gulf Stream.

Hah. Interesting.

You've remarked that "Hemingway probably laid the prose foundation for everything I try."

Probably.

Can you elaborate on that?

Well, when I was learnin' to write, I just fell under the sway of Hemingway. And I wasn't in my teens, either. I was probably like twenty-two or twenty-three before I really got involved with Hemingway. The myth of Hemingway and the priestliness of his dedication to being a writer, it was just the perfect hook to suck me in. I just love his sentences when he's good. I love the look of his pages. I was talking to an interviewer once and I said, "Sometimes, I don't read it: I just take those old Scribners out and just look at the type on the page and I get a pleasant sensation." [*Laughing*] And the person knew exactly what I meant.

It's funny: his name seldom comes up in reviews or anything, which I find interesting, whereas Faulkner does a lot. And I love Faulkner, but I'm more short-sentenced and direct, probably.

See, I would put you more with Hemingway. I suspect the Faulkner thing would be the regional aspect and the fact you have these kind of recurring characters and overlap.

Probably. I even read most of Hemingway's posthumous stuff with some pleasure.

I've waded through a good deal of it myself.

I hate it when a dead guy out-publishes me!

I'm not sure it's doing Hem a lot of favors in the long run, though.

No, it *isn't*. There are big stretches of *Islands in the Stream* that can stand up and so forth, and so on. But if someone happens to grab one of these and it's their introduction to Hemingway …

That's the thing—they may never get to the stuff that was great.

They may never try book two.

Apart from these great titles of yours, I've also been struck by the range of sources for your chosen epigraphs: Joe Frazier, Minnesota Fats, Marilyn Monroe, Carl Perkins, Oil Can Boyd, Dutch Schultz, to name a few. Do you search for these to match or evoke a novel's theme, or do you keep a book of favored quotes, as some authors do?

I scribble 'em down when I stumble across one. I remember reading Minnesota Fats' autobiography and I'd see things pop up and I'd realize, "He said that better than plenty of professors."

I've never seen much put out there regarding your work habits, and perhaps that is purposeful on your part. I'm wondering if you're a morning or an evening writer?

It's evolved over the years. When we lived in California I didn't start writing until two or three in the morning. Here, it's the opposite. I get up and go early. At one time, it had to always be the afternoon. So it's kind of flickered all over.

Do you write longhand or ... ?

I always have, but I have become comfortable now with the keyboard on the computer. I find I'm doing over half of it directly there, then more or less sketching things longhand. I still like being able to go off and sit somewhere with a notepad. But I'm no longer seeing the drawback to the keyboard.

Is there a typical proportion of the written to the kept?

Now, *Winter's Bone*, there's not much that got wasted there. When it's happening right and feels right, I'm usually pretty close on the first draft, actually. And then I read everything from the beginning again, which is an old Hemingway trick that I learned early. I prune it as I read from the beginning. And, even when I get to a couple of hundred pages or something, I still will read almost every day from the beginning. So I'm really rewriting a little bit.

Kind of a constant state of revision that keeps everything of a piece?

Yes.

Do you have a sense if any of your neighbors read your work?

Not most of them. I think a lot of people have learned what I do, for a living, but I don't run into a lot of people who have read them, nor do I want them to feel required to give me their capsule reviews if they have read them.

It would be difficult if Katie wasn't a writer, too. We can really have intense literary conversations and open that part of ourselves up and deal with it. If it wasn't for that, it would probably be too difficult here.

Speaking of Hemingway, I always wondered if that was something that kind of messed him up, because the great work came in Paris and when he was moving among all those writers, and then he went to Cuba, and became his own island, so to speak ...

Yeah, he may be someone who profited from that. I've lived at different times in situations where there were lots of writers around, and I'm never sure which is more beneficial. Utter isolation, eventually, will get you. But other writers will get you, too. You feel like you have to be up on the new thing of the minute instead of hearing your own thing. It depends on who you are. I know plenty of writers who couldn't stand the idea of isolation.

Anything you'd like to get out there?

It's funny: I saw you interviewed Alistair MacLeod, you know. One of the things I think about here all the time, and actually getting it from his sensibility there, with his background, was this linkage of the people here with Celts and other British Isle citizens and how closely related it is.

I was interviewed by the *Glasgow Herald* not long ago, and I was saying I was reading all this George McKay Brown, WS Graham. You realize the kind of blood connection between different parts of the world. I was feeling that in this one [*Winter's Bone*] pretty strongly, and I don't know if I used to feel that, or not.

Have you read much MacLeod? I mean, there's not a lot out there to read—he's got the big story collection and the novel ...

I've read just about all I reckon. I love the short stories especially. Very strong. And you know, he's a guy who grew in the dark, kind of.

He's an interesting guy in that he really didn't have to cow-tow to any of the rules, in a way. He's never even had an agent. But he's had the advantage of writing from a teaching position, and that sort of subsidized the writing for a long time.

Yeah, I often wonder if that is a plus or minus. In his case it was because he didn't have to have any commercial concerns, but I always wonder about that one, too.

ALISTAIR MACLEOD

The Tuning of Perfection

(June 25, 2001)

Alistair MacLeod was born in 1936 in Saskatchewan. He was raised "by a large extended family" in Cape Breton, Nova Scotia which is the setting for most of his short fiction, as well as his acclaimed novel, *No Great Mischief*, which earned him the IMPAC Award. The novel was also awarded Ontario's Trillium Prize.

MacLeod's short stories began appearing in small magazines in 1968. The first of these was "The Boat," and it effectively staked out the writer's territory: a story written in the first person and focused on a family of dislocated Scots living in Cape Breton. The tale turns, as MacLeod has said, on "choice."

His first collection of short stories, *The Lost Salt Gift of Blood*, appeared in 1976 to wide acclaim.

In 1986, *As Birds Bring Forth the Sun*, appeared.

The stories in those two volumes, and two more recent long and uncollected stories, were gathered in a single volume and published in 2000 under the title *Island*.

MacLeod's short fiction earned him a selection as one of the Modern Library's two hundred greatest writers in English since 1950.

The sixty-five-year-old author retired from teaching at the University of Windsor in 2001. MacLeod taught creative writing and nineteenth-century British literature.

In the summer of 2001, MacLeod's oeuvre stood at sixteen short stories and one novel.

Each of his works is written painstakingly to plan, one sentence at a time, with little, if any, revision.

If his writing habits have in any way contributed to a reduced body of work, they are worth it: MacLeod's stories are individual triumphs. It is as if Hemingway's short stories gathered in *Men Without Women* were all of the caliber of "The Killers" and "Hills Like White Elephants," with no "To-Day is Friday" or "Banal Story."

For MacLeod it seems, perfection precludes prolificacy.

Yet, the slow, methodical manner in which MacLeod writes is, perhaps, too often dwelt upon.

A woman at a reading I attended the evening I spoke with MacLeod asked him if his short stories and novel were written "concomitantly." MacLeod explained that many decades separated the first of his short stories and his novel.

"Then," the woman said, "when you wrote the novel you were a much older man?"

"Yes," MacLeod said, shrugging slightly. Then he smiled. "But my heart was the same."

Her question, in a sense, was understandable. MacLeod's reply, too, was apt:

The thing that strikes one upon reading the short stories and the novel is the consistency of voice, subject matter and style. Someone unfamiliar with MacLeod's oeuvre, presented with his short stories bound out of publication sequence, would be hard pressed to distinguish between the author's "juvenilia" (a treacherous term to apply to the work of an author whose first short story was published when he was thirty years old) and his "mature" work.

June 2001 found Alistair MacLeod touring in support of the paperback release of *No Great Mischief* (Vintage Books). The book was steadily climbing the bestseller lists in several major American cities. I interviewed Alistair MacLeod on the evening of June 25, 2001 at Shaman Drum Bookshop in Ann Arbor, Michigan.

• • • • •

A couple of weeks ago, by my reckoning, you were in Dublin to accept the IMPAC Literary Award.

A week ago, Saturday.

Are you coping with the magnitude of that?

[*Laughing*] I'm trying to. It's nice to be so recognized. Sure, it's very nice.

You met the Irish President, and the Lord Mayor of Dublin in the Eighteenth Century Hall. One writer present wrote, "Standing at the podium beneath the gold-leaf dome, surrounded by stone pillars and marble floors, the author seemed a little awed." Can you share some of the things you were feeling that day?

[*Smiling*] Well, I don't generally hang out in Dublin Castle. It was very splendid and of course they were very nice to me. They described me, I think, in that press release you quoted, as "a diminutive author." I don't think of myself as tremendously diminutive. Maybe we lose weight when we go to Ireland. Maybe, with those big, big buildings, we seem diminutive. I think maybe we all seem diminutive in Ireland.

You are not diminutive.

Well … It was very, very nice. It's nice to be recognized in that way. So long as you write a novel every sixty years, by the time I do my next I'll be 120. Best to take advantage of these things when they come along. One of the nice things about this award, I think, is that the judges are from all over the world—from Nigeria, from Guiana, from Ireland and the chairperson is from the United States. So you sort of feel it's a truly international award, not the voice of one country or of one continent.

You obviously couldn't have foreseen the scope of the acceptance.

No, no. When I was sitting down writing I wasn't saying, "I'll bet this will win me the IMPAC Award." I hoped that it would be good.

I generally write short stories. One of the things that I like about short stories—one of the things that I try to achieve—is a kind of intensity. I like them to be intense. In track and field terms, I think of them as a 100-yard dash. I thought of the novel as a marathon. I obviously couldn't run as hard as I could all the time … as hard as I wished to. But I think the novel did sustain the intensity pretty well, so I'm quite pleased with that. It's been tremendously well received. It's been bought by the Germans, and by the Spanish and the Italians and by the Scandinavians and by the Israelis and by the Japanese. Israel and Japan are kind of a long way from Cape Breton. I'm pleased the novel is able to, I guess the term you would use is "travel." Because sometimes you say, "Well, this would just appeal to people in Canada, or this would just appeal to Scotsmen and Swedes because they're used to lots of snow and ice in the winter," and so on. But its appeal has been much greater. Writing is a communicative act. Maybe some people just write under their beds and read their stories to themselves. But I think you're kind of sending out letters to the world, and it's nice when someone out there receives your offerings.

You famously worked as a miner and mining is subject matter in some of your short stories, and, of course, the novel. It was recently announced the Canadian government would close Cape Breton's last working coal mine. Did that news stir any feelings?

I worked in the mines most of the time I was going to university. I worked pretty nearly every summer until I was finished, virtually. It's unfortunate, because there are a lot of people who are very dependent on mining for life. It's hard work, but a lot of people enjoy it. I don't know if I'd say "enjoy" it, but a lot of people are used to it. When I worked in the mines, I never hated it. A lot of people say, "How could you bear that?" Well, all kinds of people "bear that." If there were, say, fifteen mines to open tomorrow in Cape Breton, there would be hordes of people applying for the jobs—going back there to work. I certainly don't mean that in any condescending way.

You taught nineteenth-century British literature. Would you say your writing derives more from that tradition, or perhaps that of the twentieth century?

I don't know. I think nineteenth-century British literature was great literature. But I think the literature of that time—people like Charles Dickens, and Thomas Hardy and the Brontes … and Mary Shelly's *Frankenstein*, which everybody likes—I think it was interesting because a lot of it was kind of literature of ideas. It was simultaneously kind of entertaining because it was pre-radio and pre-television. Dickens was making some very strong social statements about this and that, but he was also this kind of great suspense writer. I think when you teach that kind of literature it probably rubs off on you in some way. It's always hard to know how a writer *gets to be* how a writer *is*. I think you look inside yourself and find all kinds of things and you don't know just where they came from. You don't write something and say, "Boy, this is just like Dickens." But I think when you teach Dickens, or you teach Thomas Hardy, you're talking about literature and if you don't learn how to do it, you learn how *not* to do it.

You've commented that you were drawn to write a novel because you found your short fiction becoming not quite so short. Has the novel sated that for you? Is there another novel?

No. Not today, anyway. The novel went on too long in the sense that I was working at it for over ten years. I wasn't working on it eight hours a day, but I was working on it summers and then I would set it aside and it would languish there for a year and I would pick it up again. When you're writing over that length of time, it becomes kind of tedious. You're just glad to get it done before you die.

From the perspective of a literary instructor, and a well-respected author, is there an advantage, or even a necessity, for a fledging writer to move through writing short fiction before attempting a novel?

I don't think so, no. They're different forms. Some writers do more than one thing and some writers don't. I don't think length or shortness is necessarily an apprenticeship. There *is* a tendency to think that novels sell better. It's more so in the United States. Or at least it was. I don't think that's so much the case now, after Carver and the others who have become very, very adept at the short stories. I think if you can do anything well you should be sort of graceful about it.

Is there a passage or narrative thread in your novel that you take particular pleasure in from the standpoint of composition or, if you prefer, from the standpoint of storytelling?

No. I like it all. It's of a piece. I read certain sections here or there.

Are there some sections you return to more than others?

Yes ...

But you won't identify them?

[*Smiling*] *No ...*

What would you assess to be your greatest strength as a writer?

[*Long pause*] When I wrote this novel I wanted to try to write a novel in which I wouldn't have any villains, so there is nobody in this novel who is evil. I think it is too easy sometimes to build up a strawman and kind of knock him down.

As in Dickens, for instance.

Yeah. There are certainly evil people there. I like to think that everyone in my novel is trying to do his or her best.

Your writing process has become rather famously discussed. You write on the right side of a notebook and record impressions, or notes, or sketches on the left side that may or may not find their way into the story. What was startling to me, though, is that you have said you never write "drafts" in the plural sense. You're said to write one sentence at a time until the work is finished and never go back for significant rewriting or revision—is that accurate?

Yes. I think that's why I'm so slow. Before I begin I really know what I'm going to do. When I'm halfway through, I write the end. I have a plan. Some people think it is strange. But I think almost everybody who does anything has a plan. You don't have to be dictated by the plan forever. You can change it halfway through if it doesn't work. But the last lines and the last paragraphs I have. In the novel and in the short stories, I have an idea that, "This is the last thing I'm going to say to the reader and this is going to be it." And I work toward that destination. I write in longhand and I am interested in sound, so I read it aloud as I write.

It's funny you should mention that. You're one of those rare writers whom I find myself reading aloud as I go along—you want to hear those words spoken.

That's very nice. I'm one of those writers who believes storytelling is older than literacy and I think of myself as a storyteller. People could tell their stories long before they could read or write. It's a kind of a conceit, but I like to believe that I am telling a story. This is why I use the first person quite a lot. I use the first person so long as the persona that I want to adopt can know all of the things that I want to talk about. Sometimes, as in a short story called "The Tuning of Perfection," or in another called "Island," about the isolated lighthouse keeper—in those stories, there are things going on around those people that they would never know of. Because they are in those contexts—in situations where they don't understand or know things that are about to change their lives—I have to get the information out some other way, so I used the third person there. But I prefer the first-person because there is that sense that, "I'm going to tell a story about what happened to *me*."

The good news about that—well, I think it is good news—is a lot of people think that I am an autobiographical or a confessional writer. [*Smiling*] But, I'm *not* an orthodontist you know. But sometimes when it works that way, where people believe I am writing about myself, I think of it as a triumph of technique. I *want* you to think that it is true. If you go to a play, you don't want sit there and say, "Well, that's Mary Smith playing Lady MacBeth." You want that suspension of disbelief.

Your discussion of the level of detail and planning in a sense short-circuits one of my questions.

Oh no …

But I'll ask anyway: Some writers speak of being surprised by a character, or a turn of events in their novels or stories. That a character suddenly takes them off in an unexpected direction. I don't sense that has ever happened to you …

No. I wouldn't let them do it. I'm too old-fashioned a Scotsman for that: "You do what I tell you or I'll kill you on page twelve.

I'll drown you." I like to be in control. Writers are different. I know lots of writers who say, "Well, I thought I was writing about the grandmother, but then I learned it was a story about the granddaughter." I begin all my work with an idea. When I began *No Great Mischief*, I said, "What I'm going to do is try to talk about loyalty and belief as my ideas." In the short story, "Vision," I was going to write a story about sight and blindness. In "The Boat," I was going to write about choice. In the short story "In the Fall," I was going to write about the tension of when we want something to happen very much emotionally but it can't happen: Wishing your grandmother would become young again, or she would recognize you—that her Alzheimer's would go away. I want this, but in real life it can't happen. I start with the idea and then fit or invent people that will flesh out the idea. That's the way I write. I plan. You can't just drive nails in a board and say, "Well, it will come out as something." I don't think so. Better take out your tape measure and make a plan.

Your first short story was published when you were about thirty. One assumes most of your creative writing students are somewhat younger than that. Were you attempting fiction writing at the age of most of your students?

I was always interested in literature and writing. I think maybe I was like somebody who could sing, or who had athletic ability, but I never sang, or played professionally. Then, when I saw I could catch the ball rather well, I thought, *hmm*, maybe I should take this catching the ball more seriously. I went to Notre Dame for the Ph.D., and one of the things you do when you study for the Ph.D. is analyze other writers. In the midst of forever analyzing James Joyce's *Dubliners,* I began to think that maybe I could write my own. Then I wrote the first published story. The other thing is that because I was away from my home landscape, I thought about it more. I don't know if absence makes the heart grow fonder, but it makes the mind more thoughtful. I was away from my own landscape and looking at literature for a long time, and it combined to make me take it seriously when I was twenty-seven in a way that maybe I didn't take it seriously when I was twenty-one.

Is there MacLeod juvenilia hidden somewhere?

Maybe. And it will remain hidden.

A lot of academics, particularly, are mourning the rise of the word processor and personal computer because it means you start losing drafts—for those who write drafts. Have you saved your notes and working materials and so forth?

Oh yes.

That leads to my next question. After making a career of teaching other people's writings, how does it feel to be on the receiving end? I assume there are already or soon will be universities teaching the novel and the short stories? I assume the stories are already anthologized in college texts?

Yes, they have been.

Are you okay with that?

Oh sure, sure. I expect the phone calls late at night from former students saying, "Well, the paper is due tomorrow and I am wondering what you meant when you wrote ..."

I was wondering more if fellow instructors call asking what you meant ...

Well, this is interesting, now, because there is this great rise in book clubs, and Vintage has put out a study guide for the novel and it is quite excellent. When I was reading the first draft of the study guide I made some little corrections, but I was reading it and I thought this was written by somebody who was really around literature. Sometimes people just come and say, "Well, I like the old man." But other people want pegs to hang their clothes on and the guide gives them good pointers.

You're now officially retired from teaching?

I am officially retired, but I still have my office at Windsor and I still have some graduate students that I work with. I still have my key to the photocopy machine.

Prior to retirement you mused about whether the cessation of the teaching career would result in increased literary output. Has it?

I go to Cape Breton next week, and I'm thinking about some things.

The phrase that gets repeated over and over on the dust jackets to describe you is "a writer's writer." Are you flattered by that term?

Sure. Sure.

What do you take that term to mean?

I've been around quite a long time, doing my little precious short stories, so I think members of the writing community in Canada were glad that I had finally done this novel. Everyone has been very supportive. Margaret Atwood sent me flowers. I know most of these people because I have been anthologized with them and so on. It's nice to receive all of this and in a non-competitive way. I have never had an agent. So when I got the big write-up in the *New York Times,* I had people saying, "You don't have an agent—how'd you get in the *New York Times?*" But I think for young writers, particularly, there is this feeling that you'll never get anywhere unless you're sleeping with the father of the editor, or that kind of feeling that talent is not quite enough and that you have to have some backroom, high-powered agent or something. I think when this happens, it leaves people thinking, "Well, maybe you don't have to do these kind of things at all. Maybe you just have to write good stories."

I was wondering about the choice of title *Island* for your new collection of short stories. I was wondering if that was your title, and if it is, if that is a reference to Cape Breton itself, or to the short story of the same name and why you would have seized on that story particularly to name the volume after?

It was the publisher's idea. I think the publisher wanted to name it after one of the two or three stories that weren't in the other collections. See, when I brought out the first book, *The Lost Salt Gift of Blood*, the publisher didn't want that title because he thought it was awkward, and it is kind of awkward. I would encounter people who would say, "Yeah, I read your book, *Bloody Old Salt* or *Lost Blood Salt*," or whatever. Publishers are interested in something shorter. They believe people can't remember titles and they're embarrassed to say they don't know the titles. I'm glad I did say *Lost Salt Gift of Blood*, rather than *The Boat*, or something and it sold rather well. Then, when the second book came out, *As Birds Bring Forth the Sun,* the publisher said, "Now I suppose you'll want this title?" and I said, "Yes." When they brought out *Island* maybe they decided we'll just give him this one word title and stop him from these long titles.

You seem to have been spared from some of the loonier aspects of the publishing business.

Yes.

You're very lightly edited, if at all?

Very lightly. I think it is because I am pokey. In the British editions there were a few things they wanted to change that I didn't change. Things that have to do with, you know, terminology. Like what we would call a "newspaper clipping" they would call a "cutting." They would want to change that and I would say *no*. Rightly or wrong, the book comes from North America and nobody would use "cutting" over here anymore. Generally, though, there is not much editing. When it is there, it is a little mistake or some error that I made here or there. The last few pages of the novel, I was writing long hand and they were setting the book from that.

I was going to spare you that question, but I had read that at some point the publisher or editor had driven some distance to pick up all of your materials because he was just so frustrated with the wait.

It was great he did, because I would just have plodded along. It was just a sense of, "Give it to us, damn it. Get it over with."

The language runs throughout the novel, so I take it that you're fluent in Gaelic?

No.

No?

No.

Good trick.

My wife and I are both from the same community and she is fluent. It's just because they were unilingually speaking in her house longer than in mine. There's a joke they used to have: My grandfather would say, "Can you speak Gaelic?" and people like me, of my generation, would say, "I can understand it, but I can't speak it." And my grandfather would say, "Ah, you're just like the dog," because they would speak to the dog in Gaelic and it would sit up or lay down, but it would never answer back.

You obviously know a great deal about Scottish history. There are some who would find a certain irony in a "MacLeod" writing such an elegiac novel about "Clan Donald." The MacLeods and the MacDonalds were not exactly getting on in certain parts of the Highlands.

No they weren't. Why I chose MacDonald was that they were the big, big Clan. MacDonalds are everywhere. I was thinking of all of that Clan's history. I would think of MacDonalds as the Celtics or Rangers football team of their time. Or the New York Yankees of their time. They were the big team and they really affected history, because if they would go, or they wouldn't go, or would support you or not support you, it would change things. They were great to have on your side. And they were not so great to have as your enemy because there were so many of them. Then all of that stuff with Glencoe and Culloden. They were *there.* They were there in a way that MacInnes wouldn't be. They were there in Cape Breton. One of my great-grandmothers was a MacDonald. One of my great-great-grandmothers was a MacDonald. My great-great-great-grandfather was a man named John MacDonald, so we are all MacDonalds.

Have you read any of John Prebble's Scottish history books?

Yeah. Tremendous. He just recently died.

Did he? I didn't know.

Yes, about six months ago. He was tremendous. He wrote the *Glencoe* book, and the Tay Bridge book and *Culloden.*

I was thinking of Prebble's description of Clan Donald in *Glencoe*: he described them as a people with long memories and short tempers.

Glencoe is an interesting story because those MacDonalds thought they would go on forever because they were up in their mountain fastness. The man who led them was a great big man with red hair, and with being big and strong and having that kind of power there was kind of arrogance. That's the way the Zulus were, until they encountered machine guns. One of the things they were always saying about the MacDonalds of Glencoe is that we will have to teach them a lesson. So he didn't get his paper there in the right time and he ran into a system that was bigger than he was. It's like Calum [in *No Great Mischief*]: a big, strong, self-reliant man who can solve anything, but when you get involved in a law case and say I don't need a lawyer, it's a mistake. It's the old saying of when a lawyer has himself as a client, he is a fool. Calum had been looking after himself since he was sixteen and he got in over his head. I was in England and I saw the Masai on the BBC and they were driving their cows through the middle of a city to make a statement. They aren't going to last either. They aren't going to allow cows in downtown Nairobi. But the Masai think, "We were here first." But as I say in the novel, "Something will be done with them. Soon I hope." It's the same thing they said about MacDonald of Glencoe and those who supported the Stuarts at Culloden.

And, of course, it all set the stage for the Highland Clearances.

It's all still kind of cloudy, although Prebble is one of the best and I am glad you've read him because a lot of things he talks about in his books is kind of new, because, well, because …

Because history is written by the winners?

It's always written by the winners. And of course the Irish and the Scottish were all speaking in Gaelic, which the British thought was gibberish: "This is not the language of the conquerors." When they don't talk your language it is easier to kill them; to demonize them.

To marginalize them.

Yes, like the American Indians. One of the things I was trying to do in the novel with the serious grandfather, given the circumstances of his birth, because he is illegitimate or whatever you want to call it, or born out of wedlock—not a good situation to be in at that time. I see those young people who lose their parents through the ice, they are always looking at pictures and trying to understand what their parents looked like. But for the grandfather, he has no picture of his father and he is always looking at himself in the mirror and trying to work backwards, trying to find his father in his own face. I think of him as asking the question of "Where did I come from?" and "How did I get to be the way I am?" and he can't find that out. By the time we get him he is in his seventies and so as a result of him asking those questions, he kind of goes out and says, "Where did we all come from?" and "How did we all get to be the way we are?" He's always asking those questions.

To the end.

Yes, to the end. But the cheery grandfather says, "Why care about all that? I just like it when the MacDonalds win." But the other grandfather says, "No, you must look at the other side, too."

The tale of the herring king …

Yes. I love the herring king. Now, the herring king—this guy, my editor, who is a Scotsman, wrote me about the herring king. I had done all of this research and the herring king is in Prebble's book, but this guy wrote back and said, "I don't think the people of Glencoe ever saw a herring and we should leave this out." Oh, I was so annoyed, so I just sent a blizzard of photocopies of herring everywhere. I wanted my herring king. I wanted it to work. When I was over there in Dublin the editor was there. The book is doing very well in Ireland and I said, "It's all because of my herring king." My ambiguous king.

Professor MacLeod, thank you for your time.

Thank you. It's always a pleasure to meet a fellow Scotsman. "My hope is constant in thee, Clan Donald."

PART III

Dark History

ANDREW VACHSS

Two Trains Running

(July 7, 2005)

In his remarkable 2005 novel, Andrew Vachss presents two weeks in the life of a small mill town that has become a kind of Midwest vice capital.

Many criminal and conflicting forces are at work in Locke City in late September, 1959. And racial tensions are running high.

Into this volatile mix strides Walker Dett, a mysterious and deadly stranger who begins to shape events toward some dark but not explicitly defined end.

What emerges is propulsive crime novel informed by a compelling undertow—a kind of secret history of American crime and racial strife with Locke City, as metaphor for twentieth-century America.

Two Trains Running was a marked departure for Vachss: a stepping away from his ongoing Burke series and a rare foray into a stylized form of third-person narration.

In *Two Trains Running*, Vachss employs an unusual narrative device in which all activities and conversations are observed. There are no chapter breaks and each vignette is headed with a stamped imprint of the date and time denoting when the depicted events are occurring. The effect is to cast the reader in the role of a kind of surveillance officer.

His ongoing series of novels is centered around "Burke," a character whom Vachss described in a recent introduction to an omnibus of books gathered from that long-running series as, "a member of that vast tribe I call 'The Children of the Secret' (formerly abused children, now grown). Burke is also an ex-convict, a hijacker, a thief, a gunrunner, a scam artist. And, some would say, a killer."

Burke is bad by design: "I wanted to show people what Hell really looked like," Vachss wrote, "and I didn't think an angel would make the best guide."

Over the course of his career, Vachss has acquired a reputation for eerie prescience … a kind of stature as a Jules Verne of the life-threatening.

Many, many years before the rise of the Internet, he wrote of predatory pedophiles exchanging pornographic materials via modems. Vachss was unjustly pilloried by many critics at the time for engaging in some form of perceived dark fantasy.

Andrew Vachss has no children of his own, but his endeavors in the fields of law, activism and the writing of fiction have long been focused on furthering the cause of children's rights.

Vachss is particularly pleased by the formation of the National Association to Protect Children. The organization Web site can be found at http://www.protect.org/.

Vachss own Web site, "The Zero"—which includes many other resources related to child protection issues—can be found at http://www.vachss.com/.

In the course of this interview, Andrew Vachss references a then-highly publicized Idaho kidnapping case in which a family was murdered and two young children taken—a brother and a sister.

The kidnapper was eventually captured after the missing girl was recognized by eyewitnesses. Her brother, however, was found to have been murdered by their abductor.

• • • • •

You've indicated that *Two Trains Running* has been something you've been working on for some time. How many years have you invested in this novel?

The period of time is probably not less than a decade, actually, though clearly not full time. What took so long was not writing it, but figuring out a way to present the material that I had put together. The eventual decision to write a book without any exposition and any introspection—just to provide a series of surveillance opportunities in a continuous track over a two week period—that's really what took so long. In other words, I wrestled much more with structure than I did with content.

Was it always your plan to use this small-town prism for this larger panorama?

Yeah. I think that town is not just a microcosm, it's a petri dish, and everything that you see there, you see elsewhere.

Walker Dett tells Tussy he's locked into his "job" for seven years. He says, in October 1959, that he has "about four years" to go. Which would set his "retirement" around November 1963 ... right around Dallas and JFK.

Very good.

I wondered if there was some intended significance to that date for his expiration, or am I reading too much in to it?

No, you're right. But I will tell you that not many have caught it.

I got my copy of *Two Trains* fairly late in terms of reading it before we were scheduled to speak. I felt like I was charging through the novel faster than I wanted to go. It's also a book that when you finish it, you feel, "Okay, now I have to go back through it and see how some of these pieces were made to come together." Do you have a problem with the notion that a reader might have to go back into the story again to study some aspects?

No. Actually, that's my wish. It's two books: It's a kind of fast-moving book that you can just pick up and read as a straight-forward crime novel. But this book is really all about its undercurrent. If I had my wish, it would be that everybody read it twice.

Do you have any plans to return to these characters or to extend this story through Camelot?

I do not. I don't. One of the frustrations that people have expressed with this book—although I admit I have no sympathy for this frustration—is that it doesn't end. It's unresolved. I tried to write something in the third person without omniscience so that it is all your point of view, and your decisions and your conclusions. If I were to extend it—and I can't believe how many people wrote to the Web site, "When's the sequel coming?"—if I were to do that, then I would be answering all those questions myself, which is what I worked very hard to avoid doing.

You use date/time imprints in lieu of chapters and page breaks and for transitions. I guess based on some things you've already said, the intended sense is that the reader is the one conducting surveillance on the characters?

Yep, or who has access to surveillance.

Obviously *you* get access to previews of reviews and so forth, but you've been on the road now for about three weeks. So the readers are getting to weigh in and they probably have much more intelligent things to say—

No. Look: it varies about as radically as people do. I would be lying if I didn't acknowledge that some percentage of every single audience I've been in front of just starts yelling, "When's the next Burke coming out?" Some people have even expressed *anger* at the book because it makes them do too much work.

Really?

Yeah. And then other people have said all the wonderfully complimentary things that you'd like to hear.

Any reactions from readers that have surprised you regarding your treatment of JFK and his election by manipulation?

Well, sure. Some of the things have surprised me … when people say, "Look, you're noted for predicting things because I read about modem trafficking kiddy porn from you way before I read it in newspapers," and *blah blah blah*, "But in this book, since you're going backwards, why do you make stuff up?" And I said, "Well, what have I made up specifically that upsets you?" They said, "Well, the idea that the federal government let people go untreated with syphilis as an experiment."

Well, that's historical fact ...

Right: "I *didn't* make that up, okay?" So reactions like that have surprised me, yeah.

The stuff with Capone and syphilis is extrapolation ... ?

Only a little bit of it is a speculative bridge. The rest of it is indisputable fact.

You've elsewhere stated that this book requires an "investment" and I take that to mean on the part of a reader. Are you getting the sense that most are making that investment?

I think "most" would be dishonest for me to say. I think a significant percentage, but the majority ... Well, let me make it simple. There is an audio book, as well. So you'd say to yourself, "How the hell could you do an audio book of this book abridged?" Because they are all abridged. The way they did it was they took out all the sub-plotting. All of it. And there's people who have heard the audio book who just plain love it.

Yeah, those drive me nuts. My wife works for the audio book industry —Recorded Books, where they do the whole thing, front to finish. Seems to me that's the only way to do it.

Well, that's for the visually-impaired and that's one of the ultimate public services.

Yeah. But these abridgements drive me nuts. In many cases, they really aren't the book anymore.

You know, I didn't mind it so much, except that it pointed out to me that all the hard work that I put in to the subtext—people could just as easily do without it. I will tell you that on this book I'm getting more comments about the writing than about the content, which is unusual for me.

What form is that taking?

It totally varies: "I don't understand why you did it this way," to "Oh my God, it's brilliant, because I've been studying"—for example—"exposition, and I didn't know you could write a book without it," that kind of thing. And, "I always love you because your style is so very lean, and when I saw a 470-page book I was convinced it would be the opposite, but, *no.*" So it really does vary. I've never had a universal reaction to anything I've written. Even the straight-up nonfiction that you'd think there might be —*no.*

You've said that you've always regarded yourself as more journalist than novelist. Given the fact that *Two Trains Running* is presented in a historical setting, would you perhaps change that "journalist" to "historian" to some extent?

No. What I was really doing in this book, the ultimate thing in this book, is that it is my ode to journalism. I really believe journalism is the most sacred form of democracy protection. I say "sacred" because heresy is being committed every day. To me, every journalist is on a pilgrimage searching for truth. The ones that go that route and do that are the ones that protect us all. If you take investigative journalism out of the mix, democracy really doesn't have a chance. Because I don't know where people would get the information on which to act. So this book is really about *that.* It wasn't so much me considering myself a historian or a journalist, or even, God forbid, a *novelist,* right? I was trying to say to people, "Journalism is *critical* to your lives—don't be taking it for granted and don't have low standards for it."

It's not in a great shape, currently.

I speak to a lot of audiences of young people and I ask them to name journalists and they name Stephen Glass and they name Jayson Blair —my *God.* Those are the ones they've heard of, you see.

They've got the book contracts.

Book contracts and movie deals. And also, journalists are way too much judged about how well they write as opposed to how well they report.

There *is* a certain triumph of form over content.

I don't like that either. So, in this book, if there is a hero, it's Jimmy Proctor. Granted, he's not a white knight or anything like that, but he dies for the truth and that is kind of the point.

A character in *Two Trains Running* says that America is "like this old horse that knows the way home but it's not in a hurry. We're going to get there, but boy, it's not a straight line." That more or less reflective of your own attitude?

I am optimistic because I've been at this for so long. I was around when my profession didn't exist. I was around when discussing child abuse—you know, people didn't do it. You wouldn't see the word "incest" in a newspaper. So, while I agree with you completely —it's hardly a straight line—we have progress. We have moved to a point where now it's kind of balanced on the head of a pin.

Print journalism to me is a special thing. There's no generic journalism. The fact that anybody with access to the Internet— which is virtually everybody—can be a journalist today, while encouraging on some level, is not on others. Because the critical standards for judging journalism—sourcing, authentication, fact-checking—really seem in decline.

There used to be desks for these tasks and there really aren't anymore.

Oh, I mean, I'm old enough, I can remember that. There have been a million profiles done around me. But I *used* to get calls from fact-checkers after the interview and I don't anymore. I've had people write entire stories about me that were clearly pulled off the Internet that are an amazing mixture of fact and fiction. And I don't think they're lying. I mean, they've got sources, but they've never validated their sources.

There is a terrible trust in the Internet in terms of material that is there ... there is some assigned weight of authority there that is often false.

Yep. I see kids in term papers citing it. I mean, literally citing the Internet. Just mind-boggling. You might as well cite graffiti observed on the corner.

Speaking of the Internet, a special Web site has been created for this novel that stands away from your official site. It includes a reader's guide/topics for discussion. Are these questions or discussion points that you prepared?

Okay, here's the truth: have you ever seen my own Web site?

Oh yes.

That's a monster. What the publisher said was, "We're not gonna let you put this book on your Web site. We know about the ridiculous amount of traffic you get, but it's going to get lost there. So you need a separate one." So the same team that designed what I'm calling my Web site, but actually belongs to The Collective that works on it, did *Two Trains Running*. The publisher's logo is on it, but except for the visual design, all the rest was done by the Zero Collective.

I wondered about the discussion topics though.

I had nothing to do with them. The Reader's Guide? Oh please, I had zero to do with it.

Were there any particular books you were swinging at with *Two Trains*? The one that's coming up a lot in the reviews is the Hammett book. Did you intentionally set out to take your own swing at *Red Harvest*?

Oh no. I don't know why, to be honest with you. I don't see the similarity; I truly don't. Not only is the era radically different, but the motivation of every single player is different. The stakes they are playing for are entirely different. I mean another thing that people have, I guess you would say "challenged" me on, is how could I make up this idea, this insane idea, that the FBI actually had assets riding in Klan death cars.

Well, you say, "Jeez, I didn't make that up." If you look at the fact that they've just disinterred Emmett Till and they've just prosecuted Edgar Ray Killin and they've got all these Civil Rights era murders now being prosecuted, the one thing they've got in common is that not a single one of them is based on new evidence. They're all opened FBI files.

Old files that I assume weren't redacted past the ability to be read.

I think they must *have been*, because I can't understand why … Well, I can understand a lot of things. I can understand the fact that the people who stopped federal anti-lynching legislation on state's rights grounds, all these years later, are the people who are saying "No medical marijuana" on federal right's grounds. The words are different but the rhetoric's exactly the damn same. I mean that's kind of the point: What I wrote was a kind of a microcosm, but if you just cranked it up fifty years, the same principles are in effect. People are playing for the same stakes in the same kinds of ways.

Do you retain fairly vivid memories of the late 1950s so that you could pretty much write this straight out?

That's a really good question. I think to some extent I did. The visuals. But I also had the opportunity to spend time in places like Steubenville [Ohio] and Covington [Kentucky] and Weirton and Harvey and Cal City as I was older. So I got to see what they really are because those towns didn't change. In other words, the difference between '59 and '65 in those towns was not measurable. So I got a lot of reinforcement there. But I was too young in 1959 to have that sort of political consciousness. So I can remember visuals and I can remember descriptions quite well, but not the other stuff, no.

I had wondered if you had to break out the old catalogues and look back at the clothes and the cars.

Actually, you know we have such a large group that there are people within the Collective who like to do all different kinds of things.

So you've got go-to people for certain things?

Oh yeah. Yeah. Really, really good people. Typically, I meet a person who writes crime novels—and that's rare because I'm not a member of any of the organizations or anything—they always complain about how gun nuts write them letters and criticize.

Because they put a silencer on a revolver, or something like that.

Yeah. I've never gotten a letter like that in my career. I just get, "Wow, that was right." The other thing, too, is I don't really favor research in the traditional way. I go to sources, so a lot of information I have there, whereas I don't remember it, I've got people who do.

The Capone story was one that was told to me.

Really?

Oh sure. As was the Dillinger story. Sure. I'm not saying they are true, but they were related to me by people who were in that life.

You brought up Steubenville, Ohio. Your career, early, was very tied to Ohio.

Sure. First of all, I went to school in Ohio. I first got married in Ohio. I lived in east Cleveland. Then, when I worked at the Public Health Service, I was all over Ohio.

You're going to be in Ohio for about three days for your book tour. Time allowing, are their places you would want to try and get back to?

Well, see, the thing is, last time I was in Cleveland, I said, "Let me go look at some places that I remember." Well, I didn't recognize the Flats. I kept staring at it.

When you were living in Cleveland they probably weren't much different than they were in the 1930s when Eliot Ness was safety director of Cleveland.

They were bad. You went there for a very limited number of purposes, none of which were shopping at Neiman Marcus. So that was great. I'd love to go into Steubenville again and stand on Water Street and look across the bridge to Weirton. I'd love to do that. I haven't had the chance to do that. Stuff's not the same in Cleveland anymore.

Cleveland is an amazing city. It's like the Underground Railroad turned into a river and flowed north, hit a rock, and the white guys went west and the black guys went east. And it just stayed like that. Stunningly segregated.

Cleveland doesn't get enough attention—not as a Blue's town, not as a sort of Delta-retreat town, not as a stop on the Underground Railroad. Not as a town with its own history of incredible racial violence. People think of Chicago, they think of

Detroit. They somehow don't think of Cleveland. Cleveland was a big player. I was there … I remember it. For that I don't need any history books.

Any thoughts about the current state of crime fiction? I ask you because many people manage to float a pretty good career for four or five years and then they just peter off or disappear.

Yeah, at least I've gone the distance. And I must admit, since I thought the first book was going to be my only chance, I would be a narcissistic liar if I pretended that I expected this. To still be standing after all this time and still have a demand for the books? Naw.

Well, you and Ellroy are about the only ones who came up in the early- to mid-1980s who are still up front there.

I remember it. I knew James real well when he was coming up. He actually got there before me—he was published well before I was.

He had those paperback originals.

Yeah. And he had writing under other names and stuff like that. He knows what I do, in fact. One time, he actually took a shot at working with one of the kids that I represented.

I can remember reading something about that somewhere.

I told him this kid was absolutely without a conscience. His life had been such that he was an ambulatory sociopath.

James wanted to take him on. I don't know what his motivation was—I didn't care. James wanted to try and work with him. And I give him full and proper respect: he did try. But nobody could have succeeded. I don't care: Dr. Phil would have blown his brains out.

I haven't had a conversation with James in probably a decade. Last time I spoke with him was when he coming to Knopf and kind of wanted me to fill him in. That was it.

Any desire to tackle third-person narration again in the near term?

You know what: *No*. Because it's not me, first of all. I desperately want to speak with my own voice. Hence, that's what I've done up to now. I had to do it this way. There's no way this book could have ever had a voice without having a point of view. If it had a point of view, it's not the book I wanted. I don't think so. If I do another nonfiction, full-length book of course, it would fit that criteria.

You've said you prefer to write short stories. Yet there is currently little or no market for short stories to speak of. Under what circumstances do you write them now?

Every six or seven years, Vintage brings out a collection of my short stories. If it wasn't for that, there'd be no point. I've sold them to every market you can think of: *Playboy, Esquire.* But it's not any way to make a damn living. It's not cost-effective in terms of the amount of effort you put into it and what you get back.

You know, I've never really written anything for myself. In other words, I really don't write things on spec. It's not my nature. I don't think of myself as a *writer* writer. And also, it's a time issue.

I ran across some articles from last month in which you commented about a recent murder/child kidnapping case in Idaho. You shared some thoughts about what may have happened and seemed to feel there was a chance the children might be found. Any thoughts at this point as it seems to be sorting itself out?

I don't think it's sorting itself out. I mean, I'm supposed to believe …

That one guy …

Well, not just that one guy tied up three people. Leave that part alone. But I'm also supposed to believe that he came to that city, was walking around one night … looked in a window. Saw this family and said, "*Hm.* Let me climb in that window, kill those people and take those kids." I'm very very curious as to whether there was any prior relationship with that family. And if there was don't bet that my original—by the way, they *asked* me for an alternate theory.

They specifically came to you—

Oh, and, what, you think I called up and—

No, no I didn't.

I get called up all the time. I was on, whatever the hell—CNN —last night about it. Typical seven-minute, they-want-you-to-answer-four-years-worth-of-questions thing. I wouldn't have done it except I was in Kansas City and I was bored. They said, after your event, come to here, so I did.

They asked me for an alternate theory, which is what I provided. Again it's reporting. What I did say was, you have to look at the fact that when you have people killed but the kids are not killed at the scene, somebody wanted the kids for something. Which is what I said. I don't feel that was wrong. But I'm not in any way convinced that this was a person who had no prior relationship with or knowledge of that situation. I just don't think he was randomly walking by and all those events occurred.

I have two young girls and live in a suburb spread over two counties. So I have two sheriff's department databases to check for registered sexual predators who may have settled close to us. At this moment, there are twenty-three registered sexual offenders in my area. Seventeen of them committed crimes against young girls. What do you think about these registered sex offenders' databases? Some have tried to close them down. What do you think? Are they of any real use?

They're a joke. They're a joke. For openers: You know about the National Child Protection Act of 1993? Well, it's very nice that [former President Bill] Clinton in his book gives me credit for writing that and all. The only problem is that it's never been funded. So, in other words, when you're checking your database, you're not checking a national database.

No, they're put up by individual county sheriff's departments.

So tell me how good it is? That's number one. Number two: Explain to me how with well over one hundred thousand registered sex offenders who have left—in other words, their addresses are no good—there is no money allocated to find them. And, when they are found, there's not political will to put them back in prison for the crime of absconding. So that's two reasons why the databases are nonsense. But here's the third one, and this is the one I put to you as the father of young girls: let's say there was no Internet, okay?

Right.

Under what circumstances would you ever entrust your daughters to a stranger, anyway?

True.

No—seriously?

I wouldn't.

So tell me how this database helped you?

That's my question. It really didn't. I mean, I know I have seventeen of these people living around me but it's not like I can do anything with the information unless I threatened them—said, "Get the hell out of my neighborhood," but then they go to someone else's.

Right, and then they would own your house. But it's *worse* than that. Because as far as I'm concerned, the public's really been chumped off with the idea that we're doing something about this. These laws exist rather than to have politicians say the truth, which is, "These people shouldn't be at large, period."

Sure. I go through, and at least three of the seventeen—they have these gradations of risk they're assigned—and three of them have been declared "sexual predators." Well how do you put that tag on someone and ever put them out in the general public?

I don't know.

The very name implies they are out stalking, hunting.

The name implies that treatment has had no impact on them. That they are as dangerous now as they ever were … probably *more*, because their time in prison has educated them to better techniques. They have more technology working for them than ever before—which is why, again, I'm very curious about this guy in Idaho. Funny: we haven't heard anything about his cell phone records, his computer. Doesn't that make you wonder?

It does particularly since my understanding is that he had his own Web site.

Oh yeah, yeah. Had his own Web site, so clearly he had his own computer. I don't want to get into a blame the victim thing, but it's critical to know if he had a prior relationship with those people. Because the only purpose of a database that I can absolutely imagine is if you were going to entrust your child. If you're not going to do that, the fact that a registered sex offender lives across the street, what would you do differently?

I mean, presumably, you already have steps in place to protect your house.

Yeah, I guess if they are literally across the street, then suddenly your kid never goes outside again.

Well, I know what I would do. And it's possible to be really subtle and explain to someone the disadvantages of living across the street from you. Especially when you have animals that you can bring with you as you make a visit. The only thing ethically wrong with that is, I can do that, but I'm just sending him to *your* neighborhood. So the fact that you know where people are —*presumably* know where people are—and you know that they're dangerous …

I asked a guy in the audience last night who was going on and on about this, I said, "You have a little boy?" He said, "Yeah." I said, "A guy just moves in down the street. You look him up on the Internet, and he's not a registered sex offender. Okay. So now he comes over and he says, 'You know, I teach kids martial arts in my basement. How about if I teach your six-year old?' You gonna say 'Okay?'" He goes, "No." I said, "Well then tell me what good it did you."

There's a danger to registries. The danger of all registries is a false sense of security. Because if you're going to follow the logic, what's going to happen my friend, is people are going to start saying, "Well, I looked him up on the Internet and he wasn't registered." This is like a seal of approval, now.

But if a guy is registered in Florida for raping babies, and he moves to Columbus, how does he get registered?

Presumably ...
Presumably what?

Presumably these files are forwarded by the agency in the place the rape was committed.
That's only if the agency knows where he went. What of the one hundred thousand or so who simply moved? There are two steps: There has to be a federal database. And the specific crime of moving or failing to maintain registration has to have specific, incarcerative penalties. And money has to be allocated for a squad to track down absconders.

What I've said, over and over again, is if a guy who raped a dozen babies moves without notifying the authorities, he will be pursued with far less zeal than a guy who fails to show up having posted a thousand dollar bond, because the *bondsman* will go after *him*.

So, before you can ask me if the database is any good, you have to show me a real one. If you're asking me what the current ones do, I think they're dangerous because they give you a false sense of security.

What's the most hopeful thing on the horizon socially or legally you see in terms of protecting children or in some way curtailing exploitation of children? Is there anything?
Yes. "Protect.org." It's something I've called for for a million years and a zillion speeches and a thousand articles, which is essentially an NRA for child protection. It's a straight-up political action committee. It's not a Christian Children's Fund; it's not a Boy's Club. It doesn't provide services. It directly advocates for child-protective issues. It just won a major battle in California, closing the incest loophole.

It's a straight-up membership organization. It costs you dinner and movie—thirty-five dollars and you're a member. It's totally transparent. You can see every single person associated with it. You can follow every action that they take. It's fully participatory.

I'm tired of people who would always give me this silly, kind of pontificating kind of wisdom like, "Well, children don't vote." And my answer always was, "Guns don't vote either, but they've got plenty of lobbyists." In this case, kids now have lobbyists.

So if I had to pick out one thing that is most hopeful, the long name is the National Association for the Protection of Children.

The next Burke is said to be about "trafficking in humans." Your books are noted for having these often eerily prescient elements layered into them. Is there something about the slave trade you'll be incorporating in the forthcoming book that you anticipate having to defend short-term until it becomes all too clear you weren't extrapolating or creating out of whole cloth?

Yeah. I know some things people are going to be angry about. Because, the prescience is a misnomer: in other words, when I wrote about these things, I'm reporting about things we had seen.

It was known fact to you, sure.

Sure. So this business about life imitating art is just so much nonsense. Because what I write is not art, and life isn't imitating it. It's life I'm writing about. There are things in this book that I hope are going to confront specifically this administration's whole trafficking initiative.

I know a bit about that, but mostly through my research on you.

[*Laughing*] You could get me started—you know I was in Biafra during the war, right?

Yeah.

Well you could get me started on Live Aid and I wouldn't stop for a few hours, because the idea that we've got these billions of dollars going to countries that are enslaving their own people without conditions attached ... I don't understand how you give a billion dollars to a Robert Mugabe. I don't get that. I don't understand how anybody gives any money to anybody in the Congo. I just don't get it. Because I don't believe, having been a participant—I don't mean in a rock concert, but a war ... I mean, the *food* actually gets passed to *warlords*. The *medicine* actually gets passed to *warlords*.

Too often the case in all of these human aid efforts ...

But you can attach conditions. When you have that much money, you have power. You can literally say to a country, "You don't get this gigantic sum of money—" You could even say, "We *know* you're going to steal some of it—this is the percentage you can steal." You know, "Here's your bribe."

Cost of doing charity, I guess ...

Yeah. It's never been accurately reported. The "Rumble in the Jungle," the Ali-Foreman fight ... what's not reported is how this propped up the regime of a genocidal maniac. So, this is supposed to be about uplifting Africa?

The only thing I'm really a fan of is not baseball and it's not poker ... it's not horseracing. It's journalism.

Are there particular reporters whose work you seek out?

Bob Herbert of the *New York Times*; Nick Pileggi on anything to do with crime. They're probably my two favorites. But I've got another favorite. His name is Jimmy Proctor. *Jag Post Tribune.* There *is* a James Proctor. You know, way, way back in the day, where I got some of my information about things that were happening in Indiana with the Klan and with the American Nazi Party. It goes that far back with him. He's been a journalist his whole life. So this is my little tip of the hat—only a few people in the game know there really is a James Proctor.

I appreciate you indulging me with all these questions and with your time.

Actually, I was thrilled to do it, because instead of saying, "What's the book about?" or "Was your first wife really a topless dancer?" or you know, this was an *actual* conversation. I really enjoyed the hell out of it.

Well, me too. Anything you'd like to get out there I missed?

Swear to God, if you get out what we talked about, I'll be the happiest man alive.

JAMES ELLROY

To Live And Die In L.A.
(October 2004; August 2006)

In May 2001, I sat down with James Ellroy in the lobby of an Ann Arbor, Michigan hotel to discuss the second volume of his Underworld U.S.A. Trilogy, *The Cold Six Thousand*. The novel, the sequel to his hugely successful and much acclaimed *American Tabloid*, had just become the first of the author's hardcovers to crack the *New York Times'* bestseller list.

At fifty-three, Ellroy was three-quarters of the way through an international book tour that had taken him across France, Italy, Spain and Great Britain. He was starting to push across North America.

It was an ambitious publicity campaign far exceeding all previous junkets attempted by an author already renowned for the most audacious of book promotions.

But Ellroy was racing toward a wall he would later write that friends and family couldn't stop him from slamming into.

As the time for my 2001 interview (see *Art in the Blood* by Craig McDonald) with Ellroy neared, I started noticing strange and ominous comments Ellroy made to interviewers in the days leading up to our exchange. He increasingly remarked about the rigors of his world tour as the campaign continued. "Really, frankly, when you're on a tour like this you're too busy staying alive. The logistics and prosaics of this kind of tour more than anything beats you down," he confided to me. He talked of his inability to get sleep, and his growing obsession with his own health.

Two days after our 2001 discussion, Ellroy canceled the balance of his tour. A few days later he issued a statement:

> *"It is with great regret that I have had to cancel appearances on my U.S. book tour. I have been on the road since March 12 and the effect of this global tour finally caught up with me in Chicago ..."*

Eventually, Ellroy would write about the psychological and physical toll taken by his *Cold Six Thousand* tour in one of his last articles for *GQ*. (Ellroy's long-standing gig with *GQ Magazine* abruptly ended when he and a host of other authors were booted following the ouster of revered editor Art Cooper.)

But his ordeal was far from over.

What followed was a five-year struggle that stalled the author's writing of the final installment of his ambitious Underworld U.S.A. Trilogy and changed his life forever.

Ellroy, who had many years before beaten back addictions to alcohol and drugs, found himself increasingly reliant on sleep medication.

As he would later describe it, his remarkable brain turned in on itself. "My mind looped obsessively ... I could not cut myself off from the world. All my compartments were sieves ... My work habits were megalomaniacal ... Anxiety drove me back to my desk at all hours ... I did interviews with cold sweats ... I was at the height of my public recognition and going insane."

As he would reveal in a long, blunt and candid essay published in *Los Angeles Times Magazine* in the late summer of 2006, in the summer of 2003, Ellroy overdosed three times. He enrolled himself in a rehab program, and, eventually, endured the end of his marriage to novelist/journalist Helen Knode.

The following exchange consists of two interviews conducted with James Ellroy. The first took place in the autumn of 2004, when Ellroy was starting his climb back. He was promoting *Destination: Morgue! L.A. Tales*, an omnibus of his uncollected nonfiction and essays penned for *GQ*, as well as three new novellas featuring L.A. homicide detective "Rhino" Rick Jenson and his al-literative inamorata Donna Donahue—a thinly disguised version of actress and Ellroy friend Dana Delaney. (Delaney was also the author's choice to portray his mother in any adaptation of his memoir *My Dark Places*.)

Jenson is obsessed by the unsolved murder of Stephanie Gorman—a particularly brutal unsolved sex crime that also receives nonfiction treatment in *Destination: Morgue!*

James Ellroy had recently resettled from Kansas City to Carmel, California when we spoke in 2004.

He had also made news when he penned an introduction for the book *Black Dahlia Avenger* in which retired LAPD detective Steve Hodel claimed his own father, George Hodel, killed Elizabeth Short—the woman at the center of Ellroy's breakthrough novel, *The Black Dahlia*.

While Ellroy questioned some aspects of the case as laid out by Hodel, he expressed his belief that Hodel's solution was likely as close to the correct one as can ever be expected.

Ellroy had also recently taken a more active role in a different medium, serving as executive producer of the documentary *Bazaar Bizarre* about now-dead Kansas City serial killer Bob Berdella.

The second interview was conducted in August 2006—a quick, rat-tat-tat exchange as Ellroy was poised to board a plane for Venice for the premiere of a lavish film adaptation of his 1987 novel, *The Black Dahlia*.

In September 2006, director Brian DePalma unveiled his film adaptation of Ellroy's novel, starring Josh Hartnett, Scarlett Johansson, Aaron Eckhart, Hilary Swank and Mia Kirshner as Elizabeth Short. Ellroy was sufficiently pleased with the adaptation to hit the road in support of the film and the special movie rerelease of his novel incorporating a new afterword.

Ellroy was newly single, and had recently moved back to L.A., vowing to write only Los Angeles-centered novels after completing the final volume of his ambitious trilogy.

Ellroy's self-revealing essay about his five-year trauma appeared just a few days before I spoke with the author.

In that piece, Ellroy asserted the essay would stand as one of his last autobiographical statements and insisted his publicist would be instructing future interviewers that Ellroy would "walk" if confronted with any further personal questions.

If Ellroy holds to that sentiment, our brief conversation conducted before Ellroy flew to Venice may stand as one of James Ellroy's last unfettered interviews.

• • • • •

October 2004

Do you miss the outlet/platform of *GQ*? I had the sense you had great latitude in terms of subject matter and the topics you focused on.

Great question. Wonderful introductory question. The answer is *yeah*, I do. A bunch of events interceded last year in June of '03. They fired Art Cooper—a legendary magazine editor, inducted in the Magazine Editors' Hall of Fame. They brought in a fella who wanted to reshape the magazine. Astonishingly, I got the boot. Odd.

Given the fact that you'd won, at least twice I think, the *GQ* novelist of the year award, yeah.

Their award for literature, yeah. And, you know, I'm a man in my fifties. They fired all the mature guys.

I noticed there are some pieces that you wrote for *GQ* after *Crime Wave* [the first *GQ* collection] appeared, that aren't in *Destination: Morgue!*. Any particular significance to that? I know there was the last piece on Anne Sexton and Dana Delaney ... something on 9/11, that was very short.

It was a short piece that was part of a larger piece on the terrorist bombings.

And the presidential piece on the 2000 Bush/Gore race isn't here.

The presidential piece, which was a hilarious piece, didn't make it. It wasn't timely. Sonny Mehta thought it wasn't timely. And my piece on Bill O'Reilly isn't there. They wanted to keep it to crime and keep it to L.A.

Anything happen recently that you'd particularly like to have sunk your teeth into as a journalist or essayist?

Actually? No. I don't follow politics. I don't watch news. I went to Vegas for a couple of fights and I didn't find them moving or explicative in any way. What I love about this book here, is that it is such a primer on me … on my obsessions … on my interests … on my fixations. And, then, those three wild-ass novellas at the end.

Let's jump ahead to those. I remember in your last piece for GQ, you were talking about maybe writing some things with actress Dana Delaney as a protagonist. And you have a "Donna Donahue" here, and they are, for the most part, a contemporary set of stories, so I'm wondering, is it okay to read anything in there?

Well, you certainly can. Dana and I are friends. I wanted a thinly disguised Dana Delaney. I wanted a Dana Delaney stand-in. Did you enjoy the novellas?

I liked the last one [Jungletown Jihad] the best. And in a way, it's funny, I wish that one had been first, because it kind of contextualizes the other two.

Well, keep in mind, there's chronology there. The first one where Donna and Rick meet, it's '83. Then you go to '04 and to '05.

And you go way out into the future.

Oh yeah, because Rhino Rick narrates this from heaven.

You've made some statements about the "crime novel" being "dead" or moving away from crime fiction. I really thought after the Lloyd Hopkins books you probably wouldn't write another contemporary cop and I think you had even indicated that that was the case. And here we are.

These are novellas, keep in mind. And keep in mind these are also deliberately comic. They are comic novellas. This is as dark as humor gets, I think, in many ways. You look at the last one— it's a comedy about Arab terrorists, you know. Half of whom want to blow up buildings and half of whom want to go to lap-dance lairs and get blowjobs.

All factually accurate, if I remember the facts surrounding Atta and company prior to September 11, 2001.

All factually accurate. And each of the three stories ties to a sex killer from the 1950s L.A. scene.

Right. In the novellas, you use something you write about elsewhere in the collection in nonfiction form—the murder of Stephanie Gorman. That's an obsessive case for your detective in the novellas, Rick Jenson. What is it about that case, particularly, that keeps bringing you back around to it in this book? I guess in terms of age, she'd have been roughly a peer of yours …

She was one year and three months younger than me. We grew up four and a half or five miles apart. She grew up more affluently than I did. We went to adjoining high schools. I recall the case very, very dimly from "freedom summer" for me, 1965—the year that my father died and I got kicked out of high school … got kicked out of the Army. It's a particularly horrible crime that should have been a signature L.A. crime—had the Watts Riots not intersected. Also, it's a one-off sex crime. They were never able—and I read the file, many times—they were never able to link that killer to any other existing crime, pre- or post-.

That's a little like your mother's murder in that sense, too.

Yeah, but this was a deliberate, planned sex crime. My mother was a date rape that went bad.

You wrote an introduction recently for the book *Black Dahlia Avenger*. You don't necessarily really endorse its author's theory, but you seem to accept it as a real possibility.

I think it's more than that. I think he did it. I say that with some reluctance. I think a lot of the underpinnings of the story don't work. He posited a great and far-reaching LAPD cover-up and conspiracy and can't prove any of it. Here's the thing that gets me about it: when I read the book in hardcover I wasn't convinced.

The alleged pictures of Elizabeth Short, alone, threw me. Those clearly were not pictures of Elizabeth Short.

Well, here's the thing: Here's what you have to believe—this is the jump between hardcover and paperback—at the very least, George Hodel was a psychopathic libertine. He was tried for incest with his fourteen-year-old daughter. A very bad guy. He had eleven kids by various women. One kid grew up to be a homicide detective in LAPD. Odd in itself. Okay, dad dies. Steve Hodel sees his personal effects and comes to the conclusion, erroneously, I think, that those pictures are of Elizabeth Short. He becomes convinced and posits in a very well-layered, circumstantial case, his theory that his father killed Elizabeth Short. I'm unconvinced.

In the lag-time between the hardcover and paperback publications, an *L.A. Times* reporter named Steve Lopez unearths the D.A.'s bureau file on the Short case. George Hodel, Steve Hodel's father, was the number one suspect. They had bugged and hotwired all his telephones and his house. They have him on tape in a certified transcript from February of 1950 saying, "So what if I killed the Black Dahlia? They can't prove it. The only one who knows it is my secretary and she's dead."

So, reluctantly, given that, I'll buy that. This feels to me, almost, like divine intervention. If indeed, as I suspect, that those pictures are not of Elizabeth Short, but he [Steve Hodel] investigates the case at great length, puts together a finally unconvincing case, and it turns out his old man was the number one suspect and admitted it on a tape, that's enough.

Have you had any feelers about replacing the GQ gig, at all? I seem to remember *Vanity Fair* courting you at some point.

They came around while I was working for *GQ* six or seven years ago. You know, what I do is very specific, and Art Cooper was behind it 100 percent of the time. I'm more or less convinced that the magazines that are out there right now have other agendas. I don't know American culture very well. I'm uninterested in the war on terrorism. I write about a very specific number of things. I have a very limited imagination. I think prudent magazine editors know that.

You've moved back to California—has that sparked anything in terms of wanting to write about L.A. again?

Naw. I just like the central coast here. It's amenable. It's very rarely hot.

It beats a Kansas City summer?

Boy …

The Robert Blake case is addressed in one of the pieces in *Destination: Morgue!* Have you had any more thoughts about that case since your treatment first appeared in *GQ*?

I haven't followed it at all. The murder occurred in May of '01. We're in October of '04. That's three and a half years.

Any loud, current crimes you'd like a crack at or are tracking?

I retain very strong friendships in LAPD. I'd bet you could cut me loose—I have several friends on the LAPD Cold Case unit—I would love to just take a walk through, to read some old files. I'm sure I could make it happen. But then of course I'd get obsessed like I did with Gorman. My life would get disrupted again and I can't afford that right now.

It really became that big an investment of your time working on that piece?

Yeah. Yeah. There were five boxes of files and memorabilia and miscellany to read through. And you better read through 'em all. In a way you have probably eight pages of reconstruction down to the most minute detail in essential chronological order [in "Stephanie"]. In order to get that, I had to read five file boxes and take notes.

That's a bigger investigative record than you went through for your entire book-length account of your mother's murder for *My Dark Places,* isn't it?

Yes.

I recently watched a screener of *Bazaar Bizarre,* about Kansas City serial killer Bob Berdella. You're executive producer for that film. Did you know much about that case before the documentary?

No, [director] Ben Meade is a good friend of mine and I was presented with material by Ben. You know, we're doing a *Destination: Morgue!* documentary together later in the year. Regarding Berdella, Ben presented me with specific pieces of film to view and then I commented on them. I haven't seen the movie, but apparently, a lot of my comments are hilarious.

You haven't seen it?

No. But he's a good filmmaker. We're going to do that documentary, called *Destination: Morgue!* later in the year. It will be dramatized sequences from the book—not the fiction but the nonfiction. Dramatized pieces, my voice, to camera narration—interviews with Steve Cooley, district attorney of Los Angeles County and maybe even another dinner with my policemen friends focused on some crime. Then we're going to do a nonfiction segment on those three killers—[Stephen] Nash, [Donald Keith] Bashor, [Harvey] Glatman—who inform the text of the three novellas.

Now that you don't have that *GQ* outlet, I just wonder what you do when you're not working on a novel. Do you continue to write short stories and novellas?

No. I do film and TV work to earn money, and to bide my time between writing the novels, which is all-consuming.

There's a lot of pressure on people these days to write a book a year. Usually to pretty poor effect. You've resisted that and actually gone the other route. Are you under any pressure to put more out there?

No. I'm fifty-six years old and healthy. I have seven more novels that I want to write in my lifetime and I'll probably write more.

But you *do* have seven in mind? I know you were talking about a Warren Harding book.

Oh yeah, Warren Harding is right after this book [volume 3 of the Underworld U.S.A. Trilogy]. I've got a book about Wisconsin a generational novel about Wisconsin.

About a family of patrolmen, right?

I'm not sure yet. But, after that point, more will be revealed. Yeah. I think I write a great book—and they're huge. And that's the kind of book I like to read. I don't want some shit fucking generic motherfucker toadstool of a book. Oh, I can't wait for the latest, you know?

How is that going? Are you fairly deep into the writing of volume 3 now?

Yeah, yeah. I'm deep into it. I'm not promising a delivery date, but you know, it's *huge*. It's bigger than *The Cold Six Thousand*.

I know you've said you want the three novels, literally, to be successively larger. I'm wondering how you sustain your concentration and your interest across this many years.

The interest is *easy*. The concentration ... you need a very, very strong superstructure. And you need the outlines that you and I discussed when we were in Ann Arbor that day [May 2001]. You know, you need a big, big superstructure and the determination to make it work. Now, one of the big revelations for me, early on as a writer when I was into writing *The Big Nowhere*, was that I realized I could execute whatever I could conceive of.

That's ... amazing. That's stunning. That puts pressure on you, though. If you have that ability, you've got to use it—not lay back.

Yeah.

Do you read a lot of poetry? You drop these lines of poetry into interviews, articles ... and I've seen you do it across a number of years. Auden, particularly.

You know, I've read through Auden. A lot of the shit I don't understand, and I don't like and I don't *get*.

I know you read Anne Sexton.

Ohhh baby! Oh man!

Hot but doomed.

Craig, you're brilliant. You've just defined Anne Sexton: hot but doomed. You'd do her, wouldn't you?

Well yeah, based on the photos I've seen of her in her prime ... *yeah*. Hah!

Have you written any poetry of your own?

Nah. But I do love Sexton. "Hot but doomed."

I know you say you don't read a lot of crime fiction, but have you read anything recently? And if so, what was it?

No. No. People tell me there are Ellroy manqués out there. I don't know who they are. I'm always getting some fucking 1950s-noir pastiche in the mail.

I'm sure. I've heard of a couple and I've picked up one or two to look at, but other than milieu, it's not doing what you do. Although I did run across a song recently by L.A.-born, Texas-based songwriter Tom Russell ["Tijuana Bible"] about Johnny Stompanato that had to have been inspired by the L.A. Quartet ...

Did you see the movie *Collateral?*

Nope.

Well, it stinks. But there is a scene where Jamie Fox and Tom Cruise were running around doing stupid riffs on life and death and Jamie Fox throws out the phrase, "The Big Ass Nowhere."

Do you go back and reread your older stuff now?

No.

Don't look back?

No. I concentrate on what I've got in front of me.

You once started and never finished a novel, I think it was called *The Confessions of Bugsy Seigel.*

Yeah. It was a dog.

It's a dog?

Yeah, it's in my archives at the University of South Carolina.

I suppose there's no possibility we'd ever get *The Confessions of Dudley Smith, As Told to Dave Klein?*

Hah! No.

It's over?

Dudley is, let's see, he's right at one hundred … no, he's one hundred and two, or something. He's still alive. I'm the guy who created him, so I can say when he's dead. Twenty years from now: "Alright he's fuckin' dead!" Evil dies with him.

Is there anything on your mind that you'd particularly like to share with your readers?

I like this book a lot. I like the illustrations. Kaya Christian [*Playboy* Playmate November 1967]: to go back and write about having the hots for Kaya Christian, and have a picture of Kaya Christian in there …

This is a big improvement over *Crime Wave* because one of the things I like about the original *GQ* articles, you did get the photos, you did get the great original illustrations, but in *Crime Wave*, the first *GQ* collection, you didn't. Some of the art and illustration in *GQ* was so nicely done.

Yeah. You know what? I miss *GQ*. God bless 'em. I miss Art Cooper, you know? I had wonderful editors there. I had Paul Scanlon, Ilena Silverman and Michael Hainey. I had wonderful friends there.

I wish you luck with the tour—it looks like another big one. I guess you've done Europe already?

You know what, I did France.

You're huge in France. What's the appeal of your stuff there?

Well, you know, they were the early discoverers of the *roman noir.*

• • • • •
August 2006

Mr. Ellroy ...

Mr. McDonald ...

I'm grateful you're taking the time for this talk. I know they've got you on the wheel for this one ...

Fuckkk ...

You're along for the press junket for *The Black Dahlia* film. The implication would be that you approve or embrace the De Palma film adaptation of your novel ...

Oh yeah. You know what it is? It's compression. It's reduction. He isolates the themes very well ... the sexual obsession and the triangulation—the one man with the two women. You know the book, intimately: You've got Bucky Bleichert and Madeleine Sprague (who's called "Lindscott" in the movie) and Kay Lake. You've got Madeleine and the Dahlia. You've got Kay and the Dahlia. And you've got Bucky in the middle. And you've got the triumvirate of Bucky, Lee and Kay. So all of that is there. And it doesn't look like any fucking movie you've ever seen before.

It was filmed in some European backwater, right?

It was filmed in Bulgaria and the only Anglo-Saxons in the movie are the four above the title. Yeah, a lot of Slavs in this one, you know. Overall, I'm well served by it. And it's going to sell me a lot of books.

In your new afterword to the novel, you venture that the film could expand your reading audience exponentially. The sense I got from that is that you regard this as a potentially bigger film phenomenon than *L.A. Confidential* proved to be ...

L.A. Confidential was a very good film. What this brings to mind though is just the power of motion pictures to reach an audience and grab 'em by the nuts very fast. That's rather astonishing to me. I don't take movies as seriously as I take novels. I think the novel is a more profound art form, chiefly because it's indigenous to only one person. And that stated, I think a shitload of people are going to see this thing.

Guy Pierce as Ed Exley seemed to be the revelation for you in the film adaptation of L.A. Confidential. Who pole-armed you in The Black Dahlia?

Listen, Josh Hartnett is by and large very, very good. Here's one of the reasons why, just coincidental: He physically resembles Bucky Bleichert, unlike anyone else has in the film adaptation of one of my books. Which is to say, physically he resembles me. It's just coincidence—tall, lanky, dark-haired, pale. He's sort of youthful. He reads the voice-over narration very well, so that off-sets his physical youth.

He's good at projecting cognition. Bleichert is a character who is always measuring and thinking, as I say in the afterword. And Mia Kirshner breaks your heart as Betty Short.

I've always liked her as an actress. She seems perfect for the part.

You know what my ex-wife said—my most recent ex-wife? She said, "I think you should go to the Venice film festival and fuck Mia Kirshner. Because it's the closest you'll get to fucking Betty Short and by extension your *mother*. *Oooh*, that's dark, huh?

That's *very* dark.

Helen Knode!

You pick your ex-wives well.

Helen Knode!

Have you revisited or reread the novel in preparation for the junket and so forth?

I'm doing a reading tour, Craig. I'm also going out with Bruce Wagner and Dana Delaney, our friend. I'm reading from Bruce's new novel, *Memorial*. Bruce is reading from *The Black Dahlia*. And then Bruce, Dana and I, at the Hammer Museum, are reading from both books.

In 2007, the Black Dahlia murder case will have its sixtieth anniversary. Your novel will be twenty years old. How do you assess the book now?

I'm a sixteen-book writer and I've got four signature books: *The Black Dahlia*, *L.A. Confidential*, *American Tabloid* and *My Dark Places*. That's pretty great. It's my first signature book. It *may be* my signature book. It is the last gasp of my pure unconsciousness as a writer. I mean I just wrote that book on instinct—and no lack of skill, certainly. But that book is my heart. That book, and *My Dark Places*, that's my heart. *American Tabloid*, *L.A. Confidential*, *White Jazz* … *Cold Six Thousand*, especially, that's my intellect.

It's just an uncommonly obsessive book. It's an uncommonly obsessive book about a certain kind of unvarnished maleness.

The Black Dahlia case crept into your first novel, *Brown's Requiem*. It's in your second novel. In *Clandestine*, Dudley Smith describes his role in the Black Dahlia case. But his actions are given to another in the actual *Dahlia* novel …

Yeah, to Fritzie Vogel. You know what that is—that was in deference to John Gregory Dunne's *True Confessions*. Dudley Smith is an Irish immigrant and that was such an Irish book [Dunne's]. And I know absolutely shit about Irishness. Or about *Catholicism*.

A number of books about Elizabeth Short's murder have been released recently, and more are set to come out around the time of the film …

We're trying to find a language for this horrible act—the murder of Betty Short. Imaginative people want to certify their language as authentic. I don't. I gave you the most psychologically sound, pathologically valid, lunatic language that I was capable of in describing Betty Short's death. And I have not the slightest idea who did it.

Some more has been revealed in recent years about Elizabeth Short and her past and her character—implications about her physical anatomy that may or may not have been true. Other novelists have revised early works; John Fowles did it with *The Magus*. Would you go back to that novel and tweak it at some point?

Nah. I already wrote it.

Does this close out the Dahlia now for you?

It closes it out. After this interview I go to Venice tonight for the Venice Film Festival—it's a tough life, but somebody has to live it—then I have a junket day and the premier on the sixth of September. Then I have bookstore appearances with Bruce and Dana and by myself. Then a court TV documentary. That's American crime writers on their favorite cases. Mine, though, is different. It's Michael Connelly, Lisa Scottoline, Jonathan and Faye Kellerman, individually. My case is my mother's case and I narrate and host it. And that's it.

After this November—roughly the ninth—I will never answer another personal question. I will never discuss the Black Dahlia or my mother ever again. *Ever* again. When I go out for the new novel when it comes out, the publicist will inform everybody no personal questions or Ellroy will walk out of the room, like *that*.

I read your long new essay in the *L.A. Times* ...

Yeah, yeah, I've had a wild five years.

It's been a lot of water under the bridge, my friend. I grasped the essay's implicit and explicit assertion that it stands as your last autobiographical statement. Honoring the spirit of that piece, I will only say it's very bluntly self-disclosing. It reminded me of a similar wrenchingly confessional piece penned by F. Scott Fitzgerald.

"The Crack Up"?

Right.

Tell me about that—he cracked up and he wrote about it?

He did. He wrote a fairly lengthy piece, and then Hemingway, for one, absolutely reviled Fitzgerald for it publicly. Hemingway thought that was something that a fiction writer shouldn't do, or that it was some kind of breach of writing etiquette, so Hemingway mocked Fitzgerald in a short story.

And then Hemingway cracked up and blew his brains out.

Yeah. Yeah. Absolutely. I wonder what your feedback on that essay has been. Or have you been in a position to have feedback on the piece yet?

Oh yeah, yeah. The woman who edited the piece forwarded it. People were floored by it. You're always kind of humbled by that. I cracked up. I fucked up. I trashed my marriage. I'm back. I'm back and I'm really back, and if you don't believe it, *fuck you*. It's my best book yet—the book that I'm writing—and if you don't like it, shove it up your ass. And I'm happy to be back in L.A. If you don't dig L.A., or dig me, fuck you and kiss my ass. There was all of that.

It's an amazing piece.

I think it is too. I don't *ever* want to write about myself again after that. I got obsessed with a woman up in San Francisco and I was going to mention that a little bit, but forget it. It was good, though.

You've moved back to Los Angeles. Do you have an eye on one of those Hancock Park big houses you obsessed over in your youth?

No! Shit no! Can't afford one, Craig. I can't afford one. I've got a two-bedroom apartment in a nice old building.

You state in that essay you will only write L.A. novels from here forward. So no Warren G. Harding novel?

No, I'm not doing the Harding novel. It was just a momentary thing. When I met you in Ann Arbor that was the big plan. But I'm not.

Do you have a sense yet whether those L.A.-centered novels to come will be contemporary, or more books set in the twentieth century?

Not yet. Haven't the slightest.

Let me ask you then about volume 3 of the Underworld U.S.A. Trilogy and how that is coming along.

You've read *Cold Six Thousand* …

Absolutely. Couple or three times. Now volume 3 is—or was—to be titled *Police Gazette* ...

You know, I don't know how that misinformation got out. It was just an idea for a title. Did you dig *Cold Six Thousand*?

I loved it.

Yeah. You know what, you're among the 30 percent and the brave.

It's a dense book. I know a few who have trouble with it. I've read it two or three times and love the book.

It's as fierce as literature gets. It's very difficult. It may be overly stylized for a book that complex. I'm going back and I'm finding a new language. It's every plot thread from *Tabloid* and *Cold Six* from '68 to '72. Some real narrative risks and a huge book.

Are you prepared to talk about the three characters who carry the book?

I'll tell you, Craig, off the record ...

On the record, Pete Bondurant—back?

Pete Bondurant, on the record, is retired. He's still living in Sparta, Wisconsin with Barb and the cat. The cat is still alive, though.

Betty McDonald's cat?

Yeah, Betty McDonald's cat—your namesake. It's the world's oldest fucking cat.

In your new afterword to *The Black Dahlia,* you assert that only you know whether Kay and Bucky still are alive. The last time I spoke with you, you asserted that Dudley Smith might still be "alive" in your world and that he will "die" at a time and place of your choosing. Ed Exley's fate also remains unknown. For a guy who's written many books regarded as noir, many of your characters' fates are left open-ended or ambiguous ...

Well, Ed Exley never became governor of California.

I'm just wondering: Do your characters live on in your head to some extent, past the books? Are you still concocting private storylines or scenarios in your head for some?

Yeah. Ed is eighty-four and healthy.

The good die young.

The good die *hung*.

With *The Black Dahlia's* release, two volumes of your quartet now have been adapted for film. Any sense of action on *The Big Nowhere* and *White Jazz*?

White Jazz is fairly far along in development with Joe Carnahan slated to direct—the man who did *Narc*. The script is good and needs some paring down. His brother Matt wrote it and it is a very faithful adaptation of my book. I think they're going out to actors now. But as always with this stuff, I'll believe it when I see it.

What I would really like to see is the three-hour *Big Nowhere*.

That book resonates for me a little more than some of the others in some funny ways.

You know what? It does for me, too.

Anything we can expect prior to volume 3 of the trilogy?

No.

Anything you'd like to share, Mr. Ellroy?

Let's see: What would I like to do? I'd like to find a woman. I need a woman, Craig. I need a woman.

You're on the road ...

That's true, I'm on the road, so I'm keeping my eyes peeled. I'm a tall rangy guy. I look good in a white dinner jacket and I've got one for Italy.

PART IV

Page to Screen and Back

MAX ALLAN COLLINS

On the Road

(November 28, 2004)

Max Allan Collins: novelist, nonfiction writer, comic book writer, comic strip writer, independent filmmaker.

If it seems like he's been around forever, it's because he started so damned young.

His first two published novels, written when he was twenty-one, were recently rereleased in paperback by Hard Case Crime under the title *Two for the Money*. His graphic novel, *The Road to Perdition,* became an Oscar-nominated film starring Tom Hanks and Paul Newman. Collins then wrote a prose sequel and penned a graphic novel "implant" expanding on the original tale, both released in late 2004.

His most ambitious project remains his series of Nate Heller novels and short stories, featuring a private investigator whose caseload includes real-life crimes encompassing the murder of Elizabeth Short, the Roswell crash, Amelia Earhart's disappearance and the Lindbergh kidnapping.

Historical personages populating the Heller novels include such diverse people as James Forrestal, Bugsy Seigel, Mickey Cohen and Ian Fleming, creator of James Bond.

Another series of historical crime novels was written around Eliot Ness during the period that Ness served as Cleveland public safety director.

• • • • •

I looked over some past interviews and I read about overlapping projects. I look at your bibliography, and the filmwork, and wonder, when do you find time to live ... to eat?

[*Chuckling*] I'm running into deadline problems right now. I have a cold right now and it's throwing me off my deadlines and I'm careening into my promo and P.R. schedule. But generally speaking, I just feel like I'm a full-time professional writer. I'm not a teacher, lawyer or doctor who writes. I'm a writer who writes.

That's put you in a group of about 2 percent of the writing population, doesn't it?

Yeah, there's not a huge number of us who don't have a day job. And even I essentially have a day job because I do a certain amount of what you might call licensing work, which is to say I've done a lot of novelizations and I'm currently the writer of the *CSI* novels. I may be a little different from some writers in that I don't hide behind a pseudonym when I do that stuff. I was advised that I should, but I said, "I'm a comic book writer ... you don't get any less respect than that. So why should I hide I'm going out and doing this work?"

And, for example, the *CSI* books: the last two have made the *New York Times* bestseller list. So why would I not want my name on it?

Well, in terms of generating cross-readership for your own novels, that makes perfect sense.

Exactly. And I think in the last five years that's really started to pay off for me. I'm not a big believer in conventional wisdom, so I flew in the face of that and it does seem to be working out.

Can you describe a typical Max Allan Collins day? How is the time apportioned ... do you calculate a daily word output?

I am remarkably undisciplined for as much as I get done. I'd say there is usually a couple of hours a day that I'm dealing with e-mail and business and editors. One of the funny things we've been dealing with the last few days is a dozen big boxes of my books showed up from a dozen bookstores around the country wanting me to sign them. For some reason there were no instructions about how to get these things returned. So we've spent a lot of time waiting for UPS and FedEx to show up and I still have about four of these boxes in my living room.

There are peculiar aspects to the writing life that people don't understand. I think the sort of cottage industry aspect of it is lost on a lot of people. My wife is also a writer, but she pretty much runs the business end of things. She worked in a bank for many years and has a strong business background. I probably write anywhere from four to eight hours a day. It's more extreme if I'm on a deadline. I generally try to get a chapter done a day when I'm on a novel. I'd say it's unusual if it takes me more than a couple of days to do a chapter. That's sort of how I apportion it. I break the book down into chapters and I have a loose outline because I like to maintain spontaneity.

It's a little harder with historical stuff because I'm very rigidly faithful to the facts. I shouldn't say rigidly, because I do compression of time and composite characters now and then, but I don't just view history as a rough draft that I get to fill in. The first of the historical books was called *True Detective,* and that became the mandate.

I do get the sense that you finesse the time here and there ...
You have to.

But you do draw a line for yourself regarding how you're going to use or not use a historical personage? Is there a line you wouldn't cross in treatment of a historical person?
I've been pretty bold at times. My detective Nathan Heller has had sexual affairs with real people.

Sally Rand ...
Sally Rand and even Amelia Earhart. Amelia Earhart made some people mad, although I think they were madder that I had extrapolated from what I read that she was likely to have been bisexual. That made a certain number of readers quite indignant, even though the portrait of her in that novel, which is called *Flying Blind,* is probably the most sympathetic and I believe, full-

bodied version—no pun intended—that's ever been done. Because she doesn't come alive very well in the nonfiction that I've read. She was kind of a mystery in that sense.

And I would say that one of the mysteries that I have to solve is to try to figure out who these people are. Who was Hauptman, for example, in the Lindbergh book I did? Right now I'm dealing with Giancana and some of the later gangsters in a book that will be the last of the Peridition Trilogy. That's called *Road to Paradise* and that's what I'm working on now.

Regarding *Road to Perdition*: Accommodations were made, as they always are, in terms of striking a balance between the needs of the respective mediums of film and graphic novel. But your graphic novel ended much, much differently than the film. *Road to Purgatory* doesn't quite carry Michael through to that ending we saw in your original version of *Perdition*. Another sequel envisioned to close that gap?

Right, the next one is called *Road to Paradise* and that indicates that in that book we will in fact get to that ending [the original ending depicted in the first graphic novel]. But we'll get there through a rather circuitous road, which might surprise people. Because people who knew the ending of the graphic novel and come to *Road to Purgatory* might be surprised at some of the things that Michael O'Sullivan Jr. does.

Just getting back to your earlier question: I tend to work on one project at a time. The only exception to that is if I'm involved in something ongoing, as when I was doing the Dick Tracy strip or a monthly comic book. If I'm doing a monthly comic book, even if it is a miniseries—five or six issues—that gets woven into the sort of main project I'm doing. I'll, say, take ex-number of days off from the main project to get that monthly work done. But I don't ever work on two novels at the same time. That way lies madness, I think.

Let's talk about the two spins-offs from *Road to Perdition*. When you did the original graphic novel, you were doing a "graphic novel." As a result of the film, and the Oscar buzz and so forth, did you find yourself coming at these offshoots with some sense of weight? Was there an extra pressure because of the phenomenon of the film?

Only in I knew that some people would come to the material, to the sequel, through the film. So the sequel had to really work either way. Although I do in the sequel touch on inconsistencies between the world of the film and the world of these novels. I do make it clear, for example, that Michael was the one who killed the hitman, not his father—that that was a romantic invention of pulp writers. So I have a little tongue-in-cheek fun with that.

The film was so faithful to the spirit of what I did. It was about 75 percent faithful to the letter. It was really only in a couple of areas that they really drifted—all of which I understood. They made more of a point of the father and son relationship between Looney and O'Sullivan than I did, but you have to also remember that when I was working on the graphic novel—originally, in the beginning of the project—probably the first two hundred of the three hundred pages that I wrote, I was operating on the assumption that I was going to have nine hundred pages.

I had been told that we were going to do three of them and that we would be on the road for nine hundred pages. It wasn't until I was basically starting the third section that I got word that this particular publishing program at DC—which was to try and do noir graphic novels—was failing, and that I would not be asked to finish. It wasn't in response to my work—my work hadn't even come out yet—but it was failing and they were going to be pulling the plug on it. I was to only finish what I was on, to wrap it up, basically. So that's why with the graphic novel follow-up that I did, *Road to Perdition 2,* I basically did what they call in comics a "continuity implant." I said, "Okay, let me try to flesh this out more." One of the things that I did was to explore the father and son relationship between Looney and O'Sullivan Sr. a little more fully.

The other thing that they did in the film that I think was apt: Because I was setting up the whole idea that the father and son would be on the road for a very long time and there would be various people coming after them, David Self, the screenwriter, combined all the various hitmen into one figure and they became the Jude Law character.

The Weegee-kind of crime-scene photographer.

[Editor's note:"Weegee"a phonetic take on the supernatural board game, "Ouija,"was the pseudonym for noted New York City crime photographer Usher Fellig, 1899–1968.]

Right. And one of the ironies is that he's probably the most comic-booky character in the film. He, if anything in the film, is the thing that might tell you that this project had its roots in a comic book, and yet it was not something that I created. I thought that was interesting. There seems to be things in the DNA of that story: When they would change it, they would change it in ways that would resemble things that I have done. I almost feel there's something about the way in which that story was originally constructed that makes it sort of impervious to removing my intentions.

A number of writers have commented on the fact that they dread film adaptations of their work because the actors might get between them and their minds-eye image of their own characters. Were you able, in the graphic novel particularly, to see the characters as they were drawn by Richard Piers Rayner, or did you find Hanks and Tucci shouldering their way into your head?

I have no trouble with that whatsoever. I was not picturing Tom Hanks at all when I wrote my middle section of this. I was not picturing Paul Newman—not at all. I have a very strong interior vision … probably am clinically an egomaniac, so, really, my vision overrides. At the same time, I love the idea of movies being made out of my stuff. I hope there's more. I hope there's many more. I hope I live to see a lot of it. I hope they make 'em after I'm gone. I'm a movie fan and I love movies and it gives me a life in that medium that I otherwise might not get to have. It does not in any way take away from what I've done. I mean, we only had about ten thousand readers for *Road to Perdition* when it came out.

It was a small printing, about ten thousand copies, and I think it pretty much sold out. It had an *incredible* sell-through. And I thought, "Great, they'll go back and they'll do another edition," but they didn't do a second edition. I said, "Why?" They said, "We really think that everybody who wants to read this story has read it now."

It had presumably satisfied its market?

Yeah. But of course ultimately, with the Tom Hanks movie poster cover on the reprint edition, we got onto the *New York Times* best-seller list. It's probably, it could well be, the best-selling graphic novel of all time. It certainly is the best-selling crime-oriented one.

So I think that's silly: even if they did a bad one [film adaptation], I'd just shrug.

You've written many, many television and film novelizations. Do you write the characters, or do you write the actors in those cases?

That's just about the opposite process. I like to know who they've cast. Because the screenplays, of necessity, are really very bare bones. In fact, even though I had done *Dick Tracy* as a novelization, the book that got me going as a writer of these things was *In the Line of Fire.* What was attractive to me was that it was a Clint Eastwood movie and that I would essentially get to write lines for Clint Eastwood. So I relish that baggage that they bring. That's been a lot of fun. Because I'm a baby-boomer with great affinity for popular culture, I have particularly sought out remakes of famous things. I did *Maverick.* I've got one coming up that I don't think I'm allowed to mention—something very famous in popular culture that I'll be doing. Sometimes it doesn't work out. *I Spy:* I signed on for that without seeing a script, just out of love for the original show. Then the script was not … *wonderful.* But I still made a good book out of it because that's my job.

My wife is a big part of this because she reads every chapter as I write it. She's the one who keeps me honest and if I'm working on material that is less than stellar, I just hand it to her and say, "If I gave this to you as a chapter of book I've written, would you say, 'Nice job and show me more'?" She's the one who holds the bar high for me. I could guarantee you right now: go out and read *I Spy* if you're a fan of my work, and you'll have a good time. Don't ruin it by watching the movie on TV, though.

When you compose your own novels, you are, for all intents, God. When you take on a novelization, are any restrictions laid down to you?

It widely varies. It can range from "don't change a word of the script"—that's fairly rare but sometimes it happens—to "please bring what you bring to the party to *this* party." A good example would be *Windtalkers*. They were aware of what I had done in *Saving Private Ryan* where I had really fleshed it out with history and character and backstory. They encouraged me to, in particular, explore the historical aspects of the Indian codetalkers. They encouraged me to research that and put it more heavily into the novel than they were able to do in the movie. With that kind of leeway it can really to a great degree become my book.

The *CSIs* have been really pretty good. They have not been terribly restrictive. They are very stingy about character growth on that show and this is the first season where they have actually started to shake things up a bit, and I think they've been on now for about five years.

It's a little like the *Law and Order* series, where you can pick 'em up at any point and not have any sense of a continuity that you've lost or need to be keyed into.

Exactly. Exactly. In fact, there was a shake-up on the show last week about breaking up the *CSI* team, and I am waiting to hear what I'm supposed to do in the next book. I've actually sort of stopped work on that because we need to know if this is just a sort of a temporary story arc or this is a restructuring that is going to last for a while. But I do try there to do things. There's a novel there called *Sin City*. And that's not my title, by the way. I had a great title that they didn't use—that was one place that I didn't win. My title was "Dead Nude Girls," which I thought was one of the best titles I'd ever come up with, but they called it *Sin City*—"they" being Pocket Books. The story explores the Catherine character whose background is a stripper. They refer to it in a kind of sly way on the show all the time, but they've never explored it in any depth. So I set a crime in that world and had her having to collide with people she had worked with as an exotic dancer fifteen years before, and that was fun.

I try to deal with characters. The one that we just finished will be out in, I think, April [2005]. It deals with a character, his name is "Brass." It was like his first case when he came to Vegas and it was one that he had not solved, so it had been a frustration to him. That's a way I can put some meat on the bones without really ... well, they certainly don't want me to do anything like introduce Gill Grissom's brother, or I couldn't have two of the characters decide to stop at a motel. There are certain things that if they want those done, they will do them on the show.

Let's veer back to the new book. Frank Nitti's life and death figures in *The Road to Purgatory*. You've dealt with him in the early Heller books, particularly.

He fascinates me.

You have this whole alternate universe within your own literary world regarding the Chicago mob. Is there a concordance you keep somewhere? You have so damned many books encompassing this history that you've reshaped ... is it all in your head?

I did make a list. I did make a time line. There was a fan who made a more detailed one, which I actually refer to. I'm not doing Heller right now. He's sort of on hiatus. But I had to be very careful, particularly with Nathan Heller. I didn't want him to be two places at the same time. There are Nathan Heller books that take place over three or four different time periods and I really have to keep track to say, "Where was he in August of 1937?" so that I don't have him meeting Huey Long on a day that he was on an airplane with Amelia Earhart. I'm trying to maintain the illusion that these are actually memoirs.

I was real loose about it for a while, then, all of the sudden it was just like, "Whoa, these things are starting to collide."

This is the first time in any of your books that I can remember where Eliot Ness is kind of portrayed with feet of clay.

Well, it's been there. The humanity, I hope, has been there. At the end of *Butcher's Dozen* is where his drinking begins. There are signs of it. There are signs of it. But my series about him, which is set in Cleveland—I did four—are in a very real sense his glory years. I've just completed, in fact, my first play, which is called *Eliot Ness, An Untouchable Life*. It's a one-man show. It was staged in Des Moines in November for one performance as a sort of way of getting it on its feet. We're going to do a more elaborate run in

Des Moines next year. I'm going to shoot that and it's going to become my next—well, whether it's a film or TV show depends on what we do with it—but that's the next sort of moving-image project.

That does his whole life. This is where I sort of put all the pieces together. I think it's a really strong piece. I've very proud of it.

You said Heller is on a hiatus right now.

Yeah, because I have to do *Road to Paradise,* then we'll see if my publisher wants to go from there.

***Road to Paradise* will be in a novel format?**

Yes.

***Flying Blind*: Does that remain your favorite Heller book? I've seen some statements to the effect you favor that title.**

Probably. But I probably had just written it. I would say it is one of my favorites. I really like 'em all. But *Stolen Away* was a kind of a watermark. That was well received, and it was massive and it was received as my best book-to-date.

A lot of people like *True Detective,* because it was the first Heller. *Million Dollar Wound* was a favorite of mine because it was the most complicated thing I've ever pulled off artistically. It does things I don't think any private eye novel has ever done. I'm also partial to *Angel in Black,* my version of the Black Dahlia murder, because I think I probably came pretty close to what really happened. And it does some things you really don't see in private eye novels. I remember one of the things that I was very proud of, was that when I turned in the synopsis for it, my editor at the time said, "Oh, but Heller is married in this." I said, "Yeah, he's married." And he said, "But, you know, you always have these really great sex scenes in the Heller books." And I said, "Well, you know, there are married people who have sex." When I turned it in, it was the only book in which they made me come back and soften some of the sex scenes.

Between a husband and a wife? Why doesn't that surprise me?

Yeah, he's on his honeymoon. He was, for a while anyway, having a good time. At least until he found the corpse of the Black Dahlia. But I liked that book. It has weird things in it. It has a detective whose wife decides to have an abortion. And it has the darkest ending of any of the Hellers, where he does something quite despicable. It always amuses me that no readers ever complain. I mean, Heller has done things that make Mike Hammer look like Mother Theresa, and nobody ever calls me on it. I take great delight in that, because it means I've really led them down the garden path.

Lee Child told me he gets away with stuff here in America, but when the books go to Europe, there are vigilante aspects to his character where he just gets clobbered.

I haven't really been published over there in a while. All my licensing stuff is over there in a fairly major way. It's going to be interesting to see with *Road to Perdition,* because it's selling in a lot of foreign countries—both the novelization I did and the original graphic novel. And *Purgatory* has sold in a lot of foreign countries. It's going to be interesting to see if that holds steady with my other stuff. But of course Perdition is not a series. It's a saga. It's set up so if I feel like doing an implant or doing a sequel, I can do that, but the endgame there is at five or six works, tops. I would have a lot of fun at some point—if there was a demand for it—to go back and maybe do a novel about Michael O'Sullivan when he was essentially being John Looney's chief enforcer. I think there's an "Angel of Death" novel that's possible. But I wouldn't want to do eight or nine "Angel of Death" novels. I'd like to do one. Maybe. We'll see.

In the early Heller books there were a lot of archival photos bound into those hardcovers. But not anymore.

We did that in the first four. That was at St. Martin's. When I changed publishers, the publisher at that time and every subsequent publisher has felt this way: that they detracted from the books; that the books should stand on their own. I have a lot of fans who miss those ... who loved that aspect of the books. But I have to say that I actually kind of came to agree with the publisher on that. Because I kept feeling like in those early books that they would review the photos. There'd be these comments, like, "Great ... what great photos." And I'd be like, "You know, the prose isn't chopped liver, either."

It undermined the notion that you were reading a novel?

Yeah. I think it helped in the beginning. I think it grounded the Hellers and it got at least whatever my core readership is. There was something fun in the first book, where maybe you have some thug beating up on Nate Heller and you kind of maybe feel like you're in a standard private-eye world. Then you turn the page and there's a photo of the thug. That gave a strange under-pinning, because I was doing something that was new—no one had ever done that. No one had ever done a private eye novel that dealt with a real mystery and the private eye was essentially the only character in the book who wasn't real. I felt it was the logical step after *Chinatown* and *City of Angels* and what Stu Kaminsky was doing. To say, okay, let's do a real crime, and obviously raise the bar for myself because I had to do all of this research.

The other day, one of the reviews—I forget where it was — but it used a term that I thought, "Wow, finally somebody came up with a term to describe what I do." It was "Pulp Faction." I thought, "Yeah, that's it, that's what I do. I do 'Pulp Faction.'"

A couple of your earlier books were just rereleased by Hard Case Crime.

Yeah, my first two books.

Was there any temptation to go into those and change anything, working as the writer you are now? Any drive to rework them in any way?

No. But they wanted me to look at the galleys and I refused.

Really?

Yeah. I said, "Look, I'm perfectly happy and proud of those books, but please don't ask me to revisit them. Because all it'll do is upset me and I'll want to rework them and tweak them. I'll want to do things that I really shouldn't do. I'm not who I was when I was twenty-one and wrote those books. So they need to be what they are. It tickles me that thirty years later they would be back out in print. I mean, they're pretty ephemeral and here they come back.

And it may be distressing that they are so similar to what I do now. It's a father and a surrogate son … the guy is like robbing banks and has a feud with a mob guy from Chicago. It's like, "Hmm, so much for progress."

I've seen that your Dick Tracy strips are to be reprinted by a firm based in Dayton, Ohio [Checker Books].

Yeah, they're up to the third volume now. That's fun: the idea that somebody who got fired off the strip, now there are books that say, "Dick Tracy: The Collins Files." That's pretty cool.

You've indicated that gig ended when you got on the wrong side of an editor.

Absolutely. He didn't like me and he didn't like my work and he'd been giving me a bad time —and I exploded. I used expletives that this guy had probably never even heard before. I just let him have it. That was probably the single worst example of me losing my temper—and there are any number of them. But that was a bad one. My wife happened to be walking by the door and she looked in at me and smiled and said, "Well, I'll be checking the want ads now." She thought there was no way the guy was going to hire me back.

In the intervening years have you ever been approached to come back and do anything with the character again?

By the *Tribune*? No, they've not come back to me. I don't think it's in very many papers now. They have it done by somebody who is on staff and being paid to do that, among other things, whereas they had to hire me as an outsider. But you know, I saved that strip. They brought me in—the head of Tribune Media Services then, Robert Reed; he's not there now. Last time I heard from him he was just about to retire, and they had done this to me and he told me he thought it was a mistake and he told them that it was a mistake. But he's the one who hired me. He and his editor—a different editor, obviously—they brought me into a hotel room in Chicago. We had this long conversation, and about halfway through, I realized that I had the job. I thought it was a feeler sort of interview, then I realized they weren't asking me what I might do, but what I *would* do.

One of the things the president of the syndicate said to me was, "We're going to offer you a five-year contract, but we have to be frank with you: we do not think there's five years left in this strip." Well, fifteen years later, I got fired after it had not only maintained, but picked up some papers and had a major film that I was consultant on. So I do think they made a mistake and probably because of the small number of papers they're in now, probably couldn't afford to get me back if they wanted to. Which I'm sure they don't.

I know you're a huge Bobby Darrin fan. Are you looking forward to the new Kevin Spacey film … and are you doing a novelization?

Oh, I tried. I put my name out. But I don't think there is one. If they knew how cheap they could have had me, they might have done one. He's an obsession of mine since 1959. In fact, there's this very bizarre thing where we had a rave review in *Entertainment Weekly* last week, and right next to my review was a smiling face of Bobby Darin in an ad pertaining to a book—a bio of him—with a Kevin Spacey blurb. So I turned to this thing—I'd actually been tipped to the fact we were going to have a review in *Entertainment Weekly,* but you never know whether it's going to be good or bad, and it's a sequel so I was expecting the worst—and I open the magazine up and here's this A- rave review and Bobby Darrin grinning at me, right next to it. So it's like, "Here you go."

I've heard the soundtrack and he's just done an incredible job. I'm so grateful to him [Kevin Spacey] because he's put Bobby back on the pop-culture radar. I don't care if it's the worst movie I've ever seen, he's gonna be on the top of my list and I think it's going to be a good film. We're going to see him in Chicago when he's out on his tour, doing his Bobby Darrin tour. This is a real good time to be a Bobby Darrin fan.

STEPHEN J. CANNELL

Hollywood Tough
(January 5, 2003)

Stephen J. Cannell boasts a staggering résumé: screenwriter, producer, director, mogul, actor and bestselling novelist.

His success as a writer is still more stunning to those in the know:

Cannell was an undiagnosed dyslexic whose condition went largely undetected until the age of thirty-five. By the time that diagnosis was made, Cannell was already one of Hollywood's hottest screenwriters and producers.

His reading/writing disability apparently hasn't affected his output—his screenwriting credits run to the four figures.

The list of TV shows he has created or co-created is staggering: *The Rockford Files, The A-Team, Baretta, Toma, The Commish, The Duke, Greatest American Hero, Hardcastle & McCormick, Hunter, Baa Baa Black Sheep, Silk Stalkings, Renegade, Wise Guy, The Hat Squad, Tenspeed & Brownshoe, Riptide, 21 Jump Street, Unsub, Sonny Spoon, Stingray,* and the list goes on …

His big break came in the 1960s, when he landed a job as head writer on the Jack Webb-produced series *Adam-12*, starring Kent McCord and Martin Milner as a couple of LAPD patrol officers.

That gig brought Cannell into direct proximity with the prickly personality of Webb. Cannell tells a story of spending several sessions working with Webb—and "Joe Friday's" daily tendency about the same time each afternoon to lash out at Cannell without provacation. Finally fed up, Cannell called Webb out: "Say that again Jack, and you better get your hands up, because I'm coming at you."

Cannell needed to be tough, going toe-to-toe as he later would with scrappy personalities like Robert Blake, Robert Conrad and George Peppard.

In recent years, Cannell has turned his attention to writing novels, determined to fulfill the unlikely goal he set with a single word selected to describe himself in his high school yearbook: "author."

Cannell has since moved to the top of the bestseller lists with several highly-praised novels.

Several of his books are currently in development for screen adaptation, as are several of his hit TV series, including *The A-Team, 21 Jump Street* and *The Greatest American Hero*.

Cannell and his wife of thirty-five years, Marcia—his high school sweetheart—have three children and what certainly must stand as one of the most enduring marriages in Hollywood.

Cannell spoke with me from his Los Angeles film production office, and again at a stop along his U.S. book tour.

• • • • •

When you were starting your career as a screenwriter, there were still several Westerns and medical shows on the television landscape— what led you to the crime genre?

When I started writing, I just wanted to write anything that I figured I could get a job writing. I was willing to write half-hour comedies. I wrote some half-hour spec scripts. I wrote a *Batman* script on spec that I couldn't sell. I was a very disciplined writer and I still am, so I would write for five hours a day, five days a week, and then on Saturday and Sunday I'd write all day long, because I had a regular job. I'd come home after working for my dad [Joseph K. Cannell, the namesake for Jim Rockford's father, Joseph "Rocky" Rockford], driving a furniture truck, and I'd get home at five o'clock and write until ten p.m. every night.

I was specing-out feature film scripts and TV scripts of all different varieties. What ended up happening was I started getting employed in the hour drama. The first company that put me under contract was Universal. I was doing *Adam-12*. I was the head writer on that show. There was a reward out for Universal's sense of humor in those days. There were no comedies on that lot. *Nothing.* They were the hour-drama shop. We had *Kojack, Rockford, Baretta* and just every show, the Mystery Movies—*Columbo, McCloud, MacMillian and Wife.* It was all dramas, even though some of them had a light take to them, like *The Rockford Files* did.

Then what happened was my success there was pretty major, which surprised the hell out of me. But then you get sort of defined by your successes. The idea that I would sit down and write *Cheers,* or something like that—even though I would have loved to have tried—they all go, "No, no, we don't want you to do that." I used to go to the networks all the time and pitch shows with female leads. I've always wanted to do a show with a female lead. They wouldn't let me do it. They just kept pushing me back toward what I had already done. Even though I ended up with shows like *Silk Stalkings,* where "Rita" was a great female character, or *Hunter,* where "DeeDee" was a great female character, basically they were male-driven kinds of shows.

To this day you haven't created a show with a female lead?

I wrote a couple of pilots over the years, but you know what? They didn't get bought. One of the things that happened in the latter part of the '90s, going into 2000 and on, was that the networks finally got hip to the fact that women were a larger percentage of their audience than men. The reason for that was men were being drawn off by ESPN and cable channels that were offering sports. So you had a higher degree of women watching television. Then, slowly, the female-lead drama began to become an important staple of network programming, but prior to that, they weren't doing it.

I find it interesting that *Adam-12* was your first major writing job in Hollywood. I tend to associate you with projects that have some overt or covert sense of humor. *Adam-12* always struck me as perhaps the most humorless show on TV.

Yes and no. It's actually not so. One of the things that we used to do on *Adam-12* was—it was a *great,* by the way, I hasten to say, it was a *great* place to start—they were half hour shows, and we would write what we called "spine stories." The spine stories were something that was generally going on between Reed and Malloy, the two principal characters. You'd hit it three times basically during the half hour. An example might be that Reed's going back to college, and Malloy isn't sure that this is the right thing, and that's part of it. So you'd have that spine story. Then there would generally be some major crime story, like some guy holding up 7-11s that they end up catching in the last reel of the picture. Then there were a couple or three of these little pieces—a lady calls and her cat's in a tree and she's got to get him down. These kind of silly little things that were like the comedy things.

What ended up happening on *Adam-12* was that those things ended up being played very broad. The woman would have curlers in her hair and she would really be this silly kind of caricature-type of person. That was sort of the way the show was being done. When I got there I decided, "You know what I'm going to try and do with these comedy bits, if I can?" Almost like in a writing class, where you'd come on a character in page seven and you'd be out of the character on page eight or nine—but that character had to exist during those three pages or four pages and be funny and at the same time, real—I sort of developed this technique of saying, "Every character has to have a yesterday and is going to have a tomorrow." What I noticed with a lot of these scripts that I had seen prior to my coming in there was that they were just played for laughs. I decided if the woman comes out there and her cat's in the tree, instead of it being some dopey thing about the cat being in the tree, I'd have this lady be late for her night school class in law. So there would be another energy in the thing beyond just, "Oh my cat's up in the tree! Can't you boys get it down?" It turned out to be really good for me, because when I started doing shows like *The Rockford Files,* I gave them a yesterday and I gave them a tomorrow and that was all part of what I was doing on *Adam-12.* So it was a very good learning process for me.

Turning to your books, you've mentioned Michael Connelly as a writer you admire.

Yeah, I love him.

Connelly, Dennis Lehane—

Another of my favorites. In fact, I was just filling out a thing for West Coast Crime, where I'm going to go, and they asked my favorite authors and I put Dennis and Michael, and Nelson De-Mille, and I like Jefferson Parker ... I thought *Silent Joe* was a cool book.

Connelly and Lehane started with recurring characters, or series, then moved into standalone novels in order to recharge, or because the characters were getting a bit stale for them. You've tended to go the other way, starting with standalones and now your recent books have centered on this single character, Shane Scully. Was that a conscious choice?

What happened was, when I started I told my publisher, "I don't want to write a series," because I had been writing series television for thirty years. I thought, "God, the fun of writing these novels is that I can create a whole new world, every time." Eventually, I wrote *The Tin Collectors* [featuring Shane Scully's debut]. It's interesting what makes an author select an area to write in. You know you're going to be writing a book for months, and you want to pick something that is going to be exciting to you. I also want to pick something that is going to stretch me, a little bit, and I want to pick something that hopefully I haven't written before, a relationship I haven't written before. One day I was sitting around thinking, "You know, I've never really done anything on Internal Affairs." I've *written* about Internal Affairs, but I don't know my ass from second base about Internal Affairs.

They're an easy heavy for a crime writer.

Exactly. Yeah, the "shooflies," the cops who go after cops. My inclination—my *feeling*—was, well, you know, they're kind of assholes who don't like the department and who don't like cops, negative stuff like that. That was my kind of stereotypical view and that's basically the way they are written in most people's novels.

Even in motion pictures, whenever they are portrayed. So I decided I'd go down to Internal Affairs in L.A. The Internal Affairs Division for the LAPD is actually headquartered in the Bradbury Building.

The Bradbury Building is this *incredible* building that was built about 1910. It almost looks like an old Louisiana courtyard with wrought iron railings and an interior courtyard that has been glassed over and these old, filigreed, wrought iron elevators. It's one of the most beautiful buildings. We shoot it all the time. I've shot it a half a dozen times, usually for '30s private eye-type shows.

I called up to find out where Internal Affairs is located, and, lo and behold, they've rented the top three floors of the Bradbury Building. So I go down there, and one of the things about LAPD is it is open, it's an open proceeding, unlike a lot of others. I walk in and I'm instantly recognized. I'm sitting in the back of what's called a Board of Rights hearing. They want to throw me out because they're afraid I'm there to write about it, but the commander—the guy who's running the Board of Rights hearing—says, "No, it's an open hearing, Mr. Cannell has a right to be here." So I was trying to convince these guys that I was thinking about writing a book about Internal Affairs.

Well, I ended up spending two and a half months down there. Anytime I had a half a day off or I wasn't doing something, I would go down there. I showed up at Internal Affairs probably fifty times over the next couple of months. Sometimes I'd just go for two hours over lunch. I got to know all of the advocates and all of the defense reps and I wrote this book called *The Tin Collectors,* which is about Internal Affairs. I thought it was going to be a standalone. Then I was having lunch one day with a friend of mine who used to be the special agent in charge of the L.A. office for U.S. Customs. I hosted a TV show for a year called *U.S. Customs Classified.* I was the "Robert Stack" of that show—a nationally syndicated show. I got to know this guy, Bill Gately, who was the special agent in charge of the L.A. office. He's a really cool character. I actually patterned the cop in *Final Victim* after Bill Gately.

We're having lunch one day and he starts to tell me about the "parallel market." The parallel market is Fortune 500 companies using their product to launder Colombian drug cash. The more he tells me about this, I couldn't believe what was happening. This has been happening for twenty-five years. The Federal government *knows* the Fortune 500 companies are using their product to launder this Colombian drug money. And, now, al Qaeda is doing the same parallel market laundering for drug money out of Afghanistan. The more I thought about it, I thought, "You know, I could use these same characters from *The Tin Collectors*, and I could have Shane Scully tackle this case. Instead of doing it as a customs case, he'll do it as an LAPD case." So I went and pitched it to my publisher, and they said, "Will you *please* write a series? Please!" And I said, "Look, I don't want to write a series, but I'll write a second book." Then *The Tin Collectors* became a *New York Times* bestseller, and so did *Viking Funeral,* and I got trapped.

Now you're on to book number three.

I have finished three, *Hollywood Tough.*

Are you going to do a fourth?

Yeah, because, you know what? People *like* him. *But,* what my publisher has allowed me to do is, well, I'm very disciplined: I've been writing two novels a year, anyway. I was starting to pile novels up. I had three completed novels that actually didn't yet have publication dates. One is a standalone called *Runaway Heart,* that will be released by St. Martin's in June [2003]. So we're going to do two novels next year. I've also written a standalone called *Love at First Sight,* which will probably come out a year from June. So now I'm doing two novels a year. I'll have my January "Shane Scullys," and my off-season standalones, and I'll do that until I fall over, I guess. I *do* enjoy standalones, but I've been having fun with Scully. I'm getting ready to write another Shane Scully. I've sort of plotted it. I know what the story is, but I haven't sat down and written an outline yet, which I'll do when I get back from my tour. It's a great idea for a story, called *Vertical Coffin.* A "vertical coffin," by the way, is a doorway.

I was about to ask.

In police jargon, any doorway is often referred to as a "vertical coffin," because when you go through them you can die. This particular vertical coffin is a very specific killing that takes place in a doorway. So, I've got a good story for that, and, *Hollywood Tough,* again, was a story that I've wanted to write about the underworld trying to take over the below-the-line film industry.

Yes, again, I found it interesting that only now, several novels in, are you taking on your old Hollywood milieu.

Well, it was just a *great* story. Back in the 1930s, Al Capone and Meyer Lansky and those guys actually controlled the IATSE—which is the organization of below-the-line film unions in Los Angeles—for about five years by running off all the other candidates and getting one of the business agents to run for president. They basically controlled the I.A. The idea was that they [the mob] would control IATSE, then they would cut special deals with producers and let them shoot on the low budget rate card, in return for which they would get ownership of the backend of the pictures. Well, that's what this guy [the villain of *Hollywood Tough*] is trying to do. He believes that by controlling IATSE, he will eventually get his hands around the $70 billion California film industry, which would make him one of the most powerful men in California. In fact, this mobster would have the power to call a strike and literally shut down the fire and police departments, because we are that dependent on taxes from the entertainment industry. A guy actually came out here with the intention of doing this about ten years ago. The police department found out about it, and ended up setting up a phony movie company to sting him on a RICO charge, which is what Shane Scully does in this novel. He ends up producing this film, which gets out of control. He's on this horse that he can't ride. He has to go back to the LAPD and say, "I need another one-hundred-and-fifty-thousand dollars...I need another half a million." They want to keep this guy out of town, but, at the same time, when they get over a million dollars in pre-production in this movie, it's pretty funny.

It is pretty funny, and it comes across as funny, but it doesn't come across as a particularly *fond* portrait of the industry. Or, at least, it didn't to me.

If you want to talk about the excesses of Hollywood, you look at something like the *Twilight Zone* [1983] film and, I'm blanking on the name of the director ...

John Landis?

Yes, John Landis. Nobody says "no" to these guys. I think it's important for people to hear "no" occasionally. If you think you can have anything you want, then pretty soon you're screaming at a helicopter pilot, saying, "Lower, lower, lower, and—"

And Vic Morrow is dead?

They forget completely there are children and Vic Morrow is under there, and you blow a charge and bring a copter down and it's bad behavior. It *is* bad behavior.

You owned your own production studio and created many, many shows, yet never found yourself caught up in those kinds of excesses?

I owned the thirty-eight shows that I produced from my company. Actually, I *love* Hollywood. My experiences in this industry have been charming, in a way. I find show business people to be fun and entertaining. There is no anger in me at all. But there *is* a high degree of lunacy in show business. It's lunacy that is created by the fact that it is not a real world. There is celebrity. You know, people are actually really, really concerned about who Madonna is sleeping with. I say, "Who *cares?*" There are articles written about it every day—cover stories in magazines. Pretty soon, the people in this industry start to take themselves a little bit too seriously. It's a very seductive thing. It's happened to me, too, and I'm pretty grounded. I've got really great parents and, fortunately, I've also surrounded myself with people who will grab me by the throat when I start to act that way and go, "What are you *doing?*"

You also have maybe one of the record-long marriages in Hollywood.

I do. And my wife is certainly one of the first to stomp on me if

I start to wander around and lose control. She says, "Listen, I remember you when you had acne," because we were dating in the eighth grade. It's great to have people around you who are not impressed by you. Even though I'd love to have people around me read every script that I wrote and tell me that it was great and actually have them be great, the greater problem was to have them tell me it was great [even if] it wasn't. I've learned over the years to find true critics, who come in and say, "You know, you may want to take another look at this—it isn't as great as you think it is." And then if I fire that guy or gal for having that opinion, then I'm liable to fall prey to this very thing you see happening with these characters in *Hollywood Tough*. But the whole thing with that *Neural Surfer* movie [in *Hollywood Tough*]—it *isn't* that far off the truth. Look at *Battlefield Earth* [the 2000 science fiction film starring John Travolta and based on a novel by the L. Ron Hubbard, founder of the Church of Scientology, of which Travolta is an adherent]. Nobody would tell John Travolta that that was a piece of shit, you know? That thing had been around forever, but he was determined to have El-Ron's piece brought to the screen. I'm not saying that there is anything wrong with John Travolta having that belief and that love for the material, but if he's wrong, somebody needs to tell him.

When you are writing a script for *Rockford*, for instance, I assume you are visualizing James Garner and hearing his voice delivering the dialogue. Do you "cast" your characters in your novels, so to speak? Do you have an actress or actor in mind when you shape the characters?

No, *never* do it.

You mentioned a friend who served as the model for a character in *Final Victim*—the character of "John Lockwood," I take it—

God, you *have* read the books, haven't you?

I've enjoyed the hell out of 'em ...

Well, yeah, Bill Gately was my take on John Lockwood. But it was just because of Bill, who was one of these guys that really, really was a guy who put catching criminals above his own career, which ended up costing him pretty dearly. He was guy who did not play politics. A guy who was willing to take on his own bosses to succeed. As a result, he was accused of stealing money by the U.S. Customs Department. They ran a whole Internal Affairs investigation on him. Basically took him off the job, sent him to Washington, made him fly a desk … never told him that he was exonerated by their own investigation. He had to file a Freedom of Information Act to find out that he had been cleared. They wanted the axe held over his head so he wouldn't shoot his mouth off to the press. He was this guy who I thought was really colorful, and, at the same time, a really heroic character in my own mind. So I didn't make John Lockwood sound like Bill, but just the [kept] idea of that character being willing to be off the page a little bit. Basically, though, I don't try to write for actors. When I created the *Rockford Files,* when I wrote the pilot script, I didn't know that Jim Garner was going to play it. I thought that we were going to get one of the people under contract at Universal [Studios].

I read somewhere that Robert Blake was up for it.

Well, actually, Frank Price [then-Universal Television President] wanted Robert Blake to play it after he read my screenplay. He called Roy Huggins [the creator of the series *Maverick,* which also starred Garner] and me up to his office. I was, like, twenty-nine years old: I didn't know my ass from second base. We go up to the office and he says—this is *exactly* what he said—"I'll tell you one little change you could make in your material that will guarantee you a five-year hit, and," he said, "it won't take you five seconds to make the changes." Now, what a *fuckin'* deal *that* is. And I said, "Well, what's that Frank?" And he goes, "You know, every successful detective show on the air today, the detective has something strange or different about him. Longstreet is blind …"

Cannon is fat.

Yes, "Cannon is fat. Ironside is crippled." He goes through the whole list. And he says, "I think that Rockford should be five-foot, three-inches tall." And I said, "Jeez …" I'm sitting there, and Roy Huggins, who was my godfather in the business and the best there ever was, he's sitting there, and I'm looking over at him thinking, "Roy, you've *gotta* stomp on this!" Roy had this thing, when he hated an idea—and I *knew* he hated this idea—he would always do this: When he hated an idea, he would always go, [falsetto] *"Ohhhhhhhhhhhhh …"* [*Laughing*] That always meant, "What a horrible idea." So Roy went, *"Ohhhhhhhhhhhh hh …"* like that. But he didn't say anything else. So Frank says, "Go see *Electra Glide in Blue*" [starring Robert Blake] and we left the meeting. I go, "Roy, if we make Rockford a little guy, when he chickens out, it's not funny anymore. It's like he's chickening out because he's a shrimp." Roy said, "No, no, I understand, you don't have to tell me that." He says, "You know, when you get a horrible casting idea, the way you overcome it, is you just get a better idea." And I said, "What are we going to do?" I'm panicking. Roy says, "You know what you've written here? You've written *Maverick* in the private eye genre." And Roy had produced *Maverick* and created *Maverick*. So he got the script over to Jim, and within hours after we had sent the script to Jim, we got a call from Meta Rosenberg saying, "We want to do this." So now we had Jim Garner and Robert Blake became a distant memory, but, as it turned out, Frank was determined to get Robert Blake on the air—and he was right—so we came up with *Baretta*.

The CBS movies—the reunion movies—of *The Rockford Files* that were done a few years ago: were those something that you initiated, or did someone come to you?

I'll tell you exactly who it was: Charlie Engle, who was an executive at Universal back all of the years ago when we were making the show. And it was still Universal who ended up selling it to CBS. You couldn't sell in to NBC [where *The Rockford Files* originally ran], because they wouldn't do it. But he sold it to CBS, which was probably actually a better place for it, because they had an older audience. So they cut the deal with Jim, and they gave him a fortune to do it. Then they wanted to reassemble our writing staff. They brought Charles Johnson in to be the executive producer, and Juanita Bartlett was the co-executive producer and they made me the supervising producer, which was what I was during the series. That was fine, because at the time, I was running my own studio and had six shows on the air: the last thing in the world I really wanted to do was to go to work for Universal, but, at the same time, I didn't want to not be part of this project. So when the thing was all over [*laughing*] they don't have any money for me. So, they say to me, "Well, how can we get you to do it?" So I agreed to be the supervising producer on those for like five thousand dollars an episode, which is like … well, everyone else is making, like, $50K. David Chase—

Of *Sopranos* fame …

Yes, who was also one of our writer/producers on the show—everyone knows how great David was—but, back when we were doing these movies, David was sort of odd-man out. His television career had not blossomed as I thought it should have, because I always thought he was one of the best writers I ever knew.

I *loved* his episodes of *Rockford*.

They were always the best.

But then along came *Northern Exposure*, which never seemed the right fit for him.

He did *Northern Exposure* and some other things, and he always had such a specific voice, you know? And I really wanted him to be part of the reunion shows' writing team, because the idea was that Juanita, David and I would come up with all of the stories and write all of the scripts, which, in fact, we did. I got paid as a writer, but I was producing for five thousand dollars an episode. So [*laughing*], they were trying to cut the deal with him, and they said, "Well, how much do you want?" and David said, "Just give me whatever you gave Cannell," thinking that I got a huge number. So David and I both ended up doing the show for five thousand dollars an episode. We did eight of them for that. He was there for all of them and he was so great. He finally came in and said, "Man, we got boned." And I said, "What do you mean?" And he said, "How come you did it for five thousand dollars?" And I said, "Because I'm really not going to be producing that much, because I've got six hours on the air and I really can't sit here and cut film, but I want to be part of the scripting." So we did 'em all. I wrote two, David wrote two and Juanita wrote three and we got one other writer to write the last one. There were eight.

It was great to have it back for a while.

Well it was a great show. And of course we had the best star you could ever have. Jim [Garner] was so respectful of all of the writers—David, Juanita and myself. He never changed a line of dialogue. It was a dream job for a writer, because he literally wouldn't change anything. Juanita wrote very short—if you looked at a Juanita Bartlett script, her lines of dialogue were very short. One or two sentences. And she had this amazing ability in a very few number of words to say so much and be so funny. David [Chase] wrote soliloquies. Some of his speeches went on half a page. I was somewhere in the middle of the two of them. My speeches were longer than Juanita's but not as long as David's. And we all wrote kind of differently. David is a very cerebral writer. I'm a very visceral writer. I think Juanita is a visceral writer. But all of us were able to write that show and make it slightly different. All of our minds were slightly different. I used to read David's stuff and go, "God, I'm never going to be as good as this guy." And he told me he used to read my stuff and felt the same way. I just talked to him the other day, and he said, "I'd think, I've done it, this show has got nowhere to go, then I'd read one of your scripts and think, oh, there's still some stuff we haven't done. There's still stuff to do on this show." We had that kind of great respect for one another, and then Jim would never change anything.

He must be the only actor I've ever heard that said of.

If a guest star was paraphrasing material, he would listen to it in the first camera rehearsal. Then he would go up to the guest star and he would say, "You know, I think we have the best writers in Hollywood working on this show, and I just never change anything, and it would mean a lot to me if you wouldn't either." So we got our lines exactly as written from *everybody* because Jim protected us. Well, there was this one time: It was about the fifth year, and David had written this script, and as I said, he wrote these very cerebral and sometimes quite long lines. They were sometimes a little hard for actors to remember, because, since they were cerebral, they weren't coming from an emotional center, they were coming out of David's head. Very much like Paddy Chayefsky used to write. So sometimes the connective tissue between one thought to the next was a little obscure, so actors couldn't remember the dialogue. It would occasionally happen with David's scripts. By the way, that doesn't mean shit—his stuff was beautiful. I on the other hand, was a visceral writer, so there was an emotional connection between one line and the next because it was all coming out of my visceral viewpoint.

So, one day I get a call from the director on the set, and he's saying, "You better get down here because Jim is going nuts! He can't remember this dialogue." Jim hated to hold up the company. He hated to be the guy booting the line. So I get David, because it is his script, and we're walking down to Stage 12 at Universal. I'm saying, "This is amazing: five years on this show, and this guy has never asked for a line to be changed. Not one. This is just the exception that proves the rule." David is kind of grumbling, and the red light goes off and we step onto the stage, and we hear Jim screaming profanities. I can just see David cringing because he wrote the material. I pulled Jim aside and I said, "Hey Jim, I understand you're having a little problem," and he said, "Yeah, I can't remember the goddamn line." I said, "Well, you know, it's an awful long speech, I can have Rocky come in and say something, and David will fix it for us." And Jim said, "What? You mean, change the line?" And I said, "Yeah." He said, "Steve! It's a great fucking line! I just can't remember it!" [*laughing*] So that was it. We never changed a line, even in that case. He was perfect. What a joy to work on a show like that. That's why we all came back for the reunion movies even though we were all busy with other things.

Let me ask you a little bit about reducing—or adapting—your own books for the screen. You've said in other interviews you enjoy the format because you can pace it your way, fill it out and take your own time, but I understand that you've adapted at least one of your own novels into screenplay format. What's that like?

It's an interesting process. I've sort of learned how to do it now.

Do you find yourself cursing yourself—the screenwriter in you cursing the novelist for coming up with something crucial that doesn't adapt to the screen easily?

No, actually, I congratulate myself, and I'll tell you why: One other time, I have adapted a book by another novelist, and one of the things that often happens with novels is that there is no second act. *All* stories need to be told in three acts, whether they're novels, whether they're screenplays, whether they're Broadway plays, whether they're *jokes*. A good joke always has three acts. It's generic. Yet, a lot of novelists, because act two is the hardest act to plot, don't. Act 2 contains the two most important plot moves: One is the complication of the original idea, which would be at the top of Act 2, and the second most important part of Act 2, which is what we call the second act/curtain, which is "the wipeout." Basically that destroys the hero's plans. And during Act 2, you should always have your heavy or adversary in motion and your protagonist in motion. Every move for your protagonist should be a move forward. In screenplays and television, even though television is written in four acts, generically, it's three acts. Every story is in three acts. So, when I wrote my books, I worked them out in three acts when I did the outlines. You name the novel, I'll give you the three acts.

They're ready to go?

They're ready to go. They're laid out. That second act is there, man, and it's the second act which is always the hardest. If you're trying to adapt a novel with no second act, then you're trying to put a complication into the novelist's original idea and you're trying to put in a second act complication where it doesn't exist and literally, the entire plan crashes. And then you're also trying to stay at the same place in the end. *Fucking hard to do,* because you can't mess with the front. And then, you've got a producer who loves the book, but you're going, "Guys, we can't be in the same place on page sixty that we were on page thirty. Something has to happen that changes all of this." It's *critical* to structure. Well, my books all have three-act plots.

What I do when I start—the first thing I do—is I write down generically the three acts. What are the three acts of the novel? Act 1 defines the problem. Pick the novel—the first act defines the problem. The complication is at the top of Act 2. Okay, I know I need to keep my complication and I know I need to keep my second act complication and I need to keep my second act wipe-out, my second act curtain. This is before I ever start writing. Now I start to say, "Okay, what in Act 1 is really not that impor-tant?" And I go back and I just start eliminating things: "You know, I really don't need this subplot. It's cool for the book, but I don't really need it."

Now I make a beat sheet, basically. Here's the new outline. It still basically follows the track of the novel, same complications, same second act/curtain, same solution, but these things are miss-ing: "I'm not going to write this subplot with the girls this way, I'm going to make the love story this. I'm going to make the changes this." And then I sit down and write myself an outline basically for the script. Then I've learned not to marry any of the dialogue in the novel. One of the things I learned when I first adapted my first novel—there were certain scenes that I really loved, so I had my novel in my lap and said, "I don't want to leave these lines out." You can't write that way. I've *never* written that way. So I just throw all of the dialogue from the book away. I don't even look at it. I write completely new scenes. They may be about the same things, but the dialogue is completely fresh. Be-cause then I can stay fresh. If I stay fresh, then hopefully there's some snap in the work. If I'm just regurgitating the novel, then it doesn't work.

That's fascinating. You see the occasional screenplay that a novelist has adapted from his own work, and it tends to be slavish to the book and—

And it's usually just a *bad* job. If you don't try to save any of your dialogue, and you start all over again, then you have the chance to let the character to grow in a completely different direction as you are writing. I just finished adapting *Riding the Snake,* and it was a great process. I found things in this guy that I never found in him in the novel. It was good.

Do you watch much episodic TV these days yourself?

Yeah. I watch some.

Can you let go and enjoy it?

Oh, sure.

I wonder if the craftsman in you is critiquing or intruding as you watch.

No it never did, even when I was day-to-day doing it. You have to be able to appreciate your calling's work instead of sitting there being a critic all of the time. I mean, that's no fun. When I watch Dick Wolf's stuff, or Steve Bochco's or Don Bellasario's, I sit there and I just let these guys take me for a ride. You can't sit there and say, "Oh, I see what he's doing," or, "I know what he's up to here," or, "I see where he's going." I don't do that. I don't try to out-think the story, I don't try to get to the punch-line ahead of the actors. I just watch it like I would any other movie. Same as if I'm reading a book. If I'm reading Michael [Connelly] or Dennis [Lehane], if I'm reading *Mystic River,* I'm not trying to figure out what is he doing, why is he doing this?

How did he pull that off?

How did he pull that off? I'm just letting him take me on the ride because he's a good enough writer to do it. The only time I get in trouble with a writer or author is if he doesn't write well. If an author doesn't write well, or when they don't know their subject matter, then I start to get angry and frustrated. If I ever have that desire to take out a pencil and correct something, then it doesn't work.

You read Michael Connelly or Dennis Lehane, and when those cops are on that murder scene, man, you are at a murder scene. These guys are taking you to a murder scene. They sign the crime scene attendance sheet. All of the stuff on forensics is correct. They know the stuff and research. When I went to Internal Affairs when I was writing *The Tin Collectors*, I learned *so* much about what was going on down there that I had no idea was happening, but which made my book so much richer.

The first thing I found out is that they aren't all a bunch of ne'er do wells down there who hate the police department. That initial concept that I had—that everybody else has—is incorrect. You know what they all are? They're the climbers. They're the guys who want to go to administration. They're the smartest and sharpest. They're the best looking. I never saw so many guys in Armani. There isn't one guy in Internal Affairs who wears his gun on his hip—they've all got ankle holsters because they don't want to spoil the cut of their clothes. It's fucking amazing.

It's like going to the networks. So, starting right there, everything changed … everything about the way I wrote this book. The first guy who did this—who really took you into the world of police, was Joe Wambaugh. He wrote those guys like they really were. You read *The Glitter Dome* and you go, "Jeez, these guys are all suicidal." Well, yeah, after I read that, I found out that one of the highest suicide rates is among police. Divorce rates, too, and all the rest of that bad stuff.

On a different subject, were you surprised by the strong reception for the *Hunter* reunion TV movie that was on recently?

No. Not at all. As a matter of fact, I would have been surprised had it not done that well. Here's the problem with Saturday night: When Frank Lupo and I went over to NBC, I walked into Jeff Zucker's office and I said, "Okay Jeff, this is going to be the shortest meeting that you will ever have. You will either love this idea or all of us are going to be sitting on our asses out on the street here in about thirty seconds." I said, "*Hunter*, on Saturday night, as a movie first, and then maybe as a series."

I said, "This is a show that controlled its time period for seven years at NBC. *Walker, Texas Ranger* did exactly the same thing on CBS. There is a market for this and it's not being serviced by—what's on *Providence*, or whatever is on … *The District.*"

I said, "You put this on and all of those people that don't want to go out and shake their booty on Saturday night—an older demographic—will be there."

He said, "I love it: can you make it for a price?" We argued about license fees for a few minutes, and I said, "You give us a number and I'll get there with a picture." He gave us a number and we actually made it for that. I would have been really surprised if it hadn't worked. Because that kind of programming is not the sexy, very fresh sort of thing. I know how to do shows like *NYPD Blue*. I can write dark material. We did it with *Wiseguy* and some of my novels are that way. Frank and I sat there and wondered, should we modernize this? Should we make it shades of gray, or should we do it back like it was in the 1980s? I said, "Do it like it was back in the '80s, because the people who are going to be watching it are those same people. They are the ones who are home." Our demographics were *horrible*—they were older than hell—but we won the households. You're never going to get a high eighteen- to thirty-four-year-old viewership on Saturday night. They're not home … they're not there to watch. So it performed pretty much the way I expected it to.

PART V

Duty & Honor

CRAIG HOLDEN
Love & Death
(January 21, 2005)

I first heard of Craig Holden on a snowy February night several years ago in Ann Arbor. I was attending a James Ellroy reading and "The Demon Dog" pointed Holden out in the audience and touted Holden's just-released novel, *Four Corners of Night* (1999).

On Ellroy's recommendation, I picked up a copy and sank into Holden's dark, expansive, elegiac examination of lost daughters and troubled Ohio cops. It instantly vaulted into my list of top ten noir novels. Irish crime novelist Ken Bruen regards *Four Corners of Night* as "a minor masterpiece."

Holden, who studied medicine and psychology while honing his fiction writing by composing short stories and editing a student literary magazine, debuted with 1994's *The River Sorrow*. Touted as a "thriller," *Sorrow* centered on a compromised doctor and drew heavily on Holden's own medical expertise.

In 1996, *Sanctuary,* another "thriller," followed—this one about an ill-fated hitchhiker who falls in with a bloodthirsty band of religious militants. The book was inspired by the then-recent deaths of Branch Davidians in Waco, Texas and the Oklahoma City bombing.

Holden's third book was the remarkable *Four Corners of Night*.

In 2002, *The Jazz Bird* appeared, a fictionalized account of the murder trial of real-life Cincinnati bootlegger George Remus, who reputedly inspired F. Scott's Fitzgerald's Jay Gatsby.

Holden completed his fifth novel, *The Narcissist's Daughter*, in January 2005. Set in Toledo, Ohio in the late 1970s, the novel tracks the bloody events spinning out of the spiteful machinations of vengeful and libidinous pre-med student Syd Redding.

Craig Holden spoke with the interviewer from his home in Michigan.

• • • • •

Your publisher is playing up some of the more obvious apparent biographical aspects of *The Narcissist's Daughter* in the press sheets … the medical elements and the book's setting in your old stomping ground of Toledo. So what was the trigger for this book? Nostalgia?

[*Chuckling*]. I'll tell you what, I think in the beginning, when you start writing, I think it's a good idea not to be too autobiographical.

But many first novels clearly do go that route.

You know when I started to have success, it was when I stopped doing that—started making up characters who were really not me. I mean, Adrian Lancaster [*The River Sorrow*] is a long way from anyone I ever was, you know. I'm doing some teaching now, occasionally, and I try to get that across. In fact, I just had a conversation yesterday with someone who has never written anything in a voice other than her own. And I said, "Try somebody who is not you and see how it works." If she'll do it, she'll be ahead of things.

But this is my fifth book and part of me just thought there is enough distance now that I could probably try this a little bit—using some material that is a little bit closer to home and see what happens. So it was a little bit of self-indulgence I suppose. And I'm not sure how it's going to turn out because of that. But I think it's been long enough now from when I was in those places that are in the book. I find that when I write about a place or a time, it helps to have distance. I have that distance now, so it was sort of fun to go back and do that.

The other thing is that *The Jazz Bird* was *so* research heavy. I just felt like doing a book where the only research was in my head. Really, the only research I had to do for this book was some research on the cars and to some extent on narcissistic personality disorder, just to inform myself a little bit about it.

The idea was never to write a case study ...

Exactly. I read a little bit, but not much, really. The other thing was finding out what VCR or what video camera you could get in 1978, or could you? How much would it cost, and those sort of things. The funny thing is, there are Web sites for all those sorts of things now. You can actually find Web sites dedicated to old video cameras, with pictures of the old video cams from every year.

They were probably the size of end tables.

They were huge, yeah. And as you can see in the book, you couldn't get a camcorder. You had to have a video player and a separate camera and tape deck. Betamax ... you know how big those things were.

I'd read that the new novel grew out of something you had written, which is a scene now in the book, involving some guys out in the woods burying a body. Was that something that started as a short story and just kind of grew? You don't strike me as the kind of writer who is writing one book, and thinking two or three books out with strong structure for future books.

I'm trying to do a little of that now. That scene though was really just a scene that I wrote probably when I was working on *Four Corners* some years ago—because that was when I was in Toledo doing a lot of that research and that's when we shot some photos there down along the Maumee River, where that scene came from. It's a real place on the river. It really was just a scene. It was something that I wrote while I wrote *Four Corners,* but I don't think it ever really had anything to do with that other book.

Interesting. And interesting in that *Four Corners* was your other first-person POV book, too. Do you play with voices in writing some of your other books, and then end up not using a voice? I'm wondering how it affects your writing in terms of shifting voice.

I do it a lot. I spend a lot of time working with voices. This book took so long to write because I couldn't get the voice right. This book, *The Narcissist's Daughter,* was in third person for a long time. It was actually in the third person from multiple points of view. I really thought that's how it was going to get told. I liked it enough that I sort of kept going with it, but it never gelled. I finally understood that it needed to be in first person. I think part of the reason I was so insistent on trying not to do it that way is because a lot of this—the place, not the actual events, but the place—is so autobiographical out of my life. I think I felt like I needed not to write it in the first person because I didn't want it to be seen as me, or to risk that perception.

Ultimately, I realized the story had to be told from the kid's point of view and that he wasn't me. Then I wrote a draft or a couple of partial drafts in which I sort of switched third-person stuff that I had to his voice, but it still had a third-person sensibility. My editor and agent kept telling me, this is just too, what was the word they used?

Too outside?

Yeah! Like an observer. That's a kind of classic problem you can get into with first person. I didn't think I had made a mistake in giving the voice to him, but I was still holding something back … still guarding something. Finally, I just had to let him go as a character and let his language flow. So in the book, I have this voice that I've never used before. I think the feel of the language is quite a bit different than any of my other books. And it doesn't feel autobiographical. The voice doesn't feel autobiographical.

You seem to have a really enviable situation in that you're allowed to find the book and take the time to really craft it. There's so much pressure on people to do a book a year, usually, and often to really unfortunate results. Do you feel that pressure at any point?

I do now. That's the problem with publishing when you're not a bestseller: it's hard to make a living. You know, I make my living at this and it's getting harder. This book just took way too long. My publisher and my editor, they love the books, but they just tear their hair out over how long it takes. They like the good reviews and all that, but really they essentially said to me this year, "You really need to publish more books." I know for my editor it is very difficult, because he is a very literary guy and he wants good stuff. And he knows fast stuff is maybe also not going to be as good. But he also knows that you need to build a writer. He's someone who pushes me to write leaner books and I think that's probably a good thing and it's a direction I've wanted to go in anyway.

My previous editor really liked big, thick books. I think that's fine if they're complex and so forth, but I also think they can get kind of long-winded. And something I wanted to do, when I was at Dell, was to write short novels. I'm really attracted to and very interested in very short novels. I've been reading a lot of them, short stories. I've been thinking a lot about the structure of narrative and trying to become simpler—not in the language, but in the structure—and still have it be tension-filled and all of that. I've got a whole shelf of tiny little books under two hundred pages.

Are you writing many short stories yourself these days?

Not short stories. I just can't find the time for those.

I understand you wrote and sold some while you were in college.

Well, yeah. I actually had a chapbook published. Three stories, I think it was. It was published by a university in Toledo. I've got a couple of stories out right now through my agent.

Were those early stories kind of in the vein of the things you write now?

It's interesting to look back at them. Not too long ago, I was looking at the introduction to that little chapbook. The guy who wrote the introduction, my old friend Tom Barden, he wrote, "They're clearly not solely centered in action though they include a bar fight, a car wreck and a body tackle along an interstate highway. They use action more as a surface, in the way D.H. Lawrence used sex in his novels—not for its own sake, but as an opening into character … as a metaphor for human beings in general." When I read that I thought, "That really is it and I guess that's what I've always been doing." But the book I'm working on right now, I really am trying to do a much shorter novel and in a weird way that has converged with what my editor has asked for, which is more books. My presumption, anyway, is that a shorter book won't take as long to write. That may not be the case, but we'll find out.

It's a theory, anyway.

Yeah right. Well *The Narcissist's Daughter* is my shortest book by far and it took plenty of time to write.

A few days ago I spoke with Pete Dexter and I've been reading or re-reading a lot of his books in between rereading yours. He gets hung with the "noir" label a lot and people try to claim him as a crime writer. I assume that must happen with you and your books, as well. I take it, like Dexter, you probably don't have much use for such labels at all.

No, I don't really. Especially not "mystery," which is the one you hear a lot, too. The first one I wrote might have had some mystery element to it, but that's the closest I've ever come. *Four Corners* had a mystery element, but it's not a mystery. As far as genre goes, that's not what I do. I don't even think of them as crime novels or thrillers. I don't think this book [*The Narcissist's Daughter*] is a thriller. I know it's being marketed as a thriller, but I don't think it is a thriller. Not to me it isn't.

I didn't read it as such. It obviously has a suspenseful element, but I hear "thriller" and I think of something very calculated in which plot overrides character.

The term "noir," I've been thinking about that a lot. I was recently invited to a noir festival in France with my French editor. It was interesting being there. I think the French think of the term "noir" very differently than we do. We use it as a genre label—it's a crime novel, and it has got a lot of blood in it. But François, my French editor, is also a scholar and publishes a number of books on noir. He edits the series of noir titles—more than five hundred now. I got on a panel and I talked to him about the term "noir" and how they define it. It's a much different kind of definition than I believe we have here. It's closer to what I think I'm actually doing. His definition of noir is that instead of the story, it comes out of the character. It's not about plot, but almost always about character ... following some urge or obsession. In other words, what makes it a dark story and what makes the story go is not as much what happens to the character externally, but what pushes the character.

A sensibility and an attitude.

Yeah. It becomes a character study with, of course, a dark element. I now look at the early noir novels and it's certainly an interesting way to look at it. And then I look at my books, and that's pretty much how they work.

There are some unifying threads running through your novels, yet they are all quite different from one another. You've never really come close to writing the same book twice, at all.

[*Chuckling*] No.

***Four Corners of Night*—I remember being profoundly affected by that when I first read it. I've read it a couple of times since. Do you remember what the trigger for *Four Corners of Night* was? I take it that the setting is a kind of bigger, altered Toledo, Ohio.**

Well, if you place the city in that book, you'll know there is no city where I place it. I think with *Four Corners* I wanted to make it a little bigger city, or have that possibility, anyway. But you're asking about where the idea from the book came from?

Yes. After the first two, it seemed to me to represent a dramatic shift— a shift away from the first two books, which, bringing up labels again, seemed to be pushed as "thrillers." *Four Corners* seemed very much a different kind of novel.

I think to be fair, the first two probably were thrillers in a sense. I sense they went beyond what most thrillers do. But really, as those books are set up, they really are more sort of plot driven. But when I started to write *Four Corners*, I was aware of the fact that I wanted not to write a thriller. As it happens, I'd gotten a new contract after writing those first two books, so I sort of had the freedom to let it germinate instead of having to pound it out.

The actual genesis of the story was in the same way in *The Narcissist's Daughter*—one of the first scenes of that piece was that thing along the river I'd drafted a long time ago. *Four Corners* also had a scene like that, which became the scene where the boys stood waiting on the school bus. Later, when I started writing *Four Corners*, I thought it would be good to have them have to come back to their own childhood in the course of the book.

I'll tell you honestly, the other thing—I was a on a book tour in San Francisco and I had some time, so I went to see *Seven,* you know the film?

About the serial killer.

Yeah. I thought, "Oh, another serial killer thing," but I actually enjoyed the movie more than I thought I would. But, if you remember the movie, the whole thing happens, and then there is the final scene where Brad Pitt kills Kevin Spacey. The very last image of the movie is when he gets in the car after he has just learned his wife has been beheaded and he has killed this guy. The look on his face was—

Well, I just remember sitting there and thinking to myself, "That would be an interesting place to *begin* a book." In other words, after this tragic sort of thing has happened, where do you go from there? It just sort of planted that seed—how would a cop react if he faced something like that? How would he react if his child was killed, if his wife was killed? And that was really when I started thinking about that story. It became a child because I thought, "Well, what stronger reaction could you have than the murder of your own child?"

It was a hard book to write because there are really three different lines in that story: the story about the child murder, then the very current story about the girl who has disappeared and the detectives, and then the wife. I did some ride-alongs with the cops and those were very important to me in the writing.

I guess to touch on some things you said earlier, and to touch on *The Jazz Bird,* there's probably not another historical novel in the offing anytime soon.

Well given it's the 1970s, *The Narcissist's Daughter* is almost a historical novel. It's funny how much things have changed. In a sense they haven't, but some of the stuff we talked about, the little details, they've changed quite a lot. The book I'm writing now is set in the 1980s, so that isn't quite historical, but not of-the-moment, either.

I started *The Jazz Bird* initially because I was real interested in that period. I didn't know until I started reading that it was even necessarily going to be a prohibition book. That decade just fascinated me for a lot of reasons. But there is nothing else historically right now that is drawing my attention.

Did you ever hear from the current Ohio governor [Bob Taft] and your depiction of his ancestor in that book?

I actually met him. I sent him a copy of the book before his last reelection. He said, "I won't have time to look at anything until after the election, but I'll have time afterward to read it." When I met him I said, "I just wrote a book about somebody you might have heard of, a guy named Charlie Taft." He kind of laughed. He sent me a note.

The funny thing about that book was doing the readings. There are still a lot of people around who knew them—well, especially who knew Charlie Taft, who lived into his eighties and practiced law. I did a reading in Cincinnati at a library and there were all these lawyers there and I realized at some point they had all worked with or known Charlie Taft. The audience was sort of half lawyers and half really old people who as children had known or known of Remus, or whose fathers were involved with Remus. All kinds of ninety-year-olds would come up and say, [feigning a cracking voice] "My dad was a lawyer and said Remus was the dirtiest guy." One after another, it was so funny. And they loved to talk about it. One woman said, "My dad called him 'Dirty Remus.'"

I read somewhere you were actually writing much of *Four Corners* while you were out on a book tour. Do you succeed in writing much when you're on the road?

You know, it depends. I don't have a laptop and I'm thinking about getting one for this tour because I would like to try, anyway. It really depends on where I am in a book. When I went on tour and was writing those scenes in *Four Corners,* I had just gone

on those ride-alongs and had been working on the book for probably six months, so I had a lot of material—though nothing had
really gelled storywise. The voice wasn't really there yet. But then
the voice just started to come and then if I was on a plane or
whatever, it didn't matter because it was there and I needed to
get it down. I can sit here in my office and there are days when
nothin' happens. But then when it's ready to happen, there's not
much you can do to stop it.

PETE DEXTER
The Poetry of Violence
(January 17, 2005)

Pete Dexter's first novel was *God's Pocket,* a tale set in South Philly about a badass construction worker who not-too-surprisingly gets himself killed.

In that novel, a reporter who writes about the death ends up confronting some angry locals in a bar. In his own life, then-newspaper-columnist Dexter gamely went into a South Philly bar called Devil's Pocket to confront some local critics regarding a column he had written about another dead local.

James Sallis once wrote: "Another homily, another of the commandments we live by, says a man steps up to you, you have to put him down."

It's an uncompromising sentiment that appeals to most men—or we kid ourselves that it does—but put into practice: "It was like a building fell on me," Dexter remembered for one interviewer.

Next came *Deadwood* (1986), Dexter's acclaimed novel about Wild Bill Hickok and the North Dakota mining town where he was shot to death.

Paris Trout, a Southern Gothic released in 1988, won the National Book Award. Dexter adapted his own novel for the screen in a vehicle starring Dennis Hopper in the title role (other Dexter screenplays include *Michael, Rush* and *Mulholland Falls*).

Trout centered on the brutal murder of a young black girl and the ensuing trial and its devastating effects on the small Georgia town of Cotton Point. William Styron compared Dexter's third novel to the best of the works of Flannery O'Connor.

Cotton Point is plagued with rabid foxes, and the novel's haunting refrain "poison fox bit you, you were poison too" would be appropriated by Bruce Springsteen to inform his *Trout*-inspired song, "Big Muddy."

Dexter's own newspaper background came to the fore in *The Paperboy*, an elegiac exploration of a wrongly won Pulitzer Prize and a motherless family of Florida newspapermen.

In October 2003, Dexter released *Train*, a triangular novel set in 1950s Los Angeles about a talented black caddy, a left-leaning civil rights campaigner who is raped and mutilated by two black attackers, and the shadowy alleged L.A. cop who saves, beds and weds her.

January 2005 found Dexter about to embark on a winter book tour from his home on Whidbey Island on Puget Sound to promote the trade paperback release of *Train,* which he was also adapting for film.

No airplanes for Pete Dexter, though. Not fear of flying: all the metal in his body to repair various injuries sustained from beatings and accidents has made post-9/11 metal detector screenings at airports an unbearable ordeal. (Dexter has called leg operations "a hobby"—he's purportedly on his sixth artificial hip).

So the author planned to drive an estimated ten thousand miles to talk about his novel.

Pete Dexter was interviewed from his home on Whidbey Island.

• • • • •

I once drove solo from Seattle to the other side of the country. Swore I'd never do it again. I see you're driving yourself about seven thousand miles for this book tour.

Probably more than that when it's all over. I'm going down to Tallahassee and up to New York. Last time I did this, last year, it ended up being ten thousand miles.

I take it you're a guy who doesn't mind driving.

Well, I wouldn't be doing this if it were six months from now. I'm learning to fly. But I don't have an airplane yet and I don't go through airports. I'm not looking forward to this one because I'm worried about the weather.

You probably don't even have the consolation of seeing much of the country—it must be a lot of interstate driving to make the dates and the times they've set up for you.

Nah, I get off the interestate. I make it a point to get enough time in between. It's not unpleasant. It was really nice last time because it was during the fall. I think it will be okay this time, but I can't take one of the good cars, because the only car we've got that has four-wheel drive is an old Honda. So I guess I've got to take that instead of one of my road cars, but that's all right, too. I'll putt around in that.

This time out you'll be promoting _Train_, which is now moving into trade paperback. The critics have had their way and say about it. Have you had any new thoughts or revised thoughts about the book since _Train_ first appeared?

Not a thought in my head. For me, you know, once they're out of the house they're pretty much out of mind. As far as the critics go, they were pretty kind to this one overall, but what they say doesn't make much of a difference to my own attitude about the book.

Do you go back and reread your own books from time to time?

No.

Never look back?

I've never actually sat down and read one of my own novels. Same thing with movies I write. Of course, those usually end up like shit anyway. I just can't sit there and watch something that I've supposedly written. And I cannot read my own books.

You've described _Train_ as a kind of meditation of what might have happened to Tiger Woods if he had been born many years ago.

Well, that came up in a conversation. I think the only thing wrong with that, well, it wasn't intended as a "meditation." It could be that, but it is not intentionally a meditation.

Eight years lay between *The Paperboy* and *Train*. There's been some indication that filmwork contributed to that longish interval. Were you working on *Train* incrementally in the time between? Can you juggle film and book work?

I do that all the time. I work on a book in the morning and I work on a screenplay at night and then go to bed. Now I'm also working on a nonfiction collection of my stuff so I'm trying to figure out what we should run … what we should keep and what we should toss.

I was going to ask you just that—if anyone had ever approached you with the notion of some sort of collection or anthology of your journalism, of your columns. Is there a timetable for when that might be released?

No … I don't even know when we'll get it finished. I thought I'd be past it by now but I'm not.

Are you tempted when you go in and reread your own early stuff to tweak it or adjust the language? Because all of it would have been written on pretty intense deadline, I would think.

I only will do that if there is some obvious problem with language or something there that isn't clear. But I don't have any misgivings about tweaking it. I just don't want to spend my life rewriting myself.

I know you've written some short fiction, too. Is there enough there for a collection yet?

Nah, I've only written two short stories.

Were those stories that you wrote because you felt like writing them or were you approached to write them?

No, it was just something I felt like doing. One was a part of a novel that got cut out and the other was a "meditation," as you call it on this island where I live. I like short stories, I like to read them. I like to write them. But it doesn't feel like real work to me, in some way. I mean, it is work, don't get me wrong. But it doesn't feel like what I am supposed to be doing.

How long does it take you to write a novel, typically?

It depends on what else is going on. If I were doing nothing but a novel, I'm sure I'd have it out in a year … depending, of course, on the novel. If it's a big old long novel … I'm working on one now that looks like it's going to be pretty heavy. I mean literally heavy … you-don't-want-to-drop-it-on-your-foot heavy. It seems to be taking longer than I thought it would.

There was an indication you might be working on a book tied to an event from your experience that was described in *The Paperboy,* in which you underwent a medical procedure awake, but were unable to communicate your consciousness to the surgeons …

It touches on that. That's not the main thing it's about, but it is a part of it.

The title aside, when I was reading *Train,* the character I was really fascinated by was Miller Packard. I was struck by something about him. Miller Packard is described as a police officer. Well, he describes himself as such … but there is precious little other objective evidence of that fact. Were you playing with something here in terms of his reliablity?

Yeah. You're not supposed to really think that he … well, he's not *really* a policeman. You never see him do police work. He's got some kind of a connection with stuff … of that I'm sure. But he obviously has all the money he wants. He doesn't work on a routine schedule. He does and pretty much picks and chooses to do what he wants to do. Except for that bit on the boat, you never really see him in an official role. You're supposed to wonder about that.

Packard is established as a surivivor of the sinking of the battleship *Indianapolis.* I know of that ship's fate, first and mostly, perhaps like many others, from Robert Shaw's monologue in *Jaws.* Did you research the sinking to get a handle on how it might have warped or changed Packard?

I'd read a lot about it, but it was something I did before I went into this book so I didn't really research it like that. I had hold of when it happened and how it happened. But I pretty much had that scene in my head for a long time.

You've said you didn't "read a real book until I was maybe twenty." What were you reading up until that first "real" book?

I wasn't reading anything. I just wasn't interested.

So you weren't one of these people who as a kid knew you were going to be a writer?

Oh, Christ *no*. That would really have been depressing. That would have been the last thing in the world that I would have thought of. I sort of fell into it.

You credit something by poet Robert Frost for finally turning the tumblers for you as a writer. Do you remember the specific piece by Frost you were reading when it clicked?

It wasn't one particular poem. Robert Frost, he is an enormously complicated writer. There is nothing simple about those poems. It wasn't a sudden thing for me. I'm just trying to remember as we talk, which ones really did it for me. I'll tell you … something like "Birches." And so many others. It's not like he did one great piece and then settled back down.

Journalism is not in the best state right now. In your book focused on the newspaper business, *The Paperboy,* you have a passage that draws a sharp distinction between "reporters" and "journalists," with some disparaging weight placed on the latter. Anyone working now you would point to as a "reporter" in the classical sense? Anyone you go out of your way to read? A columnist?

I don't read any columnists. I mean, I read the columnists in the *New York Times* because I get that in the mail. I used to think Maureen Dowd was good when she started, but I think now she is kind of coasting on being Maureen Dowd. I don't get to see many other of the city columnists. There's nobody in Seattle that I particularly want to read. There are a couple of sports columnists who are pretty good, but I can't get those other papers even delivered to where I live and I don't go out of my way to buy them.

You've described the island you live on as having a couple of stoplights.

Yeah, the south end of the island. It's got more than that now. It's got four stoplights. It's not entirely rural. The part of the island I live on ... well, people don't want to come up the hill to deliver papers.

Were you deliberately trying to get yourself as far away from the New York literary scene as you could and still be in the continental U.S.?

No, but I was trying to get myself as far away from the crowds— all the yelling and the traffic. The kinds of things you put up with when you live in the city. There's none of that here. I love this place.

There's a tendency on the part of a lot of critics to hang the term "noir" on you. Is that a tag you can abide?

Naw, any kind of label ...

People like their handles?

Yeah. It's the critics reading each other. The state of literary criticism right now isn't a whole lot better than the state of film criticism, which to my mind, is awful. I was just thinking about this. You know, this movie just came out, *Spanglish*.

Sure.

I know James L. Brooks. James Brooks and I had worked on something together for a long time. The reaction to that movie at the *New York Times*—that critic A.O. Scott called Brooks a woman-hater and said it was racist. Just making a clown of himself as far as I'm concerned. I mean, I don't know who this guy Scott is—I've never met him—but I do know that he is a little smarter than that. I look at the reaction and a lot of it just got really kind of personal and bitter and for reasons that were never really apparent if you go see the movie. And it was really personal toward the guy who directed it, James Brooks. Saying he is the "angriest man in Hollywood." That stuff—all that does is show that these people think that these jobs with newspapers have endowed them with a certain power, and they start to believe they are powerful. That they can say that kind of stuff, and throw that shit anyplace, and there is no consequence for it.

Well, short of walking into a bar for a conversation about a piece you've written and getting hit with a club or a bottle, which you've experienced.

Yeah. So anyway, I'm not too enamored with the whole critical field right now. I don't know how I got off on that, but I don't think too much of it. All the people often are is somebody sitting in a newspaper office and the paper needs a critic. That's how much training they've had.

You adapted *Paris Trout* for screen. Have you adapted others of your books, or is that something you would even do at this point?

I'm doing it right now for *Train*. I did it for *Deadwood*.

Is there a director for *Train* at this point?

No, we're doing it without a director right now. I wrote a screenplay for *The Paperboy* which is sitting at some studio and they won't make it because it's too much money. So, yeah, I've done that for most of 'em, but not all of 'em.

You're obviously comfortable taking your own book apart and recasting it. I'd think that could be very difficult in that you get maybe a third of what you wrote in the book up onto the screen.

No, you have to go into it almost like a businessman. You have to say, "This is something different." You try to make it as close as you can, but you don't try to make it the novel. The novel is there, it's sitting on the shelf and if somebody wants to read it, there it is. But this is something else. Once you realize that, and accept that, then you're not trying to protect anything, you're just trying to make a movie out of it, which is an entirely different thing. Then you're fine, I think. I mean, it doesn't bother me.

Are there novelists you go out of your way to read? Is there a particular writer or writers working today you feel any kinship to?

Padgett Powell. I'd never miss one of Richard Russo's books. There's a whole bunch of people.

Do you read any crime fiction at all?

Yeah, nothing really jumps to mind, but I do.

I know particularly with *Mulholland Falls,* there were many comparisons drawn with James Ellroy's novels.

Actually, I haven't read much of his stuff. I read the book about his mother.

His memoir. Is that something you would ever contemplate doing—writing a memoir?

Well, I'm working on that novel now—that is probably as close to something like that as I'll ever get.

You used to have parrots for pets. What's the best or worst thing you ever taught one to say?

I only had one parrot and this bird never said a word. But he was a stonekiller. He was really my wife's bird and we finally found some guy who really loved parrots. He was building an addition for his house and Archie's living over there now.

Those things live forever.

Yeah, yeah. And they're just stonekillers. Their eyes turn orange and all of a sudden they've got your finger.

And they can do some serious damage with those beaks.

Yeah, you're typing with nine fingers.

How are you doing, by the way? All these interviews your publicist sent over seem to dwell on your injuries over the years.

Yeah, I haven't had a run like this in a long time. I shouldn't say it, but I've been really good. I tore up my shoulder a while ago, and my back. But generally I'm good. I usually work out about an hour and a half a day and I'm always walking around a little sore. But I'm generally in good health.

I remember reading a biography of Hemingway by Jeffrey Meyers that included a list of Hemingway's known injuries. It ran to *pages*. Have you ever contemplated making a comprehensive list of your injuries to assist—or awe—future biographers?

I once sat down with Evel Knievel when I was writing a piece on Knievel for a magazine. We started talking about broken bones and stuff and I was trying to add up the ones that I'd broke. At that point, I'd broken considerably more bones than Evel Knievel had. You know, Evel tended to break a lot of bones at once. I'd break one or two just regularly.

It's a war of attrition.
Yeah, oh God! If I'd ever known …

Anything else you'd particularly like to get out about *Train*?
Oh no. It is what it is.

Any timetable for the next novel?
I'm late already.

PART VI

Thriller

RANDY WAYNE WHITE

Perfect Law
(June 3, 2004)

Randy Wayne White has traveled extensively and spent many years as a fishing guide in Florida. He has written highly praised accounts of his travels, as well as a series of adventure novels under the pseudonym "Randy Striker."

He has appeared frequently on television as a host and correspondent.

But White is best known for his crime fiction novels featuring marine biologist Doc Ford, a man with a nebulous and violent past linked to covert operations.

Ford's rag-tag crew of misfit friends around Dinkin's Bay, Florida, include his "drug-modified" chum Tomlinson, a guru of steadily-growing influence and following; he also has surprising computer skills. Tomlinson's past—made hazy by his own spotty memory—is slowly being revealed to be at least as dark and bloody as Ford's own.

In his 2004 release, *Tampa Burn*, Ford's son is kidnapped and more revelations about Doc's and Tomlinson's respective pasts set them on a potential course toward an eventual confrontation.

White has also recently opened a new rum bar inspired by his character, and his award-winning documentary on Ernest Hemingway and Cuban Little League teams, *The Gift of the Game*, was recently broadcast on PBS.

Shortly after this interview was conducted, a Category 4 hurricane struck the area of Florida where White makes his home. His home sustained severe damage. In 2006, White published the Doc Ford Novel *Dark Light*, which explores the aftermath of a hurricane.

Randy Wayne White was interviewed while the author was on tour in Arizona.

• • • • •

Tampa Burn goes into your characters' pasts a bit more than some others. Why did you feel this was the time to start going into their backstories more aggressively?

You know what? In every book I try to reveal a bit more about the characters in terms of their histories. I drop little hints here and there, even from the first book. So I guess this book just required it. Plus, this book has Doc Ford's son and you have to go into the backstory there to explain how he got his son. It was neat. I like the characters very much. They're interesting.

You seem to be poised in the books to follow to maybe make some significant changes to their lives. Is that because you're still just discovering the characters, or because you're about a dozen books in now and it's time to start shifting some dynamics for the characters?

Well, the characters change. People change. But they're not going to change too much. They're essentially boat bums and roustabouts and nerds—kind of like me, really. They change, but they're not going to change too much. I like the people they are, except the bad guys.

Do you have some sense of your characters' larger arcs as you move along or are you going book to book for the most part?

Oh, you know, when I wrote the first novel, *Sanibel Flats,* I wrote long dossiers on three of the main characters—Ford, Tomlinson and Tucker Gatrell. So I've long known their inner-workings and inner-weavings. It's fun, like a striptease—you reveal a little bit as you go along. And the backstory, as you find out in this book, Ford long ago was assigned to terminate Tomlinson.

Yes, we're starting to put together some more of the pieces of the puzzle and the hints you've dropped. I assume that unfulfilled order might be the focus of a book soon to come?

I'm hoping many books down, because I want to write a lot of Doc Ford books. I want to write a standalone Tucker Gatrell book—that's one I'm really looking forward to. A standalone Tomlinson book. Maybe do some books that take place in Ford's past.

At the end of *Tampa Burn,* and without giving too much away, you obviously have to finally have Doc confront the villain. He makes a choice there that some who are a little more blood-thirsty—in the way I like to think I'd be in those circumstances—might wonder at. Did you have a strong sense early on that his decision was probably going to fall along those lines?

I did, yeah, I did. In the previous book, *Everglades,* the bad guy was just evil, just asshole evil. This guy, though, was damaged as a child, so there's an ethical/moral quandary there that I like the idea of Ford wrestling with. One thing I found interesting about the villain: I worked with a pharmo-psychiatrist who is an expert on the chemistry of the brain and behavior in terms of drawing these characteristics. It's very carefully drawn. Everything about him is accurate, as best as I can make it.

You seem to research things very, very diligently. Do you write to a plot outline?

No, I don't, but I love the research and the danger of research is that you get so involved with it. And the other danger is—and I do this and I'm trying to get better at this—I include too much stuff in my books, which can put some people off. But then other people like that, so who knows?

There's an unusual medical transplant central to this book and I wondered how technically possible that was. Then, I saw a story a few days ago indicating they may soon make an attempt at such surgeries.

Oh, complete face transplants? Absolutely, yeah.

Was that an item that you came across and decided was something you would work into a book, or did you come across that as part of your research?

Actually, I just came up with the idea and started talking with plastic surgeons. It wasn't until about the third or fourth plastic surgeon where I found a guy who said, "Yeah, they're going to start doing face transplants." I thought, "Holy shit!"

It's funny. I had just finished reading *Tampa Burn* and picked up a copy of *Entertainment Weekly* containing a review of some *Discovery Channel* documentary on face transplants. Your timing is impeccable.

It happens. There's a curious thing like that in *Everglades*. I write about that in Colombia they finance terrorism through the narco-trade and slave-trade—particularly in this one little town. About three months ago, I read some breaking story that they were discovering that that is true. *I* knew it was true, but …

The character of Ford often draws comparisons to Travis McGee, and, because you're in Florida, you get the Hemingway thing, also because of your sports fishing background. It strikes me that probably some of Doc Ford might have been based on John Steinbeck's character of "Doc" in *Cannery Row* and *Sweet Thursday*—the character Steinbeck modeled on his friend, marine biologist Ed Ricketts …

Oh, sure. Absolutely. I love Steinbeck. He's a very funny writer. I was born in Ohio, and I lived on a little farm way up in north-western Ohio near a little village called Pioneer, right on the Indiana-Michigan border. There was a tiny little one-room library there. I was a terrible student, but I discovered *Cannery Row*, or *Sweet Thursday*, and it led me to all the other Steinbeck books. I remember sitting up in the hayloft reading Steinbeck. Another great writer who I just came to admire so much and who is now a very close friend is [Ohio] writer Allan W. Eckert. Still consider myself a Buckeye. Love Louis Bromfield.

Ah yeah, Malabar Farm …

Ah, lovely, lovely. And what an amazing guy. A Renaissance guy—a terrific writer and a scientist and a farmer.

I'm sure it was gratifying to have one of your books, *Sanibel Flats*, picked as one of the 100 greatest mysteries of the twentieth century.

That was amazing.

Did you feel they picked the right one of your books?

No, but we're not always the best judge. I like that book. It's my first one. I think some of my later ones are better, but I'm just happy to be on the list for any reason.

Do you have a particular favorite of your own books? One that perhaps you feel you hit on all the points you were aiming for?

Well, different reasons. I like *The Man Who Invented Florida*, because it's just so strange, and slow and sweet. I like that, although a lot of people just hated it at the time. *Tampa Burn*, in terms of intensity of plot movement. I was exhausted when I finished the book. I'll tell you what—*God Almighty*.

You've opened a restaurant built around the Doc Ford character.

Yeah, Doc Ford's Sanibel Rum Bar and Grill.

I see there might even be another coming, so I take it it's pretty successful?

It's been a huge success. It's been amazing. You know, I've traveled so much and I said, "You know, I ought to start a rum bar." I didn't realize there are no other rum bars in the United States.

You take an active hand in the menu, all of that?

Oh yeah. I try to go out there two or three times a week and work on drinks, which is tough duty. You need to come down and help me do that. It's pretty fun, plus it's a nice place to meet people. I like doing the retail stuff—I make up the shirts, the ball caps, baseball jerseys and stuff; it's cool.

You've got the novels, the columns, you're engaged in TV and film; you've got the restaurant ... you tour extensively. When do you write?

That's the hardest thing to do now, to find the time to write. People—even friends—they don't realize what you and I well know, and that is that writing is very hard work. I've had people just stop in—I mean, all day long, they'll just stop in. I have a very open house—I've got a natural shower. Too many times, I've been up there showering and people have walked in with books to be signed.

To bring up Hemingway: He more or less fled Florida—of course he had a future wife as further incentive—but mostly because he was like Santa at the North Pole. Literally had his house in the Key West tour books in the 1930s and was just hounded by fans and aspiring writers. Living where you do, with your restaurant and popularity of the books, and all those pictures of you on the jackets, do you have any kind of anonymity or privacy left around your town?

No I don't. It's becoming problematic, too. But, I'm very lucky. I'm not complaining. And I like people—I'm not a hermit-type person.

How do you sustain yourself through your tours? There was a piece that I came across where a guy tracked you through a day or two of your tour. Pretty much fifteen hours of running and one meal wolfed down at eleven p.m. How do you sustain it?

You get on a plane every morning and there is someone there at the other end with a sign who picks you up. In this case, my friend Pierre handles it—[talking to his driver now] what is it Pierre, four for five years driving around like this? I don't like him and he doesn't like me, so it's perfect [laughter from his driver].

I saw somewhere where you had written some thrillers under a pseudonym and they're going to be reissued soon.

Yeah, "Randy Striker." I don't know how soon, but I've signed the contracts. When they bring them out is entirely up to them.

Were they standalones, or a series?

A series. There are seven of them. I wrote them when I was a full-time fishing guy. I wrote the first one in nine days. On a black Underwood, stand-up typewriter.

Sounds a little like being a writer in the 1930s for the pulps.

I know. I wrote my first Ford, *Sanibel Flats,* on it—I'm a two-finger typist—on the same black typewriter.

You wrote a really great piece that I enjoyed about boxing—well, we'll use "boxing" in quotes since it was an exhibition match for a cause and the guy was eighty—Kermit "Shine" Forbes, Ernest Hemingway's 1930s-era sparring partner in Key West.

Oh, I adored the guy. I spent the last three nights of his life with him in the hospital. A dear, dear friend.

That was something that Lorian Hemingway recruited you for. Are you often tied to the Hemingway Days event in Key West?

I go down about every year, I think. Last year I gave a little talk. I miss Shine, you know? This year we're going to dedicate a memorial to Shine. Then there are the Hemingway look-alikes. A strange but great bunch of guys.

Yeah, anyone who wears cable knit sweaters in Key West in July has to be regarded a little warily.

God, I know it, I know it. You ought to come down for it. Lorian's going to be there. I think Phil Caputo is going to be there. It's an interesting group.

You just completed a documentary on Ernest Hemingway and youth baseball in Cuba that won some awards. How'd that come about?

Well, we've gone down to Cuba the last couple of years to play ball and we always take a bunch of gear for the kids. We chip in ourselves, don't ask for donations, just simply do it. Lorian happened to mention that Ernest Hemingway started a baseball league for kids in his little suburb, but it was long-defunct because it was a very poor area there. I said, "Yeah, we can completely restart this thing." I had no idea if we really could. I got some guys, we got uniforms made, had probably seven to eight thousand dollars worth of equipment. We took it down there, and, coincidentally, these filmmakers had optioned one of my novels and I told them what we were going to do. They said, "Jeez, we should do a documentary." I said, "That sounds great guys," 'cause you hear that stuff all the time, but they really showed up. I wrote it and narrated it. First film I ever wrote.

I wouldn't normally ask a novelist about politics, but I saw something recently about you hosting a fundraiser for a candidate in Florida. I take it there are issues important to you and I'm going to speculate they are environmental?

Largely environmental. I'm middle of the road—Democrat/Republican/Independent. Occasionally I meet someone, man or woman, who just seem to be straight-shooters and who have a reasonable outlook in terms of the environment and other issues. When that happens, particularly in close races, then I'm happy to get involved. But I'm uncomfortable with anyone—even as small a celebrity as I—who comes out and makes political statements. I don't know any more about politics than the next guy. I think it's important to be involved. I've traveled enough around the world to know that our Republic is hugely valuable. Whatever issues, whatever side you're on, it's very important to be involved.

I read your piece that you wrote a few days after September 11, 2001—"An Open Letter to He Who Hides Behind the Coffins of Innocents." Is there a postscript to that now, three years out? Something that you might revise in that statement? It was a very stirring, passionate piece.

No, I don't think I would change anything. I don't think I would. Things are always, in any kind of adversity or conflict between two societies, both of which are convinced they are right, well … the party with the lowest standard of morality sets the guidelines or the rules.

That's very interesting that you should raise that phrase. I had that quote pulled out. It comes up in your post 9/11 piece, and I noted it also comes up in *Mangrove Coast*, where you dub it "Perfect Law."

What is it? What's the exact quote?

"In any conflict, the boundaries of acceptable behavior are defined by the party which cares least about morality."

Yeah. I think that's accurate.

Is that original to you?
Yeah, that's mine.

I find that particularly resonant, as some in the media try to draw moral equivalencies between the prison tortures of Saddam Hussein and the pictures coming out of Abu Grahib ...
Hmm. Heart-breaking. Absolutely heart-breaking. But, again, I don't know enough about what is going on there to really comment beyond that.

Florida crime writers are kind of a breed unto themselves. I think all of your work is very different, yet you all tend to be lumped together as a breed. There is Laurence Shames, Vicki Hendricks and Tim Dorsey and Carl Hiaasen. Do you socialize with these people? Are you a fairly close bunch?
Aw, they're the scum of the earth. I wouldn't go near 'em. No, they're great. I don't know Laurence Shames. I don't know if I know Vicki. But Carl and Les Standiford and Tim Dorsey—Tim Dorsey is a dear heart. We don't get together often, but I consider them good friends and confidants. We can talk about anything. Well, essentially, all we talk about is bitching about TV and we talk about money. Very shallow—don't let anybody fuckin' fool you—extremely shallow. I like those people I know a lot. But I don't read fiction. I just don't. My memory is not that good—I'm afraid that I would steal something.

I've had crime fiction writers concede that same thing before—fear of reading the works of others because they might subconsciously lift a plot thread or story idea.
That's it exactly.

Are there places in Florida that for reasons of preservation you just don't want to write about because it would just ruin them if people tried to reach or explore them themselves?
The place I care most about is the little Indian Mound village where I live. Without intentionally doing it, I've certainly exploited it. But I still love the place.

You've been a globetrotter and you've written extensively about your travels. Are there places in this post 9/11 world where you just don't want to go? Have you turned anything down?

Oh no, no. I'd never turn anything down. Haiti—when Haiti was bad—it was *bad*. There are just dangerous places there. I've been all over the world. I was in Cambodia during its most recent revolution … Vietnam shortly after that … Cuba, Nicaragua after the war. I've never been *anywhere* where people didn't like Americans. That's just been my experience. I haven't been in the Middle East in years, but I have been in many Muslim countries—Sumatra. It's a dangerous world. I've been stabbed … shot at with intent … and I was in a hotel that got blown up.

Where did the explosion happen?

That was in Wakaya, Peru. The Sendero Luminoso attacked the town and fifty-six people got killed. A cop got shot right in our doorway. I got stabbed in the back.

What's next in terms of the books and your writing projects?

Well, I'm sixty thousand words into a book now. I just can't write on the road—it's too intense.

I don't know when you'd have the time.

Unless I started drinking, and Christ, you know …? I think it's going to be called *In the Dead of Night*. It's Doc Ford and it has to do with bio-terrorism.

That's sadly timely.

It is, it is.

LEE CHILD

One Shot

(May 31, 2005; May 13, 2007)

L ee Child enjoyed a long and successful career in the television entertainment industry until the mid-1990s, when he was "downsized" out of Granada Studios.

Child's improbable and improbably successful response was to attempt to write a novel and launch a career as a highly regarded thriller writer.

Many books later, Child is riding high with his internationally bestselling series featuring ex-military cop Jack Reacher. Reacher is a career Army investigator and military brat downsized out of his post in the wake of the fall of the Berlin Wall and the collapse of the Cold War.

Reacher is a six-foot-five, 250-pound latter day Shane who wanders America, and, eventually, Europe—righting wrongs and helping those in need.

In June 2005, Reacher returned in Child's ninth novel, *One Shot*, investigating the case of a former military sniper who apparently went berserk and opened fire on pedestrians in an unidentified Indiana city.

Child was interviewed a second time on May 13, 2007 in conjunction with the release of the Reacher novel *Bad Luck & Trouble*, which reunites Reacher and his military cohorts.

• • • • •
May 31, 2005

What was the trigger, no pun intended, for *One Shot*?

There are a number of things you've got to do. At bottom, it had to be another Jack Reacher book because that's what the readers want—the continuation of the series. And yet from my point of view, I didn't want to make it similar to any of the others. It's always a bit of a challenge to keep them different enough to stop the author himself from getting bored. So my plan was to have not a sting in the tail, but a sting in the beginning, really, which is that something happens, and a guy is arrested and he calls for Jack Reacher. Most people are going to assume, "Okay, Reacher is going to come and help this guy." In fact, Reacher shows up not to help him at all, but to bury him. So it was a kind of punch in the gut, straight away, I was hoping. The fact that Reacher does end up helping him, somewhat unwillingly, or reluctantly, is a kind of moral statement on Reacher's part.

Yes, it is rather risky in that the man who asks for Reacher's help isn't the most sympathetic of characters and quickly becomes less so.

Yes, exactly, and that's a challenge from the writing point of view, as well. It's similar to my fifth book, *Echo Burning*. There was a woman character in that book called Carmen who everybody was going to be very ambivalent about. You weren't sure—could you trust her, or could you not? And it's actually very, *very* tough to write an unsympathetic character.

It's interesting you mention that specific book because it's probably my favorite of your books, with this one coming in just behind it. How'd you come to pick Indiana as a locale for this novel? I notice you're not touring in Indiana ...

Yeah, I don't know why that is, because I think it shows Indiana quiet sympathetically. You know, the sniper outrage that opens the book is always going to be bad wherever, but I think there is a sense in the States that somehow that if that was Baltimore or Washington, D.C., or L.A. that that would be sort of expected in a way. What I wanted to do was to transfer that to the heartland where that is a genuine outrage. It's an atrocity—not just a crime, but an offense against the decency of living there. It was really a "feel" that I was after. I don't name the city at all that it takes place in, though obviously I do name the state. What I wanted to do is get that middle-America vibe—the pure heartland vibe—to set a grotesque crime somewhere where you would not think of it occurring normally.

The book was released in Europe first. Have you been pleased with the reaction on the part of European readers?

Yeah, it's done really well. It's done great in Britain and New Zealand … in Australia. It's a building franchise, you know, the whole Jack Reacher thing. What you're definitely trying to avoid, when you've got the good will of people loving the series, is to write a bad book and let them down. So what I hope every year is that the new book people will be pleased with and they have been, yeah.

You've indicated many times in interviews that European readers in particular have some trouble with the vigilantism in the Reacher books. Has this become more acute in recent months as the gulf between America and Europe has widened?

You're right, there's a lot of tension between Western Europe and the U.S. right now. Actually, right now I'm living in France—I'm in France for a few months. But there is a huge split between how people look at Americans, and how people look at *America*, you know? It's like they say, "Yeah, we love America, we love you people, we want to go there, but we don't like the administration right now."

They do distinguish between the two?

Yeah, they totally do. Whether it is a sort of defensive mechanism because they don't want to just give up on a country that they've traditionally admired for so long, or what, there is no hostility at all to individual Americans that I've ever seen, and certainly not to anyone I've ever spoken to. My wife was just in Amsterdam last weekend. On her way back to France, she was talking to a family from Boston at the Amsterdam airport who said they'd just had the most fabulous time ... everyone was being so welcoming and kind and generous. There's absolutely no animosity at all against individual Americans. It's just entirely geo-political.

So I think in terms of how Europe is looking at the books, it hasn't actually changed at all. Which is to say, that it is what it always was: they love Jack Reacher despite knowing that they shouldn't. It throws them into great confusion.

Rumor has it that the book after *One Shot* is going to take Reacher to Europe. Accurate?

Because, as you've pointed out, I do them a year ahead, I know exactly where he's going. It's England, actually, that he goes to. At the core of the next book is a mercenary group—a private military contractor based in New York. It has ex-Special Forces people staffing it, including a couple of British SAS guys. One of them looks like he is the bad guy and the pursuit leads back to England.

And that novel's called *The Hard Way* ...

That's right.

Last time we spoke, you were venturing into short story writing. You had a piece in Karin Slaughter's collection, *Like A Charm*. You have another story out right now in the new collection *Cocaine Chronicles*, edited by Gary Phillips and Jervey Tervalon. How'd that one come about?

Well, it was the Karin Slaughter thing: it just had the most appalling effect. For years I'd managed to get away without writing short stories because I'm not especially great at them, I don't think. Do you know Karin? Have you met her?

I've interviewed her a couple of times.

She's a very appealing, friendly young woman with great person skills and the whole thing. So she talked me into doing that one, basically. I was happy to do it and I think it came out good, but the fact is that now that people have seen that I've done one, everyone is knocking on my door. *The Cocaine Chronicles* is done by Gary Phillips, who is from L.A. I've been friends with him for a long time, because as a matter of fact, my first-ever joint book-signing I ever did on my first tour happened to be with Gary in San Diego.

An interesting pairing.

Well, it was a great pairing. It was my first tour and I was just so excited about the whole thing and he [Gary] has a sort of permanent place in my heart now—he was the first guy I ever sat side-by-side with at a dual signing. So he wanted a story for *The Cocaine Chronicles*. It's a funny story, because, as a matter of fact, I really got that idea years and years ago for somebody else who wanted a short story for a hit-man anthology. Nothing ever came of it. So I had that idea and then Gary said, "Would you do this?" So I thought, "If I make that hit-man story into a kind of cocaine-trade hit-man, then yeah, I could do it." It took me one day. So, I did it for Gary, and then the very next day this original guy from years ago e-mailed me and said, "You know that hit-man anthology? It's back on now." And I had just given the damned story away, so I had to write another. I'm doing a few at the moment. I'm doing one for Bob Randisi's hit-man anthology. I've done one for Harlen Coben's *Love is Murder* anthology. I'm doing one about horse racing. And then I'm really going to try and cut back on that, because it's disproportionate effort, you know? It's actually a lot harder to write a short story than a long story. It's a big investment in a well-polished idea for not much return.

I have to ask you the obligatory question about possible films. Now, according to your Web site, New Line has optioned six of the novels …

Actually, New Line's option expired very recently. They haven't renewed it although there is still a lot of interest from certain key individuals. But just a few days ago we got an absolutely massive offer from a movie company that is not one of the usual players. I can't say who it is at this point until we know whether we will go with it or not. But it's a very interesting bunch of people. It's a quantum leap up in terms of what they're offering, so I don't know what that means: are they hopelessly naïve, or are they going to do it?

It's been reported you're shooting for twenty-one Jack Reacher books. I think that was the number of books that John D. Macdonald published about Travis McGee ...

Exactly. There's always a question in readers' minds: "What are you going to do with the character at the end of the series?" It's a great question, actually. I know a lot of writers who write series, and we all kind of agree that these old war horses are great, but they deserve an end. I firmly believe that: When it comes time for the end of the series, I want to write the *big* tragic novel in which he dies. Of course, readers don't want to hear that, because they're afraid it's going to happen next year, or the year after. And certainly publishers don't want to hear that. But I think that's the writer's instinct: you want to see your character go out in a blaze of glory.

So I picked the number twenty-one because I do admire the Travis McGee books, and if I could equal that, I would be very, very happy. Plus it means there's, what, another eleven to go? So the readers don't get upset just yet.

It is appalling to see some of these ongoing characters who are just treated as franchises and farmed out to subsequent writers.

It is. And I think you have to have the courage of your convictions: an unambiguous end to the series.

The Jack Reacher books are published in thirty-nine countries now. Is there some fortieth country you have an eye on? Some country you're surprised isn't offering Reacher to readers?

For a long time, we had no deal in Spain, which was kind of odd because Spain is just another European country—no reason why it shouldn't have. There was a sort of business reason: They got burned a few years back when they invested heavily in certain authors in the thriller field and it didn't work out. So they were kind of reluctant. But we do have a deal in Spain now. The other one was Sweden: For a long time, it was too fastidious to go anywhere near them. When the first one sold all around the world, everyone was jumping on the bandwagon, but Sweden was horrified with it: "We're not doing that ... the body count is far too high ... it's gruesome ... it's violent." Eventually they had to get on the bandwagon about three books late. Now they just this year brought out the fifth book, *Echo Burning*, the one that you mentioned. You know the peculiar way certain things happen in certain markets? For some reason that book this year became a huge, almost literary phenomenon. It got a review in a very, very serious literary journal and became a big, respected bestseller. So I've been invited to Gothenburg Literary Festival at the end of September ... so I'm going to go, but I have no idea what it is going to be like, because you know what European intellectuals are like—they're probably expecting some furious discussion, and what can I say? But I'm going to go just for the fun of it.

It's been a few years. Will you read the book again to prepare?

I'm gonna have to. That's something I have to do before each tour, because the newest book is a year old at that point. I have to reread it so that I can answer people's questions.

I'm fairly stunned at the level of touring that authors are expected to undertake now. Particularly you, and someone like Ian Rankin. You guys do world tours. I look at the tour schedules and wonder when the writing gets done. How long are you on the road this year?

It generally works out that you're going to do two whole solid months in the spring. There's probably a month's worth of other stuff scattered through the rest of the year. So it's probably three months of the year that you are on the road. It's weird. Structurally, it's weird. We become writers because we have some performance DNA in us: we want an audience. We want to please an audience. But we are essentially shy people, you know. We have no talent to be on stage, which is exactly why we pick the medium of books, because the book is the perfect middle-man: you can perform, but you don't have to be visible. Yet, we *do* have to be visible, because publishing now is so heavily into promotion. As I say, for three months of the year, you are literally on stage. It can be a bit of a strain, you know?

Can you quantify the impact touring has on your writing?

Not me, really. And I bet not Ian Rankin, either, because we're both of us fast writers. Ian is probably faster than I am. It takes me from September to March to do the whole book. Which effectively gives me the spring and summer then to tour and to take a break. It's not impacting me in terms of time.

The upside of it is that you go to places that you would never otherwise go. It's programmed that you never see anybody who doesn't already like you. You show up at a bookstore: why would anyone come if they weren't already enthusiastic about the book? It's a warm bath, basically.

Reacher travels with little more than the clothes on his back. I notice on your Web site you have a shot of your luggage. How much time do you spend trying to decide what to take?

Really no time at all. First of all, I figure out what the weather is likely to be. The last one I did was London in the spring and then New Zealand and Australia in their fall, which is basically the whole of the April. I figured that was not hot, but somewhere between cool and warm weather. Then I just pick out four identical outfits. Anything I ever buy, I buy in groups of four. I wear one, and carry three. I recycle them through the hotel laundry. What it means is that I never have a decision about what to put on, because it's all the same stuff. That's why you look at the Web site and the photographs of the tour, and even though the tour is a month long, I'm wearing the same stuff all the time.

I'm trying to get as close to the Reacher spirit as you can get in the real world.

Have you ever had any good travel tips from other writers?

The best one I think I got was from Barbara Kingsolver: "Never, ever, ever check luggage." Otherwise you're bound to have your suitcases a day behind you everywhere. Apart from that, I've developed a habit of wherever I am, I go out for walks last thing at night. Because that's a great way to sample wherever you are. I'm a night person. It might be eleven p.m. or midnight but you can go out for a stroll and look at the neighborhood. It's good fun. It is tiring, but I'm glad I'm doing it.

Do you afford any attention to the literary blogs that have kind of come into their own in the last year or two? Are those things that you look at at all?

I look at 'em, yeah, pretty much obsessively.

You do?

Oh yes. It's a bit like reading the newspaper. Given that writers themselves are geographically so dispersed, you read some of those blogs and it is like reading a hometown newspaper. It's all about people you know and things that you know about.

A bit like a trade journal, I guess.

It is—it's exactly like a trade journal. It's organized by trade rather than locality, but it is your hometown paper. So yeah, I read a lot of them. I don't know that I really pay any attention to them, because that's a bit like reviews, you know. I'm not sure that I would be influenced by them in any way. But certainly I look at them, yeah.

When we spoke last year, you indicated that you'd been one of the writers who had been pulled in after 9/11 to provide some scenarios to perhaps plan against and so forth. You mentioned one unnamed scenario that you had provided that had gone unaddressed. Has that potential threat ever been addressed?

No, it never has. I know that it hasn't. It's kind of illustrative of the problem, because to address it would be a massive inconvenience for the people involved. It's that balance: exactly how far do you go? It's a fairly obvious threat in my opinion and there's a fairly obvious solution to it, in my opinion, but to put it into practice would be hugely disruptive to something that people are used to doing in a certain way. As I said, it illustrates the problem of "how far do you go?" and clearly they've chosen not to go all that far.

Have they come back to you since for further input?

It was kind of ironic in that two agencies came to me in the first place, kind of unaware of what the other one was doing. Again, I thought *that* was a bit illustrative of the problem: they hadn't even coordinated their mailing lists. As I thought at the time, though, if you ask hundreds of writers and screenwriters that kind of question, you're going to get overwhelmed with possible scenarios. I think they probably did just get overwhelmed with it. There's probably a filing cabinet somewhere actually bulging with everything that anybody could ever think of. It may have become too big to ever deal with.

Any closing thoughts, about *One Shot,* or about anything else that might be on your mind?

Just my usual: My only aim is to entertain people for the however-many-days it takes to read the book. I sincerely hope you're entertained and if you are, thank you very much for buying it.

• • • • •
May 13, 2007

By my reckoning, this is the tenth anniversary since the publication of your first novel. What are your thoughts on the decade?

It's come a long way. That book [*The Killing Floor*] was a relative success for a first book, but now it appears tiny in terms of initial sale and so on to what's happening now. What's interesting is that obviously when that book was written I was the only person on earth who had heard of Reacher. As soon as it was for sale, increasing but small numbers of people had found out about Reacher. Now, after ten years, it's as if the ownership of Reacher has migrated outward to a kind of public ownership. Certainly I've written them all, but by fact that people have read them all, they've invested a lot of themselves in him. In a sense, he's created now as much by the reader as by the writer.

Obviously he's evolved and you've revealed more about him as you've gone along, but does he remain for you essentially the same character you started out with?

He is essentially the same. That is a lesson I learned a long time ago in storytelling really, which is that people have to feel comfortable. To an extent they want to be *slightly* surprised, but not *too* surprised. To coin a phrase, you've got to give them the same but *different*. This goes way back: I remember when my daughter was a very little girl, she would literally want the same story every night. I think that instinct is still with us. Although adults are too overtly sophisticated to literally read the same book over and over again, they need to have something that is comforting, familiar and welcoming.

You've quoted your agent elsewhere as saying it takes ten years of hard work to be an overnight success. Ten years in, do you feel you've exceeded that axiom? You did have that initial success that's much bigger than most debut authors can really ever hope for.

Yeah. True, so to say it didn't happen for ten years sounds ungrateful. I think what he means is, and what is certainly true is, there is a certain tipping point where it just becomes an everyday reality. This morning, flying down to Nashville, the guy sitting ahead of me in the plane was reading *The Hard Way* in paperback. To see that on a regular basis, that does take ten years to sort of build up to.

Your books are in every airport on earth, virtually, and you travel a lot, so that must be a fairly routine experience for you by now.

Statistically, I stand a good chance now.

Was this latest a tougher book for you to write in that you're effectively writing five Jack Reachers in terms of his crew and the fact they're this very hyper-effective group of über people in a way?

What was a challenge was managing the relationship between them. Specifically, this time I wanted Reacher to be a little tiny bit insecure about his own choices. As you know, he's been very confident up to now. I thought it was time to see him evaluate himself just a little bit. Of course he wouldn't do that for anybody except his old buddies who he had been so close to. I wanted to see how he would measure himself up … thinking, "Have I made the right choice, or have they made the right choice?"

Then I also wanted to see without the formal command structure of being in the Army, would his natural authority kind of assert itself in a free-form situation. I had a lot of fun, actually, writing from the point of view of four old buddies. The banter, the self-deprecating, sort of between-the-lines thing where nobody actually says that they care about each other but it's perfectly obvious that they do.

He does sort of go through this kind of high school reunion level of crisis, which he compounds in a way in terms of a really questionable haircut. Is that something contained to this book, or has he been shaken enough that these insecurities could track him into other volumes?

It's really only those three who could have that effect on him.

In the past you've shied away from bringing back characters from earlier novels, although you do that somewhat in this book. Do you envision doing more with this team at some point?

I think what might be fun would be go back to do another prequel to when they were all still in the unit together. That could be good. In general, yeah, I'm against repeating characters. But Neagley herself, obviously has come back, and some of those others got minor mentions in *The Enemy*. If you have a great character in one book it is kind of nice to bring it back later.

Are you near the point now where you almost have to have a concordance of past books to keep from shooting yourself in the foot with contradictions?

Yeah, you've pretty much got to because readers pay attention to that kind of stuff. I remember when we used to work in television—and, of course, in every movie—there are continuity people. For long-running television series there were archivists. That was their entire job—to keep track of what people had done in the past so they wouldn't do anything out of character in the future. So, yeah, I'm reaching that point.

You're your own archivist?

I have to be, yeah.

I'm pretty phobic about math. Mathematics are central to this book. Is that something you have a natural affinity for?

I don't think I'm exactly phobic like you, but I'm pretty far down that road. What I was trying to do was to shake it up a little bit as I've done in the other books where on first glance it's all about physicality—fighting, violence, fists and all that kind of stuff. But in a couple of other books, the clues have been fairly subtle, and to do with grammar and punctuation and so on. I wanted to find another thing that was similar. We have this image of these very hardboiled people pouring over the arcana of arithmetic just to bring in a bit of variety. I am a bit like you, a bit hopeless at numbers, to be honest, so it appeared all the more exotic to me that they would be doing that.

Terrorism also is an element in the novel. Do you see that increasingly as a necessary factor in terms of writing the sorts of books that you do?

It is. Fortunately, I'm not writing generally the sort of big government-type thrillers where I think it would be completely impossible to avoid.

With Reacher's military background, I wonder if it becomes a harder thing to explain why he's not more directly involved in the war on terror.

Technically I suppose his status would be reservist, though he's been out for a long time now. I don't know how long he'd be subject to recall. And of course he'd have to have an address to be recalled from. I think it's easy enough to get around that explicitly.

The terrorism question is very interesting. How far do we go with it? At what point does it become uncomfortable? At what point does it become a cliché, frankly? It seemed the inevitable conclusion to a story that involved a new defense contractor that was involved in shenanigans. So I approached it really through the weapons manufacturer rather than through starting out with terrorism.

You and Reacher have had to make some accommodations in terms of his nomadic lifestyle in that he now has an ATM card. Does Homeland Security concern you as Reacher's creator in that it's going to be increasingly difficult for him to maintain that kind of nomadic, off-the-grid life?

Kind of, yeah. What really happened there is his lack of baggage was always kind of metaphorical in as much as it was a symbol of the type of person he was. But there's a sort of uneasy boundary between metaphor and reality and readers were getting unhappy that it's just simply not possible to travel without I.D. I've found from experience it's just simply not possible to phone a bank anymore and have them do anything. Therefore, in the sense that we have to be somewhat realistic, I have to update it a little bit. But it is a problem. At what point are we going to stop? Reacher kind of addresses that in the book. One of them asks why didn't he save his shirt, which was still wearable. It's a good question. The answer is you have to stop somewhere, and the safest place to stop is the absolute beginning.

You've remarked, "Thriller writers can't help but to reflect and influence their times." Would you venture an opinion about what your influence has been to this point in terms of your body of work?

My influence on the reading public in general?

On the reading public, and on culture …

I think I'm too modest to think that I've made any at this point.

That's why I was trying to drag it out of you.

If anything, what I'm hearing from people is what they are more and more valuing about Reacher is come what may, he will do the right thing. That's what people are saying, and I'm thinking, "What lies behind that feeling?" Are they thinking that in the real world more and more people are not doing the right thing that they should be? I'm wondering if that would be a reaction rather than a proaction, but I'm wondering if that is what they are seeing: that government, society, times are getting more and more compromised and therefore they're valuing a hero who is simply prepared to do the right thing.

In a previous conversation or two we've had, we've talked about the European audience being a little different than the American audience, particularly about Reacher's rather vigilante persona at times. I wonder if you've seen a stronger reaction to that in this book, because that quality in him comes across stronger in this book? It is, at base, a kind of revenge quest.

It is. It's a revenge story, pure and simple. We don't know about this one yet, because it's only just out here. It's not out in Europe yet. The closest to this one is probably *Persuader,* which is again a pure revenge story. They were pretty appalled about it. I went to Sweden where *Persuader* became a big, big bestseller. For the sort of fun of it, I had bought a very, very nice suit. I wore my suit to the event in Sweden. The discussion was all about his vigilante methods, how awful they were … How can we like him so much when he does all these awful things? The headline in the paper that reported about the event had a picture of me talking and it said: "Only the suit is proper." That sums up their attitude. It wasn't like they were condemning the book, because it was just falling off the shelves everywhere, but they were horrified at their own enthusiasm for it.

A little different experience for you, I take it.

Yeah, but again, they take it so seriously. We all understand this is a metaphor essentially. The fact that we put it in fiction is a tacit admission that we know that we can't do it in real life. That's almost proved in my opinion. If we enjoy something in fiction, it's exactly because we *can't* get it in real life. The American audience and British audience is actually more sophisticated in that sense because they understand on a subconscious level if we're enjoying something in *fiction*, that condemns it in *reality*. Whereas the sort of Western Europeans and Scandinavians aren't making that distinction. They're taking fiction for being a textbook for how you should live, and really it's the opposite in my opinion.

Your editor is Kate Miciak. You hear about different relationships be-tween authors and editors. I assume with your first books you were more or less left to your own devices ... you could follow your own in-stincts and write the novels you wanted to write. At a certain level of success, it seems some authors must run plot outlines or story pitches by an editor before knuckling down to write. Are you in a situation where you still do that?

Pretty much I'm completely left to myself. It's a close thing ... you grow toward the same goal in a way that is not overt at all. Kate would never dream of calling me up and saying, "Don't do this," or "Don't do that." But I know what she wants and she knows what I'm capable of, so the whole thing becomes almost an un-spoken contract. We get along really, really well, which is fortu-nate because she is a very. very perceptive editor. Certainly, it would be very difficult to get something unsatisfactory past her.

You've indicated before that after each book you're at a loss of ideas for the next. Is that still the case for you, or do you have a general idea a book, two books out?

I don't two books out. That's still true: I finish one book and feel pretty bereft. But I don't have to start the next one for two or three months. I've come to rely on the fact that in those two or three months something will build up in my head. But at this point, for the next one, I have absolutely no clue what it will be.

Do you ever toy with a standalone not featuring Reacher, or are you committed to the series?

I really am. The way the series is set up, there is a tremendous amount of flexibility, given he doesn't have a job or a location. Those are the two things that tend to suffocate a series. If you've got to write your twelfth book about a police lieutenant in Chicago, already you've cut your options down drastically. The fact is, Reacher can be anywhere and do anything. It's really not very restrictive so I don't feel the need to break out of the straight-jacket.

Plus, there is a kind of unspoken contract with the reader. I was thinking about this in terms of baseball. I go to Yankee Sta-dium: I expect to see Derek Jeter playing shortstop. I'm sure that Jeter is in a position where he could go to the Yankees and say,

"Hey, I want to play center field tomorrow," and they would probably scratch their heads a bit and let him. But that's not the deal; he's a shortstop, and I'm the guy who writes Reacher. If the public wants something different from Reacher, well, great, there's fifty-one other weeks in the year, they can read somebody else's books.

You've written non-Reacher short stories. Conversely, have you ever thought about a series of Reacher shorts?

I would love to do that. That would be a very good idea for fulfilling short story commissions. There is a minor tactical problem—a kind of industry-level problem—with that, which is with the character rights being sold to the movie industry, what you're essentially doing there is giving them more material for free. If you wrote a Reacher short story, that becomes their movie material. So generally speaking, business-wise, that would be regarded as a bad move. But it would be fun. The short stories I've done so far have typically been favors for friends who are doing anthologies. If I get an idea, then I love to do it. It's fast and easy to do. But short story ideas are very hard to come up with. It sounds counter-intuitive, but it's *much* harder to write a short story than a novel.

You brought up film. What's the status of the Reacher film franchise?

The status is "in development." The industry reality is that right now the rights are jointly owned by Tom Cruise, Wagner and Paramount, who have of course split. It's had a bad effect. Essentially, the rights are now like somebody's Labrador puppy in a divorce. They're fighting each other with anything they can for absurd reasons and therefore it's pretty much in limbo at the moment. Until that resolves itself, I don't think anything will be done.

You've acknowledged a couple of times that you've been approached to write a James Bond novel or to continue the character, but you've labeled it a kind of impossible task, citing Bond's rather dated characteristics. What was your impression of the new film, *Casino Royale*, starring Daniel Craig?

I thought it was a great film, actually. If you look at it on two levels: First, as a business project—how can we revitalize a moribund franchise? I thought it was sensationally well done from that point of view. The grittiness, the physicality … the specific rejection of the various Bond movie clichés that it did—I thought was terrific. And it was a great thriller. But in a sense, it was *so* repositioned that it almost wasn't a Bond. It could have been anything … a Jason Bourne … It was *so* contemporary in the way that it felt that it didn't feel like a Bond film. I can't really prove it in any way, but I bet those guys have read my books. I felt there was a lot of Reacher influence in there somehow.

My first impression was that it's moving back toward the Bond character as written, but then I went back in and read the novel—which I hadn't read in probably twenty years—and found that no, it really wasn't Fleming's Bond either.

That's interesting, because I did the same thing. It tempted me to go back and reread some of the books. That was *really* fascinating. We forget in some ways how good they were and in some ways how bad they were. And, in some ways, how unreconstructed they were—just blatant racism, sexism … all that kind of stuff. But a lot of writers from that era are the same. We've really moved on.

You're a founding member of the International Thriller Writers Association. How are things going with that organization—does it seem to have found its feet?

We predicated early on that it was really the first five years that were really going to make or break. If you look at our main—we don't like to call it "rival"—but MWA [Mystery Writers of America], which is the other sort of main organization, that's sixty-two years old. You've got to take your hat off to that. We're effectively about three years old and we're heading toward our second convention. The first one was a spectacular success. Really fresh, energetic and so on. The second will be even better. But it's easy to get seduced by that. The first one and the second one, that's all very well. But two weeks ago, I just went to MWA's sixty-second one. Let's see where we are down the road. Really, we're heading toward a critical period. Things are looking great, but it's about momentum now. Can we keep it going?

There's been a lot written about the thrillers of late, and the fact that they are dominating the book market and bestseller lists. Do you get the sense that there's some increased respect or regard for the craft?

The respect issue is very difficult to articulate. ITW's mission statement for instance says, effectively, when you boil it down, "We have four hundred members. Our combined sales are two billion books. We want some respect." I'm thinking, "Now, wait a minute. Two billion books? How much more respect do you want?" But I suppose what we're saying is—and actually what we're seeing—is that reviewers are looking at an apple as an apple and an orange as an orange and don't confuse the two. It used to be very difficult to find a review where a reviewer did not say, "Well, yeah, *but* ..." You know? "This is great, *but* ... but the characters are a bit thin," or whatever. That to me is apples and oranges. You cannot expect the kind of English literature character development that you get in a leisurely classic novel. But I think more and more at face value are saying, "This is a really good thriller," and there are no "buts" in there, and I suppose that's the kind of respect that we're looking for.

The obligatory question: can you preview the next book?

Play Dirty is the title. It's a small-town book set in Colorado. The best way to sum it up is it's Reacher's take on the Iraq War—the various consequences back home of what's going on in Iraq. It's a risky book, but I think it is a book that is honestly written and also is true as far as I understand what I am hearing from my friends in the military. Just to preview the theme, which is summing up what I've heard from a lot of people, at one point, Reacher says, "I *loved* the Army. I *hate* what's happened to it. It's like I had a sister and she married a creep." I think that is sort of how people feel. If you go up to general officer level you're going to get all kinds of political nonsense, but basically for people who love the institution, that's how they feel.

PART VII

Troubadours

TOM RUSSELL

Tough Company
(March 7, 2005)

Thomas George Russell: one of America's greatest living singer-songwriters.

An abiding love for the land; an unerring eye for the telling detail; a gift for fashioning lines that fall *just right*.

And quite often, Russell's tunes are noir set to music.

Check the man's résumé and you'd be forgiven for deducing he must be nearly 230 years old.

Russell had early ambitions of being a novelist.

He has a degree in criminology and taught it in Biafra, Africa, where Andrew Vachss also spent some time.

But Russell also heard Bob Dylan; he heard Buck Owens on his uncle's "tube-driven" radio. Russell eventually drifted into songwriting. And drifted away.

He traveled with circuses in Europe. He drove cabs in New York City. He married. Had two daughters. Divorced.

He veered back into music while driving a cab, when a fare—someone with ties to the recording industry, and, *ahem,* the *Grateful Dead*—struck up a conversation and eventually asked Russell to play something. So Russell strummed out his composition "Gallo del Cielo," a borderland tune about Pancho Villa, stolen family land, cockfighting and a cyclopean, broken-winged rooster that would do crime novelist Charles Willeford proud. Russell's famous fare asked him to sing the song four more times.

That taxi performance kick-started Russell's dormant musical career.

At least three rich veins run through Russell's body of musical work. He's the last living king of the elegiac and brainy cowboy ballad—Marty Robbins' truest heir.

Born in L.A. and educated along the borderland country— a California, Mexico and Texas nexus—and now living in El Paso, Tom Russell has recorded three albums of superlative cowboy music: *Cowboy Real* (1992), *Songs of the West* (1997) and 2004's *Indians Cowboys Horses Dogs*.

But Tom Russell is also a purer, more courageous noir voice than many of our current crop of so-called "neo-noir" novelists.

For starters, Russell has that criminology degree. He was born in the City of Angels in variously the late 1940s or maybe 1950. Russell deliberately puts out conflicting information about his real birthday, asserting that giving accurate birth dates assists critics and media-types in their drive to sort and assign titles rather than judging music or an artist on their own terms.

But Tom Russell is a contemporary of James Ellroy's—they share a 1950s-60s Angelino milieu. Russell's "Tijuana Bible" (*Modern Art*, 2003), is James Ellroy's entire *L.A. Quartet* distilled down to a single, intoxicating song:

L.A. mobster Mickey Cohen's stooge Johnny Stompanato gets shanked by movie queen Lana Turner's daughter, Cheryl Crane. "Stomp" rides "an ice truck down the brand new Harvard freeway." A MacArthur Park-based P.I. investigates. Seeking a treasure map, the Eye digs up Johnny's corpse, looking for riches ... and finds an *L.A. Confidential*-style "Tijuana Bible" full of smutty sketches of Cary Grant doing the nasty with Donald's drifting squeeze Daisy Duck "in a Tijuana bedroom."

"Hong Kong Boy" spins on Chinatown crime: an Irish cop, walking that "Mah Jong" and opium-salted beat ... "he's seen it all from Precinct 4."

"Blood Oranges," dedicated to writer Paul Bowles, is another chilling piece of work: a folklorist goes searching for "a rare nomadic tribe" of mysterious blue men and finds them, to devastating effect.

Russell's 2001 release was a revelation: *Borderland* is a Tex-Mex masterpiece. Russell keynotes the album with an excerpt from Raymond Chandler's *The High Window*: " ... nobody cared if I died or went to El Paso."

The songs include "Touch of Evil," a brilliant and wrenching examination of male/female relationships with Orson Welles' noir film standing as cockeyed metaphor for love and sex, where all the players "are tragically miscast."

"Hills of Old Juarez" is about drug-running along the border—flying bullets and bloody betrayals.

"California Snow," written with Dave Alvin, is a ballad of illegal immigration gone repeatedly wrong—the song that Springsteen's "Sinaola Cowboys" achingly wanted to be.

And that third vein: Tom Russell is our last great mythographer-folklorist-balladeer and the credible heir to John Steinbeck. He's written songs about FDR-era abuses against Japanese-Americans ("Manzanar"), about the collapse of the American steel industry ("U.S. Steel") and about Vietnam ("Veteran's Day").

Russell has also penned a collection of rich and resonant biographical tunes encapsulating the lives of writers, outsiders, athletes and real-life outlaws. William Faulkner, Edward Abbey, Edith Piaf, Jack Johnson, Bill Haley, Mickey Mantle, Muhammad Ali, Roberto Duran ... Claude Dallas and Geronimo: they've all been captured—and definitively captured—in song by Russell.

This vein of the songwriter's work reached an apex with the release of *The Man From God Knows Where (An Immigrant Song Cycle,* 1999), the first in a projected trilogy examining the American experience.

Part two debuted in March 2005: *Hotwalker: Charles Bukowski and A Ballad for Gone America* is a startling montage of songs, voices and riffs on the American experience in the twentieth century; moving monologues and wrenching ballads about outsider artists and vanquished American culture. The CD includes audio captures of Charles Bukowski, Harry Partch, Jack Kerouac, Lenny Bruce, Edward Abbey, Dave Van Ronk and, maybe most affectingly, deceased carnival legend Little Jack Horton—"circus midget" and "the voice of the midway." Horton was a salty-mouthed little man who seems to have been everywhere and to have known everyone who mattered.

A companion book to *Hotwalker* was released by Mystery Island Publications in 2005. *Tough Company* includes interviews conducted by Tom Russell with Charles Bukowski, correspondence with Bukowski, and Russell's own distinctly noir poetry and short fiction.

About the same time, Russell launched a new enterprise, taking part in a series of "songwriter trains" through Canada and down into Mexico.

In 2006, Russell released *Love & Fear*, a cycle of love songs in the vein of *Borderland*.

In concert, Russell is a riveting performer—very much in the moment and singing each song as if he is performing it for the first—and perhaps the *last*—time. Between songs, his patter is charming and funny and smart.

But hawking products between sets, making "the lunch money," as he terms it, Russell can at times seem a bit prickly or standoffish. Fans sometimes "slag" him, to use his own term, on his Yahoo discussion site for perceived brusqueness when they've met him in person.

Some of it may stem from Russell's own painful shyness growing up. On stage, he's the consummate performer.

One-on-one, the extrovert vanishes. As he commented in an interview in *Tough Company*, in a quote James Ellroy might have given, "I was a weird kid. I lived in my head. I went through the motions in the outside world. I felt painfully shy and unable to talk to anyone until I was in my thirties. I felt like a budding serial murderer. It wasn't until I began writing that I became centered."

I spoke with Tom Russell on March 7, 2005. Russell was on the road, touring for *Hotwalker*.

· · · · ·

I'm just changing strings on my guitar while we speak. Gettin' ready for another show.

They've got you on the wheel, huh?

Yeah, but it's better than not bein' on the wheel.

Hotwalker is such a complex and nuanced album. I feel there were intimations of it with Charles Bukowski's "Crucifix In A Death Hand" on Modern Art and your song about Edward Abbey on the most recent album [Indians Cowboys Horses Dogs].

Yeah, definitely.

So is Hotwalker something you've been thinking about for some time? And why now?

I liked the form. You caught that—a lot of people haven't caught that—that I've made intimations at this before. It even goes back to a Ramblin' Jack [Elliott] song, basically, called "912 Greens," where he plays a guitar and talks about a trip down to New Orleans. It always influenced me. I started doing that on my records, like "What Work Is" on *Borderlands* and then the Bukowski piece. People liked it. It's different. It has the warmth and sort of musicality of a song, but sort of the vibe of a Beat poem. I think *Hotwalker* is a real extension of that. But I hadn't really been thinking of it for a long time. It really came out of the book, *Tough Company*, that's coming out about the letters back and forth with Bukowski from the '70s and '80s.

My understanding is you kind of rescued a book for Bukowski because you had collected his columns [Notes of A Dirty Old Man].

Yeah. Nobody else did. A guy named Sanford Dorbin who was putting together a Bukowski bibliography at the University of California, Santa Barbara, was chatting to me in the '60s and I said, "Well, I have those columns." And he said, "Well, Bukowski would dig that if you would let him borrow 'em." That's what happened and that's where the correspondence started. Later on I interviewed him by mail a couple of times for an arts journal in Scandinavia. They were pretty spiky interviews. Those are kind of the basis of the book, along with some vignettes from me about the early days working in bars. It's a small book, but out of that the record grew.

I understand you have a number of short stories in *Tough Company*, too.

Little pieces. They're written as poetry and then extended into short stories. I've written a couple of books. This is sort of a little Beat poetry book.

I've read your songwriting book written with Sylvia Tyson, *And Then I Wrote*. I understand too that you've written a detective novel. I've tried like hell to find it.

Instantly forgettable.

Oh. *Okay ...*

It was published only in Norwegian. I think the same guy that's publishing *Tough Company* is going to publish an excerpt along with a Dashiell Hammett excerpt, coming up soon. It was a thing I did for money. I'm always working on some prose. But tracking that one down wouldn't do you any good because it is in Norwegian.

Are you still writing poetry in addition to songs?

I don't really write poetry now. There is stuff in there that is very Bukowski-esque. It's sort of short story-like, but it lines up kind of in a long line.

An excerpt has been posted on the Web, called "Getting Off Work At the Topless Bar," that you wrote in 1971, I think. It's very noir.

Yeah, that kind of thing. I don't know if I wrote it in 1971 but that's when it happened. There's a lot of stuff like that. I'm trying to finish up sort of an apology or closing for the book by saying, "Look, this stuff was really influenced by Bukowski and some of it holds up for me." But you know he ruined a lot of writers, too. They thought they could write drunk about screwing somebody.

Yeah, I pick up his posthumous books now and then and it's pretty uneven.

Yeah, some of it holds up and some of it doesn't.

A lot of crime and crime fiction seems to creep into your songs. You have a degree in criminology and taught that, as well. Was that something you did with an eye toward a career? And I read also, that you regard yourself as a frustrated novelist and set out on that course, too.

I did very well [in criminology] and I had a good teacher. I went to Africa with him and taught over there. But I didn't like academic life at all. I knew that was very beat. I didn't like the people, so I went back to music. But I like the street-level thing about it. I think I found it in the bars when I went back to the bars and played music. I wrote about street-level problems of Native Americans at first.

You have a song about Johnny Stompanato on *Modern Art* that reminds me a lot of crime writer James Ellroy's stuff. But you guys are about the same age and from the same part of L.A.

Yeah, yeah. That's in the same vein. I used to read a lot of true crime, too, if it was well written. Not so much because I was fascinated by violence, as fascinated by character. Which you don't get in a lot of modern American fiction writing.

Now, *Hotwalker* is a tribute to outsider art and outsider voices. Do you really view yourself within that context?

Definitely. In this culture, I'd hate to be an insider. I'd be playing eighteen holes of golf a day and listening to country music. This other crap. A fear-driven culture. If they call me an outsider that's fine, because it leaves me alone to do whatever I feel like, really.

Songwriter Gretchen Peters concludes *Hotwalker* with a performance of "America the Beautiful."

I can't say enough good about Gretchen. *Halcyon* is just about one of the strongest records I've heard in years. Someone gave it to me in England last year and I just went, "Holy shit." I wrote her a fan letter—e-mailed her—and she wrote me back. I said, "Man, I don't listen to Nashville music, but this record ... if you've got a wild hair, come over and sing with me on these two projects I'm doing." She goes, "You know what, I do." So she came over and sang on *Hotwalker* and *Love and Fear*. We've become friends. She's a unique writer who not only wrote hits and could have retired on that, but she's a great performer and she's going to get out there. I think she's strong across the boards and just a great singer. I'm a big fan of Gretchen's. She's written with Neil Diamond, and that's a little weird. But Gretchen is a really, really great person. I put her in my top five.

What kinds of reactions are you getting to *Hotwalker* so far?

Very strong. I think there was one pan in *No Depression,* but that's as it should be. You know, the people who should understand it don't. The *London Times* is doing a page on it and it is probably the best newspaper in the world. Mojo is doing a feature in *Uncut* and I respect them a lot. Of course the English press loved it, and the Canadian press and radio loves it. In the States, it's been a little bit slower because of the fear factor—because it takes a shot at America. Radio is playing it … smaller stations … but they're afraid of the so-called "strong language," which I think is hilarious: "Goddamn it."

One of my favorite phrases.

Yeah, really. "Goddamn it" being considered "strong language" is hilarious. It's a question of that sort of thing. But overall, the reaction has been very strong. There's a lot to write about there and there is quite a bit to play. NPR did a ten-minute segment on it last week and that was cool.

I read where there were early proposals to have people like David Carradine and some others like Sean Penn read some of the Bukowski materials.

Well, the book publisher came up with that and that was on. But the Bukowski estate wasn't going for it. Which in the end was fine with me, because I would have just been leaning on some actors.

Well, you have that great riff on *Hotwalker* that I took to be in reaction to that notion about actors being "flim-flammers" and "magazine faces."

Well, definitely. It spurred me really into my own story, which is basically what I'm supposed to be doing anway and not leaning on people that are more famous. It wouldn't have been that much fun, really.

You corresponded with Bukowski for, it sounds like, about three decades?

Yeah, the '70s and '80s, mostly. Then, right before he died I think, I interviewed him. It was sporadic. Sometimes he wouldn't even remember who I was. Usually when he wrote letters late at night he was drinking quite a bit. They're pretty funny letters. But they're very short. He put a drawing on them, which was kind of neat. There would always be a dog or a bottle … something running across the bottom. And the two or three written interviews I did with him are very spiky and funny.

Did Bukowski ever hear your music and if so, did he comment on it?

I gave him my first record, *Ring of Bone* [with Patricia Hardin, 1976]. I met him once on the street in Hollywood. We came out of Capitol Records, Patricia Hardin and I. We'd made a record and we were trying to get a deal, some ridiculous thing, and we came out of Capitol Records. I looked down the street and I said, "Damn, there's Charles Bukowski, man." It was like 1975 or '76. I said, *"Wow!"* He was buyin' an underground paper out of a vending machine with his girlfriend. I said, "Let's go down and give him a record." So we walked down there. He was very friendly. He wasn't like you'd think. People think he was drunk like twenty-four hours a day. Very friendly.

I said, "Listen, do you want to go to a bar?" He said, "No. I appreciate you sending me that stuff [the columns]. We have to go on an errand right now." He took the record, although I don't think he listened to stuff like that. He listened to a lot of classical. But we split, then got on the freeway in our truck. About a minute a later, this little VW Bug came racing up alongside. It was Bukowski and he rolled the window down. He pointed to his girlfriend, Linda, and said, "Hey, this is Linda!" and then he took off. He'd forgotten to introduce her and she'd probably given him a bunch of shit. That was funny. She told me later—I met her a couple of times—he had written something about this, a poem, but I've never seen it. But that was the only time I met him and he was quite gentlemanly and funny.

I love what you did with Buk's "Crucifix In A Death Hand." How'd you come to link that poem with Warren Zevon's song "Carmelita"?

That just sort of happened in the studio. It's my favorite piece of his [Bukowski's] because it really portrays the L.A. I grew up in. Alvera Street … the train station in downtown L.A. where I was born. It's really a different city than any other American city. All of the sudden, I thought of Zevon's "Carmelita," which really portrays the same thing, and threw it in there.

Now, *Hotwalker* is billed as part two of a trilogy.

You know, I kind of dreamt that up. I wasn't thinking that when I was doing it, but *Man From God Knows Where* handles my ancestors back a couple of generations to Norway and Ireland and it ends on my father's death. *Hotwalker* picks up really at my childhood influences. The third one I have worked on quite a bit, but I shelved for a while. It's a view of the American West through the eyes of a woman, my sister-in-law, Claudia. It's a really great, unique story. I've written seven or eight songs around her growing up on this Spanish land grant ranch in California. She's a unique person and she has her whole history mapped out and has all these scrapbooks. She shot two bears in her kitchen that were coming after her. She lives way out isolated in central California. It's a great, great story and has epic quality.

She sounds like she's right out of your song "Hallie Lonnigan."

Well, that's who I wrote that song for. So I'm going to get back to that and that would be part three. You would have three very musical histories of America.

You work from a lot of historical influences and biographical sources. I love the track "Woodrow" about Woody Guthrie on this album. But it's not the *Bound For Glory* depiction of Guthrie you tend to get.

Well, no. You know my agent books a Guthrie show and this and that and I've always declined. I said, "I don't dig a couple of things that people have done." People that have finished his songs—I don't get that angle. I wouldn't want my kids to be finishing my lyrics. You know, I'll burn 'em all. And putting political sloganeering in a dead man's mouth? I got at Woody by talkin' to Ramblin' Jack a lot, who knew him as good as anybody. Probably better than his kids knew him. And Jack really gave me this very unique view of Woody—and I talk about him every night, as you saw. I'm more interested in the individual. I mean, he did jail time. He was a real womanizer and he wrote great songs. I'm more interested in that than his family saying, "Woody would have voted for Kerry, man." Give him a break. Let him have the life that he had. That's kind of why I wrote the song. And all the other people on the record who I was talking about are of the same ilk, I think.

Your Mickey Mantle song, "Kid From Spavinaw" is one of my favorite songs, period. That line about God throwing change-ups is about as terse and perfect a definition of Manichaeism as could be hoped for. You've written about Ali and so many others. Ever thought about batching all these together at some point?

You know, I've never thought about it, but I have boxing songs. And I've always liked characters. I just finished a book on a plane today about Bobby Fischer the chess player and that match in 1972 in Iceland, and he reminds me a lot of Ali. Just these incredible American characters that invented themselves and triumphed.

You read pretty widely, I take it.

Yeah, yeah. I enjoy reading. I'm not a TV guy. I get to read a lot when I'm traveling.

What do you tend to read?

I read the de Kooning bio [*de Kooning: An America Master*] this year, which is big and great, and the Dylan book. I think those two informed me of two unique American artists who—in spite of intense and constant criticism—reinvented themselves and are part of our culture. They are deeply rooted. Dylan has a huge catalogue and you can't deny him, no matter what you think of him. And de Kooning, too. He snuck aboard a boat when he was sixteen and came to America illegally. By the end of his life at age eighty-five with Alzheimer's, he was still painting million dollar paintings. It was just a great story, a great American story.

You've taken up painting.

In the last year, year and a half, yeah.

And you're using them as illustrations on your CDs. You're down to the point now where you're almost an auteur in terms of your packaging.

Yeah, and I like it. I sold the cover painting to a fan. We did that as an auction and it got some bucks. I have a show coming up at Yard Dog in Austin that handles a lot of folk art. They have five of my paintings. I'm kind of thinking on the next album of steering away from it for a record. I'm doing a record called *Love & Fear* that has twelve or fifteen new songs. I'm thinking of really just doing black and white photography like the picture that is on my Web site now. It was taken with a woman in a motel room.

It's a great shot.

Yeah! I *like* that angle: don't look back, kind of grainy … what it's like on the road and love and fear. I might get away from the art cover just so I don't lean on it all the time.

I take it these songwriters trains you're doing lately are a little more satisfying than just the grind of the road.

Yeah, I'm looking forward to that. Last year's was a little rough because my ex-girlfriend was on it.

There's no way to get off that sucker ...

Yeah! It ended on the train, but I got some songs out of it. This time, I've been pretty girlfriend-free for eight months and I'm just going to enjoy the ride.

When you're songwriting, do the lyrics or the melodies come first?

They come together in a really weird way, although I'm pretty lyric-driven. I throw away a lot of lyrics. I struggle a little more with the melodies so they're not cliché. But the lyrics seem to imply a melody all the time.

You're such a writer's writer—I wondered if it was word driven.

It is pretty word driven but I have to watch that. I want to be a melodist, too. It helps writing with different people. I've learned a lot writing with Dave Alvin, Ian Tyson, Nancy Griffith. They all come from different melodic angles. It helps also to write on a piano instead of the guitar ... get away from your limitations a little bit.

Do you have a particular favorite among your albums?

Not really. Once they're done, I don't go back and listen to them because I've put so much into them and I'm always thinking of the next one. I think I'm going to like the next one, *Love & Fear*, because it's so unique. I haven't written a lot of love songs before this and I have written ten or twelve that I really like. I think they're really different sorts of love songs. That will be a favorite album. *The Man From God Knows Where* is very personal. It would probably be that one. But a lot of people like *Borderland*. That was a very painful period for me. Like *Blood On the Tracks* or something.

I love the song "Touch of Evil" ... such an inspired and strange and wonderful song.

I like that movie *a lot*. Reminds me of Dylan's "Desolation Row."

You do a lot with your Web site.

That's my guy in Kansas City—always coming up with something.

How has the Internet affected your career?

It's important now. When you're an outsider person you don't have access to major market radio. You gotta *scuffle*. We're revamping our mailing list. We had ten or fifteen thousand people on that snail mail list and now we've gotta go to e-mail because that's the only way to go financially and we're up to two or three thousand. But you've *got* to be there. You've got fans that want to know what you're doing. You've got to keep your Web site updated.

There's a chatroom—I don't get involved with that—where people can slag me, or whatever they want to do. "What Tom did last night," and they do the set lists and all that. That's kind of cool. And we send out e-mails of where we are appearing. That's real important. It's like a drumbeat across the world. And people who are into it live a lot on the Internet. You can't get away from e-mails and the Internet. It's like a newspaper that comes out every day. I value it. I've *learned* to value it 'cause I know the power of it. They can tell about us going to London with the band, they can tell about the trains. Now people are getting to the soundbytes that have little movies with them. As long as I don't have to do it, I'm fine with it. I've got guys who help me. Basically, I'm a guy who likes to read and paint and write, and that's where I'm coming from.

One of your earlier songs is about the recently released convict Claude Dallas. Any thoughts about that?

I would be real interested sometime in talking to him. A few people I have known know him and they think he got caught up in a situation and he did what he thought he had to do. I think that had he not overreacted *so* much he would not have done *any* time because the guy was definitely pushing him. It was a volatile situation. A lot of cowboys liked him. I tried to even out the song because I had a police officer in my family blown away, so I know both sides of the story. I was trying to make it a little more even.

But from everything I read he just wants to disappear now. He didn't exploit any of it and he did his time. He'll disappear back into the wilderness, you know. He was basically out there trapping stuff, out of season, but just to live on, and the guy pushed him and that's what happened.

You wrote a screenplay based on your song "Mineral Wells" about a film critic and an aging movie star. Any prospects of that happening?

It'd make a good movie. We haven't been shopping it recently, but I have people shopping some of my songs to films these days.

You have a DVD coming soon.

Hearts On the Line, done by Canyon Productions and Eric Temple. He did a great film called *A Voice in the Wilderness* about Edward Abbey. It's finished and it should come out in May.

KINKY FRIEDMAN
Independence Day
(March 9, 2005)

Richard "Kinky" "Big Dick" Friedman wants you to know that he is serious.

He recently stood in front of the Alamo—the most hallowed structure in his home state of Texas—and announced his candidacy for the seat of governor. He'll have to defeat Richard Perry—George W. Bush's successor.

When I spoke with him, Friedman said the "Pat Paulsen/joke phase" regarding his Independent candidacy for Texas governor was finally shaking out in the minds of the media types seeking him out. It had finally dawned on them, he said, that he was a serious candidate with issues of real concern that he meant to address if elected.

But the hurdles were high. He was running as an Independent in a state whose election laws are seemingly devised to discourage Independent political bids. And the amount of money spent by the major parties in the previous Texas governor's race was simply obscene.

But Friedman was giving it an honest shot, collecting donations, volunteers and potential cabinet members.

He'd just left his post as columnist for *Texas Monthly Magazine* lest anyone cry favoritism, and in his new novel, *Ten Little New Yorkers,* Kinky killed off "Kinky Friedman," the Greenwich Village troubadour/detective.

That Kinky Friedman and the Village Irregulars debuted in 1986's *Greewich Killing Time*. Seventeen volumes later, character Kinky was seemingly taking his final bow.

Before becoming a successful mystery writer, Kinky toured with his band, The Texas Jewboys, penning songs like "Top Ten Commandments," "The Ballad of Charles Whitman" and "Nashville Casualty and Life."

He was born on Halloween Day, 1944. He was a chess prodigy—that photo on the back of the dustjacket of *Blast from the Past* of little Richard Friedman playing chess against World Grandmaster Samuel Reschevsky in 1952 is the real deal.

Kinky was one of the pioneering Peace Corps members.

Now he runs an animal rescue ranch partly funded through the sale of his own brand of salsa.

The author's official Web site, once used to peddle his books, CDs and DVDs, has been given over to the campaign for governor.

In June, 2006, Kinky stunned political watchers by successfully earning a place on the November ballot in the race for Texas governor.

Kinky Friedman called the interviewer, and dead on the scheduled time (no pun intended).

• • • • •

This is Governor Friedman.

You're maybe too punctual to be a politician.

I'm too punctual to be a musician, that's for sure.

Well, to paraphrase one of Kris Kristofferson's lesser-known songs, "My God, you killed him." Why did Kinky "step on a rainbow"?

Because I think it's time for literature's loss to be politic's gain.

Is it really linked that directly to the race?

Ah, no. I think the characters have pretty well run their course. They were starting to irritate the Kinkster. Actually, I was just starting to like the guy—that Kinky. Yeah, but you know the mystery field is as narrow as it is deep. When you write mysteries, the mystery element is what keeps the whole genre trite and limited sometimes. As I've said, cheap, dog-eared death is not as interesting as the question: "Is there life before death?"

You went off the res' and used a different character in *Kill Two Birds & Get Stoned*, and in *The Prisoner of Vandam Street* Kinky the character was pretty ill. Have you been toeing up to this for a while?

It's a blessing. It's a blessing that Kinky was killed. But if I hear the literary community clamoring for his return we'll see what we can do, but he is going to be pretty hard to resurrect.

Well, this last novel reminds me a lot of *The Final Problem* by Doyle. Doyle didn't leave himself a lot of wiggle room when he sent Sherlock Holmes over the falls. You kind of have. Without giving away the ending, in terms of the obit and its author—and you didn't leave a cadaver—so the path seems open.

[*Chuckling*] No. If he ever does come back, I promise it will not be a dream sequence. Or a twin Kinkster.

You're apparently not too worried about the karma of offing your namesake.

It's all right. It's time to move on. Seventeen of these books is a lot to write.

It's a hell of a run.

I never would have dreamed it, yeah.

When you go into writing the books, do you go in with some general notions, or are they plotted pretty closely up front?

No, I never do that. I go in with an ending. It's the Joseph Heller method. You've got the ending, so you write the ending. Then you write the beginning. Then you go back and write to that ending. But I do it all by cowboy logic and Jewish radar. I don't have any plans or scripts. I don't plot it out. That's really what keeps the mystery field so narrow: You've gotta have a corpse in the library, you've gotta have the usual suspects. And no matter how good a writer you are, that's limiting.

You have described yourself as "a prisoner of genre," but you've gone outside that field as well with some non-mystery books.

Oh, we may well do some more nonfiction. Maybe the governor's race. We may come out of this thing probably with a book, a wife and maybe the governorship.

You have your eye on a potential First Lady at this point?

No, I'm married to Texas.

You and Sam Houston.

Yes, it could happen. I would be the first Independently elected governor since Sam Houston in 1859. If it happens.

Now, you've made many comments about the plight of Texas death row inmate Max Soffar. And in fact there are some long passages about his case in *Ten Little New Yorkers*. I've seen you refer to him in some other articles and interviews. Is his case a part of the foundation for this bid for the governor's seat? I've heard you say you're not anti-death penalty.

Right, I'm not anti-death penalty, but I'm damn sure anti-the-wrong-guy-getting-executed, and Max is the wrong guy. They got the wrong guy. The system took twenty-four years and still they haven't admitted that they've made a mistake. But Max does have a new trial and he's got a real shot at it this time. Because, man, if anyone was innocent of this crime, it's Max. As I pointed out, we executed an innocent man named Jesus Christ two thousand years ago, and my question is, "What have we learned since then?" And I think the people have learned something. But I think the government has learned very little.

How's the campaign going so far in terms of the money?

It's a circus with a purpose. Things can be fun and important at the same time. They can simultaneously be fun and significant. I think the money is starting to roll in. Of course it won't be anything like what the others have. They spent $100 million last time out for governor of Texas.

That's ... obscene.

A hundred million for a job that only pays a hundred thousand. I mean that's why the campaign is all about the coin of the spirit. It's about Seabiscuit. It's about David against Goliath and it is a spiritual calling, not a political campaign. I'd rather talk about Jesus Christ or Martin Luther King or Ghandi than I would about Kay Bailey Hutchison or Rick Perry or Kinky Friedman.

Have you contemplated a first act as governor if the world turns your way?

The first thing I'm going to do is get a listed phone number. I'll be the first governor with a listed phone number for the governor's mansion that anybody can call. It'll be one of those big answering machines that can take lots of messages in case I'm not there *all* the time, but I will get back to everybody. And I want to give everybody a voice and a choice besides plastic or paper.

I think the first thing I'll probably tackle is Texas' lack of life without the possibility of parole. The fact that here in Texas it is either eject or inject, you know? It's a sick thing that we are first in executions. I don't think Jesus Christ would like that.

Are you prepared to cope with that in the sense that before all of them go for final injections, their cases go before you for review and you're going to be the final arbiter of their lives?

Yeah, I'm totally prepared to deal with that. I mean, I'd *like* somebody to deal with it, for a change. I don't think the governor or the Harris County D.A.—that's where all the executions have taken place—I don't think either one of those guys is a real crime-fighter. I don't think they're truth-seekers. If they were, they'd know that there's a killer—in fact, we even know where the killer is, he's in another prison. This is in Max's case. They haven't looked into it at all. They haven't investigated it. All the detectives and all the people are saying there's witnesses who saw this guy. There's no witnesses who saw Max. In fact, there's no evidence against him. How can you sustain a mistake for twenty-four years? Well, if you're politics as usual, I guess you can do it.

Going back to the writing: You've peppered the series with references to other detectives and other series such as Doyle and Agatha Christie and Rex Stout, among others. Do you read much now in terms of contemporary crime fiction or mysteries?

You know, Craig, I don't read anything anymore. It's really sad. I watch Fox News Network about twenty-four hours a day.

You recently quoted another crime author who said, "If you like a book, never meet the author." What kind of crowds do you draw for your appearances and signings?

We've been drawing really good ones. They're kind of half political, half literary. I think the crowds have been really good, wherever we go. I do think people are kind of getting over the joke phase of it and realizing that being first in executions and forty-ninth in funding public education ... well, we're in a race with Mississippi to the bottom. And we're winning. As Dr. Phil would say, "How's that workin' for you?"

I've caught you on a few cable news programs recently, and the tenor of the approach by the talking heads does seem to be a little different in recent days in terms of how they handle you.

Well you're beginning to hear the passion of the candidate. That's what that's called. Or so they tell me. Not writing for *Texas Monthly* anymore. That's over. That's what they call "journalistic integrity." That's what they call it, but I thought that was an oxymoron. I thought people read *Texas Monthly* for the Neiman Marcus ads, but maybe I was wrong.

You've said it's easier to write a novel than a country song. Was that hyperbole?

Oh yeah, it's much easier. A country song is one of the toughest things in the world to write ... I mean to write a good one. Because you've got to be really miserable. It requires a lot of self-pity and divorce and alcoholism and drugs. All that stuff.

Do you ever sit down with a guitar and dabble at it these days?

I haven't written a country song in twenty years. Too happy. Well, I haven't really been happy, but I haven't been able to recreate that ambiance. And, on the other hand, a lot of great writers like Kristofferson and Willie Nelson and Bob Dylan probably haven't written a *great* song in fifteen or twenty years, either. I think success kills greatness. I mean, it makes you not what you're supposed to be. To really write well, you do have to be, I think, pretty unhappy and unfulfilled. If you're signing books for a hundred people at Barnes & Noble, well … that's the kiss of death, yeah.

I interviewed a Texas neighbor of yours the other day, singer/songwriter Tom Russell, and he has spoken with real disdain about Nashville and the music coming out of there now. I've heard you make similar comments. When you're home spinning the discs, what gets played?

I'm kind of like Elton John, who said he would never go to a concert unless it was a friend of his. I'm kind of like that and I don't listen to music much. And because I've heard so much of it, anyway, I guess. And, you know, Shel Silverstein and Roger Miller are dead, so country music is not very clever, to put it mildly.

I know you maintain ties and are in touch with Billy Joe Shaver and Willie Nelson. Are there others you stay in contact with in that world?

Yeah. And those are the kind of people I want to have in a Friedman administration. I want the state to be run by musicians, not politicians. It will be a damn sight better. It'll be more honest. And a lot less corrupt. So I'm kind of looking forward to that aspect.

You know, a lot of what I think you can do as governor falls under the realm of spiritual lifting. All this means is inspiring people. Getting them to be the best they can be. Getting them back involved. They've become very apathetic because they haven't had any choices but plastic or paper.

I was rereading your book, *'Scuse Me While I Whip This Out,* and your passages about George W. Bush and Laura. Have you heard from W. now since you've formally announced?

No, I haven't. Except a very close friend of the Bushes told me I have a better friend in the president than I know. I don't know what George can really do except humorously straddle the fence. If he does, that will elect me.

That posture *could* be pretty telling.

That would be telling the Republicans to go ahead and follow their heart, do what you want to do. I don't see how he could actually do anything but just crack jokes about it.

I haven't heard him asked anything yet.

Not yet. But it's coming … it's coming. And then what he does will be really telling. I don't know. But I think he'll be funny about it. He is very witty. A lot of people don't know that, but he's very funny. Laura might help. That would be great.

She's done some fundraisers for your Utopia Rescue Ranch.

Yeah. And if Laura were to get involved, that might be enough to throw the thing over.

You haven't been invited out to Crawford yet, then.

If they invite me to Crawford or the White House, that's almost stamping me with approval, so I'm not sure they can do that.

How are things going at the Rescue Ranch?

Very well, Craig. I just talked to Cousin Nancy. We've got a whole string of adoptions happening, which is the best, of course.

How many animals pass through in a year? Do you keep records like that?

I don't know in a year. In six years, I think fifteen hundred, around that area, have been adopted to really good homes. We really vet them carefully—no pun intended. We screen them carefully. The animals are very happy. It's a happy orphanage. A very, very happy place to be. And it's a never-kill sanctuary, of course. Now we're only really taking dogs that are at death's door. And we've got donkeys and pigs and chickens. Of course our rooster, Alfred Hitchcock, crows precisely at noon.

You've got a book coming out called *Texas Hold 'Em*. Can you tell me a little about that one?

That one is more like my *Guide To Texas Etiquette*, maybe. It's

got some good stories. It's got some illustrations by John Calla-
han, the paralyzed cartoonist in Oregon who is a genius. This has
hysterical, very, very dark cartoons. It's *Texas Hold 'Em: How I
Was Born In A Manger, Died in the Saddle and Came Back As
A Horny Toad.* When you read the whole thing, you get a good
feeling for how I feel about Texas. It's almost my *Charge To Keep,*
you know?

A mission statement?

A mission statement, that's right. And really I'm only influenced
by two things: my fellow Texans and my heart. That would be a
really novel idea to have a governor that way.

I've got to ask you about immigration and the border.

I'm conflicted about that one. I'm looking into it more. I'm just
going to have to say, "Read my lips: I Don't Know Right Now."
George W. has the same problem. I think he's awfully conflicted
about it. I think what I can do, immediately, is shine a light into
the darkness of criminal justice and education. Those are two
things we can get going on. And then bio-diesel is something I
want to take up with Willie Nelson, my energy czar. We would
make Texas lead the country in bio-diesel, which is a renewable
fuel that cuts eighty cents off every gallon of gas. And it runs
beautifully. The farmers love it, the truckers love it. And it smells
like French fries. It's totally biodegradable and friendly to the environment. I think Texas will lead the country in bio-diesel as it
led in oil and gas exploration once.

In ten years, a drop of gas is going to cost ten dollars. It'll be
a dollar a drop, the way things are going. We got that, and we've
got the anti-wussification program, of course. You know, where
people are ashamed to say "Merry Christmas." I want prayer back
in the schools. What's wrong with a kid believing in *something?* I
want to take things back to a time when the cowboys all sang and
the horses were smart. So I'm gonna fight this wussification if I've
got to do it one wuss at a time. I see Texas as the last stand. The
last resort for America.

Well, you announced your campaign at the Alamo.

Right. Once I get rid of the career politicians in Texas, I'm gonna get the Californians out of here.

Are there any campaign laws that preclude you getting campaign funds from out-of-state sources?

No, no. We're getting contributions coming in from everywhere. Because anyone who hates politics as usual is drawn to us. My goal is to knock down that windmill of "politics as usual." Get rid of these insider games. Make that Lone Star shine again.

Apart from the campaign, what's next for you?

After *Texas Hold 'Em* I think that's going to be it for a while. When you publish as many books as I do, Craig, well, that's an index of an empty life. That's all it can mean. I'm going to get back to working for the people of Texas. The campaign is going to be long and arduous. The petition drive occurs in March '06.

My understanding is that you're in the position of having to encourage people to sit out a primary in order for them to support you.

That's right! It is so perverse. The ribbon-cutters have devised a way where nobody that votes in the primaries can sign the petition. They're not only not sending the elevator back down to us, but they've cut the cable.

Well put.

We've got to go out to a universe of people who don't vote in the primaries. But we'll get 'em, and we'll get a lot more than fifty thousand, because right now we've got thousands of volunteers already pouring in. Make no mistake: Just because humor is the weapon that I use to joust at the windmill, that doesn't mean I'm not going to knock it down. Will Rogers and Mark Twain were very important cultural leaders in this country even though they weren't in politics. So humor is just a device for sailing as close to the truth as you can without sinking the ship.

I have to ask you a question about this film, *A Case of Lone Star,* that was to star you and Willie Nelson and some others.

That's pretty dead. Hollywood is smoke and mirrors and Kinky is merely smoke. We're talking about doing a documentary on the governor's race. I don't trust Hollywood, and I hope the feeling is mutual. Although a lot of Hollywood people *are* helping us.

It's funny: I think we're almost over the joke hurdle—the Pat Paulsen hurdle—here. We'll see. You wouldn't believe the sincerity of the volunteers. And the zealousness. I don't want to let them down. That's why I'm running in the spirit of Seabiscuit. I want to be every man's horse in this race. And I don't want to show or place. I intend to win. It would send a shiver up the spine of every career politician. It would be so much more significant than a Democrat beating a Republican or a Republican beating a Democrat.

Anything else you'd like to get out there?

Only, may the God of your choice bless you.

Likewise.

Well, thank you and stay tuned.

PART VIII

The
Desert
Dialogues

CONVERSATIONS WITH
James Sallis
&
Ken Bruen

"Memory, too, is a kind of a storyteller,

often more poet than reporter,

selecting and rearranging details to correspond

to some image we have of ourselves,

or simply to make a better story."

— JAMES SALLIS

"After he died, beside his bed,

I found copies of all my books.

Interspersed through the well-thumbed pages,

was every review I'd ever had."

— KEN BRUEN

WESTWARD WE GO

The stars in their courses sometimes afford opportunities. A rare convergence presented itself in March 2005: James Sallis and Ken Bruen ... within a few miles of one another ... way out west in the Arizona desert.

Henry David Thoreau wrote: "Eastward I go by force; but westward I go free... This is the prevailing tendency of my countrymen. I must walk toward Oregon, and not toward Europe."

Slide into the passenger seat.

Ride shotgun into the desert.

Meet James Sallis and Ken Bruen: like Daniel Woodrell and a handful of others, they write crime novels that will endure.

James Sallis was born in 1944; Ken Bruen in '51. Both have worked as teachers. Both aspired to be poets. Poetic cadences, structures and allusions inform the novels of both authors.

Sallis' first Lew Griffin novel, *The Long-Legged Fly,* takes its title from a Yeats poem; the title of the last of the Griffin novels, *Ghost of a Flea,* echoes William Blake. Bruen has written several crime novels keyed to poets: *Rilke on Black, Her Last Call to Louis MacNeice* and *Dispatching Baudelaire.*

Sallis has published volumes of his poetry. Bruen remains steadfast that his own poems will never see print. (That said, a few poems of Bruen's own composition *have* found their way into several of his crime novels and a recent chapbook.)

And here's something: poets don't make commercial concessions.

Sallis and Bruen have been accused by some critics and fellow crime writers of allegedly attempting to subvert, or even undermine the "mystery" novel. The stylistic flourishes and touches that endear them to their most passionate readers are the very elements various critics, editors and publishers have disparaged or even attempted to strip from their works, charging these flourishes threaten to condemn authors such as Sallis and Bruen to cult writer status.

Both men subordinate plot to characterization. They fill their books with allusions to the works of other writers: stray epigraphs taken from essays, novels and songs.

Despite pressures to conform, they remain true to their own impulses and tastes. And both writers continue to publish with small presses. Bruen says that he can envision a time, not too distantly, when he will return to exclusively publishing with smaller houses that will print his works as he envisions them.

Sallis has published more than one hundred short stories. His first novel, a mystery, appeared in 1992. He quickly drew several genre award nominations. Bruen's first, *Funeral,* debuted the same year. Bruen toiled in obscurity for several years, not widely known outside the UK. But in January 2003, St. Martin's published Bruen's *The Guards* in the United States. That novel, featuring the alcoholic and bookish Irish private investigator Jack Taylor, collected several awards nominations, eventually netting a Shamus.

In March 2005, Bruen's third Taylor novel, *The Magdalen Martyrs*, was published in the U.S. Bruen's publisher sent him on his first American tour to promote the book. The pace was punishing.

The touring, the crime conventions—Bruen's fame for graciousness and support of up-and-coming fellow writers—all of these began to squeeze Bruen.

James Sallis has commented on the phenomenon: Just as one's own books begin to make a mark, the pressure to write blurbs for others' books, to give interviews, to tour and promote … these conspire to cut into the time the writer should spend writing.

When I spoke with the authors, and composed the following account of our time together in Arizona, their lives were in different places than they are now.

Sallis' public profile has changed dramatically since I sat with him. The short novel discussed in the following narrative, *Drive*, went on to become Sallis' most widely and enthusiastically reviewed work of fiction and was optioned for screen by Hugh Jackman.

Bruen's public profile was just beginning to peak and he was searching for a publisher for his first novel to be set in the United States, the controversial *American Skin*. Some publishers were deeming the novel to be too dark for American audiences. Since this piece was written, the novel has been published by Justin Charles.

Rather than revise the following piece, it stands as written: as a snapshot of two of crime fiction's most remarkable stylists and writers richly deserving of wider audiences. Authors committed to writing their books, committed to their visions—swimming against the dark, dismal tide of chain stores, formula blockbusters, publishing house consolidation, mid-list decimation and the age of the so-called "no-style stylists."

PART I

JAMES SALLIS

Of Time and Memory

Arizona may be mostly desert, but it's the dusty land of sprawl; there are no commercial and residential breaks between Scottsdale and greater Phoenix, where James Sallis, America's finest crime writer, makes his home.

And homogenization has set in, even out here: there's not much grass and all those cacti, but the twenty-five-minute drive from the hotel to Jim Sallis' house reveals an unbroken strip of chain stores, fast food restaurants and Walgreen's pharmacies. Later, driving with Sallis, I'll remark on finally seeing a building more than six floors high. "They don't build up," he'll say, "because they can build out." It's all held together by a canal system that keeps all the Hummer-driving wealthy folks of conservative Scottsdale/Phoenix in water.

I exceed Yahoo! Maps' arrival estimates to James Sallis' house by many minutes. I swing past his place once, then pull into the lot of a neighboring bank to kill twenty minutes. I slip in a CD of acoustic guitar music by Andrew Hardin and browse over my Sallis notes and questions. An old woman wanders by my car, taps on the window. She's wearing a white cotton T-shirt covered with polka dots reminiscent of a Wonder Bread bag. The blue jumper she's stretched over the shirt looks like it must have been designed for the world's largest toddler. She has one bare foot; there's a red sock on the other. She's carrying a big bag full of God-knows-what and cursing to herself. Another, younger woman calls after her. The elderly woman gives her pursuer the finger. Just then, a nursing home van swings into the bank lot. The driver and an orderly wrestle the elderly woman into the van and tear off.

Okay …

I check my watch: Sallis time.

I pull into the driveway behind a green pickup truck I've been instructed to look for. As I pull out my duffel bag, James Sallis walks out the side door of his house to greet me.

They say we eventually begin to "look like" our careers. Sallis looks like a writer: tall, bearded, bespectacled. Despite the melancholy tone of his books, he laughs easily and often.

You go through a stunning range of temperatures in the course of a mid-March Arizona day, so the canny strategy is to "layer": when I meet him, Sallis is wearing a purple corduroy work shirt over a Hawaiian shirt.

James Sallis lives in a small home on a quiet street in an older neighborhood with his wife, Karyn, and a white rescue cat named "Grace," for her reported lack of same. Grace, Sallis says, bending down to rub her head, has more canine than feline sensibility.

The house is filled with books: books and a stereo system in the living room, more books in his office, some more volumes visible in the portion of the bedroom I see. Sallis writes in a small study in the back of the house. Everything is neat and orderly. He writes on a computer.

In his study is a bookshelf filled with American and foreign translations of his own works. It's quite an array. In addition to his seven crime novels, America's last true man of letters has translated Raymond Queneau's *Saint Glinglin.* He has published volumes of poetry, several volumes of essays, a wonderful biography of Chester Himes, an avant-garde novel (*Renderings*), a spy novel (*Death Will Have Your Eyes*) and he has edited various anthologies.

Sallis now writes and reviews for the *Boston Globe* and the *L.A. Times,* among others. A few galleys, photocopied typescripts and advance reader copies of forthcoming books are stacked on a low table by the door.

The room is also stocked with stringed instruments: six- and twelve-string guitars, a banjo and mandolins (Sallis has written/

edited books on the guitar). Chrome finger slides rest on the shelves with the books. He plays from time to time in jam sessions and the occasional club.

There is a critical distinction between "living as a writer" and "making a living as a writer." Sallis has remarked on the difference on more than one occasion. Living as a writer has made it necessary over the years to do things other than writing to make a living. Right now, that involves teaching several classes on fiction writing.

For many years, Sallis worked as a respiratory therapist. But the hours are long and a recent hip replacement has made it impossible for him to endure the too-typical twelve-hour shifts. Apart from the physical demands, it must be, I say, emotionally and psychologically crushing. Sallis says he found the work *exhilarating*:

"I worked with newborn babies. One-pound babies. We ran the ventilators, the machines that breathe for them and keep them alive. It can be emotionally very draining, but it can be incredibly rewarding. I did this for twenty-something years. Before I started working with babies I worked with adults and I worked critical care. So I was dealing with chronic lungs, chronic hearts … people who are abusers. That was rewarding, but it was also extremely frustrating. It ground you down. It was kind of like working as a policeman, or a lawyer. Then I found that I loved working with neo-nates. Nobody else wanted to because everyone else was afraid of them. Afraid of the machines."

Sallis reasoned if he could run an adult ventilator, it wasn't that great a reach to operate the same machinery for a newborn. So he signed on for the very duty many in his former field shun.

"I found that I loved it," Sallis said. "Yes, it is grueling. Yes, it can be taxing. It was very demanding work. You have to be on top of it; you have to think very fast. You have to move very fast and you have to really know what you're doing. I like that."

The strain of the work was eased slightly over the years as Sallis saw medicine make strides in treating these youngest of patients. "When I started, we were lucky if we saved babies who were thirty-two weeks and they were okay," he said. "We are now routinely saving babies who are twenty-two, twenty-four weeks.

They're okay. It was good knowing that you do that and it was good seeing the level of care progress."

Sallis' experiences in the field inform the opening pages of *Moth,* when detective/author Lew Griffin goes to visit a crack baby born to the daughter of one of Lew's former lovers. In *Cypress Grove,* a therapist kidnaps the patient he has been caring for—a young woman in something like a "persistent vegetative state." He takes her to his home where he can give her more attention. The vignette again draws on Sallis' medical expertise.

"I love that scene," Sallis says. "That is something that I had in mind to do and I just couldn't find the right place to do it. I always tell people that my work in the hospital has given me a special take on things. It has somehow exempted me from a fear of death. And it has somehow exempted me from a lot of the presuppositions that people make. I get very angry when someone is making a decision according to dogma rather than information."

As we're speaking, a bitter legal battle is being waged in Florida between the husband and the parents of Terri Schiavo, a luckless young woman who has been in what is termed a "persistent vegetative state" for more than a dozen years. Her husband has won a long legal battle to have the woman's feeding tube removed and she has now gone several days without food or water. Congress has stepped in, and the president and his brother, the Florida governor, have also weighed in. I ask Sallis if he's following the case.

"Oh yes," he says. "With tremendous anger. My feeling is that any of the congressmen who voted for that should have to take care of a brain-dead person for about a month. Do all the bed care. See what it is like. They are making political decisions. They are making intellectual decisions and they don't know what the hell they are talking about because they haven't been there, they haven't seen it and I have, *a lot.*"

After a short discussion in his house, Sallis suggests coffee. We take my rental car, driving into the city of Phoenix, Sallis supplying directions. In the course of his life, Sallis has lived in many cities—in Europe, across the U.S. I share my surprise to find him living in Arizona. The Lew Griffin books are set in New Orleans, that least American of U.S. cities and the one to which

Sallis has expressed the strongest affinity. In the Griffin books, Sallis often remarks on the near daily rain that lashes New Orleans. Here in the desert, where Sallis now lives, rain is a rarity. "I miss it," he admits. "I miss seasons." But in Arizona, he explains, one can live at the level one chooses.

In Ken Bruen's *Magdalen Martyrs,* Bruen's bookish hero Jack Taylor—a James Sallis reader—is confronting a thug about an author. Taylor says, "Listen, sometimes you hear about 'a writer's writer.' Well, he's been described as 'the writer's writer's writer.'"

Taylor/Bruen could be speaking of James Sallis. He's the author that the crime writers' crime writers—Pelecanos, Rankin, Bruen, Woodrell—all admire.

His masterwork is the Lew Griffin series: six remarkable books that focus on time and memory and the ways in which the two exert themselves on identity.

His most recent novel is *Cypress Grove.* The "hero" of that book is "Turner," a damaged man who has been a cop, a convict and a psychotherapist. Turner retreats into a rural idyll to lose himself, but he is drawn back into the fray by a small-town cop faced with a brutal murder he knows is over his head.

Sitting in the shade outside a coffee shop in a Phoenix mall, we start our discussion with that book. I express surprise to hear that Sallis is working on a sequel to *Cypress Grove,* which was touted as a standalone. The follow-up will be called *Cripple Creek.*

Sallis, too, is surprised to be writing a follow-up:

"I've never intended sequels. *Long-Legged Fly* started as a short story, turned into a novel, then mutated its way to six novels. *Cypress Grove* was going to be a standalone. I realized that I had always written about cities, which is where I've lived since I've been an adult. I grew up in a small town in Arkansas. I thought that maybe it was time to write about rural life, the kind of life that I grew up in, just more or less to see if I could do it."

Hemingway wrote: "For a true writer, each book should be a new beginning where he tries again for something that is beyond attainment."

Sallis, like Hemingway, is leery of leaning on one's well-learned lessons: "One of the dangers of writing is that as you write you learn how to do stuff," he cautions. "You know how to do things and it's very perilous, because you have to keep challenging yourself. You have to keep refusing to do the things you already know how to do."

The challenge that James Sallis set for himself in *Cypress Grove* was to write about a rural backwater … a place of silences and stillness.

"Well, I didn't know how to write about this certain place that I came from," he said. "So I thought, 'I'm going to do it.' I really had no idea what I wanted to write. I was just talking about this to friends: 'Oh, my next book is going to be … ' We all say these things and we have no earthly idea what we're talking about."

Wordsworth famously composed his poetry while walking. Sallis, too, gets many of his ideas while pounding pavement: "I was walking one day and I had this visual image—which is the way that most of my books start—of a person standing by a cabin with woods behind. There's a body of water and he hears a Jeep engine bouncing off the water the way it does in wooded, still areas. It's a very particular sound. And that's all I knew. As I tell my students, you ask yourself 'Who is this person? Why is he standing there? Where is he standing? Who is this person in the vehicle coming up around the water? Why is that person coming up there? Have they met before?' As you start asking yourself questions, the story starts forming."

By the time Sallis had returned to his home, he said he had much of the first chapter of the novel worked out in his mind. "At this point, I had no idea where it was going. I just knew this guy had moved back to a town that was sort of like the place he grew up … maybe *is* the place he grew up."

Sallis envisioned his narrator as a man who had moved through many passages in his turbulent life—"a very complicated life. At one point he had been a homicide detective or a detective in a major city, so he had that training. The person who had come up is a local sheriff who has a murder to investigate. And he doesn't have a clue, no pun intended, how to do it. He's come to enlist this guy's help, and it becomes apparent that he has known this guy is out there all this time."

Then Sallis began pushing forward: "They used to take gold and put it into 12-gauge shells and shoot it into the ground," he says. "I started doing that with the story: planting these little things. I didn't know where they were going, but I knew I would pick them up and use them later. The whole thing just develops by asking myself questions. I did intend it to be just one novel, but as happened with *The Long-Legged Fly,* I finished and I was still intrigued by this guy. As we end *Cypress Grove,* Turner is serving as temporary sheriff."

The sequel, Sallis says, will pick up with Turner still operating under color of authority.

"I said, 'Wouldn't it be interesting if a year later, he's still temporary sheriff?' And that's how the next one started. Again, I had absolutely no idea where I was going with it. I had an idea that probably one of his children would show up because he had mentioned that he had had children. So this is definitely just going to be two books." *Maybe.* Sallis shrugs, says, "We'll see."

Cypress Grove takes its title from a Skip James song. The working title for that book had been "The Hollow of the Heart and the Hand."

"Again, I didn't have a title for the second one," Sallis said. "I was just using a working title and I just got up one morning and I thought, 'Cripple Creek'—it's perfect. It fits with the first title. It's an old song, an old mountain song."

The acoustic string music that Sallis loves will move front and center in the sequel: "Turner's girlfriend, Val, plays a lot of banjo in this and "Cripple Creek" is a great banjo song. I thought it worked—it's got the same sort of sound: 'Cypress Grove,' 'Cripple Creek.' But it was not planned. Now the insect names—the 'bug books'—that wasn't planned, either. I used the first one, the quote from Yeats, because I thought it was a cool title and I had had it in mind to use for a long time. And it fit the book thematically. Then I decided I needed to find something that tells readers this is that kind of book—that it is 'salami' and not 'pepperoni.' So I hit on the bug titles. Same thing here—finding things that fit and alert the reader."

The emerging main theme of the Turner novels appears to be that of identity. Sallis has mentioned urging his students to ask themselves who they are writing about. I passed through *Cypress Grove* again on the flight out to interview Sallis. I remark that I'm not sure upon finishing the book—for perhaps the fifth or sixth time—that I "know" Turner any more than I did after my first reading of the novel.

Sallis indicates the sequel may not clear things up for me on this front.

Turner's creator says, "I don't think that Turner is probably knowable in *Cypress Grove* and again in *Cripple Creek*. In *Cripple Creek* he talks about why he stopped doing therapy, and one of the reasons he gives in *Cripple Creek* is that, 'I thought it was really going to let me understand things and I found out that it is just really another language. It's just another shibboleth—another secret language that made me think I was understanding things but it really just shrouded my understanding of them.' I think he feels that way about himself. So I don't think he's ultimately knowable. He's a patchwork. There's just too much in there."

Cripple Creek, Sallis says, will take Turner back into the darkness. In the sequel, Sallis says, he is unleashing Turner's demons.

"It's inevitable if you're writing a sort of a thriller or genre book," he says. "At the end of *Cypress Grove* he seems to have everything under control and he's constructing a life much like Lew Griffin in each of the four sections of *Long-Legged Fly* and most of the other books, but then that collapses. In *Cripple Creek,* Turner becomes violent again and that's interesting to write. He's thinking a lot, not about the cop business and prison, which occupies him in the first book, but more about when he was a therapist and what was going on in his mind as he sat with people. I originally planned in *Cypress Grove* to include some more about the people he saw and have them have those wonderful little novelistic/structural connections. I'm doing that more in this one. It didn't seem to feel right or to fit in *Cypress Grove*. But there are several subthemes running through *Cripple Creek*."

I ask for elaboration on those subthemes.

Cripple Creek, Sallis says, will focus more attention on Turner's childhood. Turner also befriends a veteran—one who didn't make it back intact. Sallis describes Turner's new friend as "a completely scrambled vet" back home who "used to be a fiddle player and now can't do much of anything. He works in an ice house."

Another subplot turns on an unsual collection of people living in the hills. The group's members memorialize the Holocaust. "They have all tattooed their arms with numbers and they are living in a communal situation," Sallis says. "One of the people is a deaf-mute and there is one who runs the group—he runs the family money. They're being looked over by the old mountain guy who always comes to sit with Turner and get drunk."

The book is listed from Walker as an October 2005 title, but it looks as though it will be closer to a first or second quarter 2006 release.

"I always start these books thinking they are very simple and straightforward and they refuse to be that way," the author says. "This one *really* has. I didn't intend to put Holocaust references in, and the soldier just came out of nowhere. It's gotten much more complicated. There's another subtheme about a person whom Turner arrested who has been on death row all this time and is finally executed. That's another story that is sort of threaded through the narrative. It's kind of like a jigsaw puzzle some days, deciding what goes where."

In *Cypress Grove,* we never learn Turner's first name. I ask if this situation will be remedied in *Cripple Creek.*

Sallis says it won't be. So I ask him if *he* knows his character's first name. "I don't," he says. "I would tell you if I knew."

Sallis also has several other books coming. PointBlank, which published a collection of Sallis' short fiction in 2004 (*A City Equal To My Desire*), will be releasing *The James Sallis Reader,* an omnibus that includes his novels *Renderings* and *Death Will Have Your Eyes,* as well as some essays, more short stories and some poems.

He also has a novel coming in fall 2005 from Arizona-based Poisoned Pen Press, called *Drive.* This is an expansion of a short story he wrote for an anthology published by Dennis McMillan, another Arizona-dwelling independent publisher.

"The story there is, I wanted to write a kind of classic noir story, a good old paperback that could have been published by

Gold Medal," Sallis explained. "We all love 'em. George Pelecanos did it with *Shoedog,* and I decided that I wanted to do it.
This was pre-computer: I had a third of a page of scribbled notes
and that was it. I carried these things over most of the U.S. I had
this idea for years and years and years. Finally, Dennis McMillan
came to me and said he was putting this anthology together and
asked if I could do a story for him. I thought, 'Boy, this is a great
opportunity for a trial run.' So, to see if I could do it, I wrote the
short story for Dennis."

Sallis' recuperation from his hip surgery also made the project a desirable one as he struggled to regain his stamina.

"My attention span was short, but I really needed to concentrate on work," he recalled. "So that's when I rewrote the story
as the novel that I always intended. It's a very short novel—140
pages. And I also wrote the draft of what will be my next novel,
which is a non-genre novel called *Others of My Kind.* The draft of
that one is written at about 150 pages. I showed it to my agent,
and my wife, my English agent, and my French publisher. They
all said, 'Expand it to a full length novel,' which is kind of what
I was planning on all along.

"So when I finish *Cripple Creek,* I'll go back and fill in the
blanks that I left there. It's a very, very strange novel. Recovering,
I really wasn't up to concentrated writing. I could just write a
page or two, go do my physical therapy and then come back. But
I couldn't do anything else. I couldn't leave the house. Even working in spurts I got an awful lot done in a short period of time.
One can only Web surf for so long."

The Man With No More Past

James Sallis' first novel, *The Long-Legged Fly,* appeared in 1992.
That book introduces the character of Lew Griffin: African-
American, alcoholic, thug ... eventual detective, literature in-
structor and novelist.

Fly is notable for its innovative structure—essentially, four novellas involving four missing persons cases. Each section of *Fly* catches Griffin at a different point in his life. It opens in 1964 with him killing a man in an oil field. We find him again in 1970, 1984 and in 1990, as Lew's life is drawing to a close.

Fly's frame, in turn, encapsulates and informs the five novels with Griffin that follow: *Moth* (1993), *Black Hornet* (1994), *Eye of the Cricket* (1997), *Bluebottle* (1999) and *Ghost of a Flea* (2001).

It is best to treat the Griffin series as a single novel and to read the entries in publication sequence. Like Yeats' fly, Sallis skims across the surface of time, jittering back and forth between past and present. Recurring phrases and shifting memories crop up in new contexts from book to book. The last lines of one book become the opening lines of another that Griffin is purportedly writing.

A bit of graffiti once glimpsed on a 7-11 wall haunts Lew, stirred from memory from novel to novel: "Convenience kills!"

"We must learn to put our distress signals in code," is another.

But time and memory are the real protagonists of the Griffin series. "Memory's always more poet than reporter" is a frequent refrain. "We go on living our lives forward, attempting to understand them backwards."

In *Black Hornet,* Griffin laments, "Mostly what you lose with time, in memory, is the specificity of things, their exact sequence. It all runs together, becomes a watery soup. Portmanteau days, imploded years. Like a bad actor, memory always goes for effect, abjuring motivation, consistency, good sense."

Because the Griffin novels are told in retrospect, recurring lines like that one serve to undermine some of the reader's faith in the story as it is unfolding. And in all of Sallis' works, there is the sad recognition that too often we recognize our moments of happiness only in retrospect—moved to do so by present circumstances we similarly don't yet recognize as comfortable, and won't, until they, too, have slipped into the past.

Another character says to Griffin: "In your books you never write about anything that's not past, done with, gone." Memory, Lew says, "holds you down while regret and sorrow kick hell out of you." He also laments, "Maybe the best parts of our lives are always over. Maybe happiness, contentment, are things we only recollect through the filters of time, elusive ghosts forever behind us."

In *Eye of the Cricket,* a vagrant turns up in a hospital claiming to be Lew Griffin. Griffin has also written several novels featuring a character called Lew Griffin. The reader begins to lose all compass points in terms of grasping the "real" Lew Griffin as the books accumulate on him or her.

The great achievement of the Griffin series is, in effect, to force the reader to ponder whether there is a distinction between a fictional character and a *fictitious* fictional character, and, if there is, what that distinction is and what difference it makes to the reader. For those who come to love Lew Griffin, that is a question that comes to mean *everything.*

After expending so many words undermining his reader's trust in memory, Sallis' final feat in *Ghost of a Flea* is to rip the carpet out from under the reader. He recontextualizes the entire cycle of books and sends the reader back to the beginning to explore the series from a new vantage point.

But, in a virtuoso feat, Sallis' revelation has rendered faulty our own memories of his books. Without divulging one of crime fiction's greatest "spoilers," the conclusion of *Ghost*—and its impact on the receptive reader—is to force a reevaluation of the reader's connection to *all* fictional characters.

In *Renderings,* Sallis quotes Wallace Stevens: "The final belief is to believe in fiction, which you know to be fiction, there being nothing else. The exquisite truth is to know that it is a fiction and that you believe in it willingly."

But all of this analysis can make the Lew Griffin series seem overly complicated ... monolithic and forbidding. And Sallis' "bug books" are not.

A tremendous sense of love and compassion and humanity comes through in the Lew Griffin series. The prose is clean and lean and straightforward. It is entirely possible to read nearly all of the Griffin books as "simple" mystery novels if one chooses to do so.

Sallis assures me over coffee and croissant that many have done just that.

"You know, a lot of what we do, it's not intended to be noticed," Sallis cautions. "It's subterranean structure. At one level, I intend the books to be read just as mysteries. But for the reader who wants to read them another way, there is a lot of stuff there. My interest is always to make a really readable genre book that is also a very readable literary book, but functions as both. And judging from the fan mail I get, and the reviews I get, it largely seems I manage to do that. I get a lot of letters—well, not letters, nobody gets letters anymore—I get a lot of e-mail from people who are reading them pretty much as straight mysteries and they are able to enjoy them and appreciate them at that level. Then there are other people like you and other reviewers who start trying to connect these things, and there is a lot of stuff there. But I don't expect that."

And he's not particularly comfortable discussing it:

"There is a great poem by Lawrence Durrell that I've quoted before, called 'Style.' It starts with him sort of looking for the perfect metaphor for style. He goes through all of these grand things like the wind and the trees and the storm and he finally comes down to 'Grass—an assassin of polish.' He describes how you reach down and you pick up a blade of grass and you look at it and you think 'that's really beautiful' and you throw it down. Only then do you notice that it's cut you. The line is 'the thread of blood from the unfelt stroke.' With a lot of really subtle writing, that is what you're trying to do. You want that thread of blood, but you don't want that stroke to be felt. The best writing to me is the writing that has all of that tucked in very well and succeeds as a story or a character piece or whatever it is, and all the subterranean stuff kind of sneaks up and kicks you in the butt when you're not noticing. That is why all that stuff is packed in there. It's not for anyone to notice. It's not to be taught in graduate seminars. It's to make the story work better."

Okay. But in *The Long-Legged Fly,* Sallis' Griffin has written a book incorporating a thinly disguised Blaise Cendrars. "I wondered if any reviewers or critics would pick up on that," Griffin wonders. "I also wondered if other writers ... play such games to get themselves through books."

And that twist ending at the last of the Lew Griffin book is impossible to discount, or to dismiss. Sallis knows this. He comments, "I tell my students that I've probably written the only six-volume series that has a surprise ending."

I ask him when he realized what he would do in the last pages of the last Lew Griffin book. "I knew quite early that was what I was going to do," he says. "As I was writing *Moth,* I realized that that was what I was going to do. But at that time, I thought it was going to be in the next book."

But the clues to that twist, I press, seemed to be there from the very start. Sallis tacitly confirms this, but says, "It took me a while to pick up on them and realize what I needed to do." It was, he says, a matter of "hearing" the book talking back to its author.

"It always does," Sallis insists. "It always does. I had a student last night complaining she was writing a story that was due and the character kept not doing what she planned. I said, 'That's the best sign you can get. Go with it. The character learns a lot more than you do what's going on in that story.'"

As he "listened" to his own narrative, Sallis' plans for a Lew Griffin trilogy derailed. The third Griffin book was *Black Hornet,* in which Griffin seeks a sniper who has killed a white female reporter leaving a bar with Griffin. *Hornet* also introduces the character of "Doo-Wop," a drifter/informer living on "Hopi Mean Time," outside the temporal flow, swapping stories learned from others for drinks. For Doo-Wop, "everything is in the present." The novel is set in the 1960s, and crime writer and Griffin inspiration Chester Himes has a cameo.

The fifth Griffin novel, *Bluebottle,* is a mirror image of *Hornet* ("same vineyard, different grapes"). Another sniper is on the loose, but this time Griffin, leaving a bar with another white female reporter, takes the bullet. It costs him a year of his life. He attempts to reconstruct the narrative, and his lost months, from memory. His lover, Verne, tells Lew, "*You're* the missing person." Griffin cautions the reader, "Bear in mind that much of what I'm telling you here is reconstructed, patched together, shored up. Like many reconstructions, beneath the surface it bears a problematic resemblance to the model."

The trigger for *Bluebottle* was rather unusual: "The BBC commissioned a story from me to be read on the air," Sallis said. "I started writing a short story. People had been asking, 'Have you written any Lew Griffin short stories?' and I'd say, 'No, I haven't.' So I thought, 'I'll write one for the heck of it.' So I started writing what turned out to be *Bluebottle*. It got rather long. About thirty pages in I realized, 'Oh, hell, this is a novel.' So I got back to the BBC and said, 'Guys, I'm going to write another story for you,' and I wound up writing another story that they broadcast and turned the first into *Bluebottle*."

The meticulous construction of the Griffin series, and that last revelation, make casual dipping into the series a potentially treacherous affair. I ask James Sallis if he's run across many poor souls who started with the last book.

"Yeah, and they always go back and start to read the series at the beginning," he tells me. "I get a lot of people asking me 'Which should I start with?' Which is a very difficult question. I can't reread them because I know too much about them. I read them when they first come out, because that is usually the first time that I can give them a fair, objective reading. But it takes a while. I'd like to think that you can read any one of the books and it functions on its own, but as you suggested, and I assented, I really do kind of think of them as one big novel. The structure, the structural elements, the way things are tied in together, it's really sort of by conception. You know, the first book is this arc of a man's life and then other books go in to sort of fill in the chinks. So it is a novelistic perception of this man's life and this man's world. I'd hate to think how thick the volume would be."

Sallis and George Pelecanos are kindred. Sallis has written introductions for books by Pelecanos.

Pelecanos also wrote a trilogy featuring black private investigator Derek Strange. In a number of interviews and reviews, Pelecanos was taken to task for presuming to write from the point of view of a black man. Sallis, somehow, evaded this criticism in his depiction of Lew Griffin. I point out the disparity.

Sallis smiles. "George is very funny," he says. "He once said someone told him that and he just said, 'Well, hell, I'll just put all blacks in my next novel.' You know, when we first started publishing, I anticipated we would get some flack. But I have had absolutely none *ever*. In fact, it's been quite the opposite. I've had congratulations and people saying, 'This is really good.' I've had people come up and say, 'How did you know that?' The only time this has been even nominally a problem was when I was in Britain doing interviews. I had one interviewer who just kept asking me, 'Why do you think you can write about a black person?' And I kept just saying, 'Well, why not?' I finally said, '*Listen*: What a novelist does, is he tries to get into other people's heads. We're all isolated inside our own skulls. What art does, whether it is literature or another art, is it tries to get you out of your skull and get you close to somebody else's view for a while. And if I can only write about a white, middle-aged person, I'm not much of a writer. So it's absurd to suggest that I can't write from a black point of view.' In *Others of My Kind,* it's the first time I've written a novel from a female point of view. And I didn't do it intentionally. I was out walking again, and the voice in my ear was 'I,' 'I,' 'I' and it's a female 'I', so I had to write from a female point of view."

The early Griffin books did not contain photos of Sallis on the dust jacket flaps. Consequently, some readers reached some conclusions regarding the author whose books they were enjoying.

"There was a lot of talk on the Internet about whether I was black," he explains. "In New Orleans, my favorite thing happened. This was after *Moth* was published or something. All the booksellers there are really active, because they are all independents. They had these wonderful parties where everybody comes and we were at one of those. I was speaking or introducing the others. We were sitting having lunch before, and there was an elderly gentleman sitting at the next table by himself. We said 'Why don't you come and sit with us?' He was an African-American and he was beautifully dressed. And he came and sat down and we just chatted through the meal and then they announced me and I went to go up. He said, 'You're Mr. Sallis?' I said, 'Yeah.' And he said, 'Well I'll be damned.' It turned out he had come to the luncheon, which was not cheap, just to see me because he had been reading my books in the library. He assumed that I was black."

I ask Sallis if his fan seemed disappointed.

"No, he was surprised, but I think he was perfectly happy. But that happened more often than anything else."

In some rather striking moments, the author's closer readers will find Sallis' characters browsing over passages from Sallis' other works. David Edwards, the reactivated spy in *Death Will Have Your Eyes,* remembers a passage from the Sallis short story "Potato Tree," collected in *Limits of the Sensible World.* In *Eye of the Cricket,* Lew Griffin is reading Sallis' *Renderings:* "They come in the dark and do terrible things to me. They go away," and, "I can tell you in a few words who I am, lover of woman and language, in terror of the history whose responsibility I bear, a man awake at night and alone."

If the six Griffin books are all one novel, one senses that Sallis' oeuvre, similarly, is an integrated whole. "Given paper and crayon," Sallis writes in *Death Will Have Your Eyes,* "the ape draws, laboriously, precisely, only the bars of its cage, again and again."

I confess to Sallis that of all of the Griffin books, *Eye of the Cricket* is perhaps my favorite. "Yes, I think that is my favorite," Sallis agrees. "I think it's the best of the novels. And novelistically, I think it is by far the best of the books."

Death Will Have Your Eyes, which appeared at about the same time, echoes some of the same sense as *Cricket.* In both books, men in search of another man venture out into the world, seeming to trust in the gravity of their own persona and movement into the world to draw their quarry to them. James Joyce's "Nighttown" sequence from *Ulysses* informs both books.

In *Death Will Have Your Eyes* David Edwards reflects, "One thing I knew absolutely was that the stories we live by are as real as anything else is. As long as we live by them. Even when we know they're lies."

Perhaps the most interior of Sallis' novels, *Death Will Have Your Eyes* is also the one of Sallis' novels to be optioned for film.

"For three years I got these really nice checks in the mail for not doing anything, which was really a good deal," Sallis says. "It's an odd story. The guy who made *The Avengers* film was in London and when the book came out there were piles of it in the bookstores. He saw it and thought, 'I'm making this spy film and here's another one.' So it was optioned for three years. The option money for each year was more than I got for the hardback, so it was welcome.

"*Death Will Have Your Eyes* was a book that I had had in mind for quite a long while, too. Sort of like *Drive.* It was something that I realized I wanted to do. I wanted to write a spy novel. Because I love Phillip Attlee, Donald Hamilton—that sort of Gold Medal genre of spy novels. I wanted to write something that would be an homage to that. I guess I had finished *Moth*—I don't have a good memory for these things. I really am on Hopi Mean Time. But I had just finished a novel and as a gift to myself I decided I would write this novel that I'd wanted to. I told Karyn at the time, 'Nobody in the States is going to buy this book, but it will do well in Europe.' And, indeed, it did well in Europe, and I had a heck of a time selling it here in the States. It came out here in hardcover, fell off the face of the earth and never had a paperback printing."

Sallis' other standalone novel is *Renderings* (1995), a book particularly close to the author's own heart. It is, to date, the closest of Sallis' novels to a full-length science fiction novel. It came into being during a period of unusually intense output for Sallis.

"I was writing a lot of short stories," Sallis says. "That was the period that a lot of stories like 'I Saw Robert Johnson' came. I had this incredible summer, where I wrote *The Long-Legged Fly* in a month. I wrote probably a couple dozen short stories. Some of my very best short stories. And God knows how many poems. And *Renderings* came out at about that same time. It was something I had sort of worked on off and on. But it came together about that same time. I was trying to write a lot of poetry. And in the short stories that I was writing at that time, I was really into language, into strong first-person point of view stuff. I think *Renderings* is as close to poetry as a novel can get. Originally, it was going to be a full-length novel. I had decided, as I always say, that

I was going to leave out the boring parts—though some people would maintain that I left out the good parts and put in the boring parts. But I basically said, 'I'm just going to tell the really important scenes and leave the rest to the reader's imagination.'"

"The word of the day," Sallis once wrote, "was 'eschatology.'"

"My wife and I are in opposition to what the book is about," he says. "She said for her, when she reads it, it is just his imagination making up this end of the world story and all these other stories. To me, the world really is ending. To me, it is a science fiction story. It was conceived as a science fiction story and you can read it that way. If I'd written it as a full-length novel, it would have been a science fiction story. But as I wrote it I realized, 'If I leave enough space in here, the events of the story are going to grow to fill that space. They're going to become what they want to.' I realized, 'If I will just be quiet, somebody else will sing in there.' I liked the way the first parts felt. I always tell my students, 'You write a draft. You do not write a story, you write a *draft*.' You look back at the draft and then you say, 'What is the story trying to turn into? What is the story telling me?' You figure that out and then you rewrite to that.

"That is what happened to *Renderings*. I wrote it, I looked back at it and saw, 'This is really different. This is really strange. I really like it; it is mysterious and it feels like music and I'm going to go with it.' So I went back and fine-tuned and tweaked—intuitively—to the point that it worked for me; that the lengths of the individual passages were right; that it didn't seem too abrupt a transition when you went to another. That the voice came back in at regular intervals. I think it's the best writing I've done in one little place and I'm very very fond of the book. Richard Martin—who started my Web site—it is also his favorite of my books. He said that everything that I have written and probably will write is in that book and I think he is largely right about that."

As Sallis has said, the text of *Renderings* moves closer to poetry than that of narrative prose in several key passages. When I reiterate this quality, Sallis tells me that he, in fact, recently read the novel aloud to his class.

"They were absolutely enthralled because most of them had never heard anything like that," he says. "And reading aloud, the euphony and the rhythms really, really come out."

Ken Bruen and Walter Mosley profess to read their own writing back into tape recorders to hear the prose and dialogue as they compose their works. Other writers read their material aloud as they revise. I ask Sallis if he does this when writing.

"I used to," he says. "I don't anymore because I actually do hear it when I'm writing it now. I do advise my students to do that. Everything I wrote—poems, short stories—I would do that. But now I really don't have to. As I'm writing, it's in my internal ear and I'm hearing the rhythms and hearing the sounds. I've just been doing it so long."

The Writing Life

Many American crime writers, going back to Chandler really, have remarked on the acclaim they receive from European readers. Chester Himes enjoyed greater support in France than in America.

I ask Sallis, who formerly lived overseas and whose books are presently more widely available in much of Europe than in his native country, if he ever thinks about moving back there.

"I think about it all the time," he confirms. "The European appreciation of the American crime novel seems more enthusiastic and broader there than here." I tell him that several American crime novelists have confided to me that they essentially subsist on their European publishing royalties.

"There are many of us that way," he says. "I live off my foreign money. I certainly don't live off what I make here. My books are now coming out in Italy. They bought them all. They've brought out three of them, including *Difficult Lives*. They've gotten incredible reviews. As a matter of fact, Karyn and I are going to Italy in September for a festival in Literatura. They're bringing us over for a week and I'm really looking forward to it.

"Gallimard has all my books in France," he continues. "They've always been a really, really good audience for me. Spain just bought a bunch of them. If I had to try and survive on my U.S. money, I'd be selling cars or something. Working as a musician … I certainly couldn't live off it. The foreign money is not a lot, but it adds up. A lot of times what happens, as it happened in Spain and Italy, is that they buy several books at once so it's an appreciable check."

Sallis has translated the works of French writers. Has he, one wonders, ever read his own books in foreign translation?

"I really only read French," he says. "I studied Russian for a long time, but it's pretty much gone. I can make my way in Spanish. I do read my French translations. I've liked my translations for the most part. I've worked with at least two of my translators pretty closely. And I'm over there, so I get to talk to them and know them. I worked with my Spanish translator, initially, and then they sort of changed horses in midstream on me and I didn't after that. *The Long-Legged Fly* was actually co-translated by a translator and Patrick Raynal of Gallimard, who was a big fan of mine and a great writer. It's the only thing he has ever translated from English and I'm really honored that he did it … that he didn't trust anyone else to do it. And it's a wonderful translation."

Although the French, the Japanese, the Dutch and the Germans have a keen appreciation for American noir fiction, one wonders how the hardboiled patois "travels." There is also the question of how much of the writer's book remains in the translation. I mention to Sallis that I recently reviewed a new translation of Cervantes. As an exercise for the review, I tell him, I picked up three different translations of *Don Quixote* and compared the same paragraph across the three translations.

Sallis winces, but I press ahead: "There were," I say, "striking variances. One version was quite stilted … truly dead writing. It was revelatory, depending on the translator, as to whether the passage popped, or just sat there. But none were truly the same." I ask Sallis, as a translator of other writers' works, if the resulting translation is the author's book, or, in a sense, the translator's.

Sallis shakes his head. "*God.* That's the question. Let me preface this with, I just taught *The Stranger.* And I first read the Stuart Gilbert translation or whatever—the one that has been around forever—when I was a teenager. That also was actually the first novel I read in French. Generally, I just read it in French. But there is a recent translation by Matthew Ward—it's new to me— that came out four or five years ago. One of my students had that translation and I was looking at it. I put down my French version and decided to read Ward's. It is really amazing, the difference. He has tried to bring it into American English and to make it less British, like the old one.

"As to your question, I always tell people I could have written three novels in the time I spent translating *Glinglin.* The work involved was absolutely awesome. This was a book I just kept putting off delivering on because I had more work I wanted to do on it. When you're writing, you feel that there is a part-kindly and part-deadly demon looking over your shoulder to see if you are getting it right. Well, that was my right shoulder. When I was translating, I felt that that same demon was looking over my shoulder and I had to be true to that demon and to myself, but Raymond was standing over my left shoulder watching me and I had to try and be true to him, too. It's an impossible task and only a fool would do it."

But that task is undertaken every day, in numerous languages … sometimes by translators of conscience, and sometimes not. And even those with the best of intentions face treacherous choices. Even if the translator is somehow perfectly in tune with the intent of the original author, language itself sometimes throws up insurmountable barricades, Sallis says.

"When you're writing, every word is a choice," he explains. "Every piece of punctuation is a choice. When you're translating, the choices proliferate, because you not only have to decide the word, it has to fit the sound of the original, it has to fit the intent of the original, the structure of the original sentence. And if you're translating from French, those Latinate phrases give you *fits.* Because we can say it in this much space, whereas the Latinate phrase takes this much space. What do you want to do? Do you want to try and keep the rhythm of the sentence? Do you want to look at the thought process behind the sentence? They are two completely different things. There is a linguistic approach and there is a thought approach: the conception of the sentence, the way the sentence is put together, which conveys the thought of the narrator or the POV—the point of view of whomever is telling the story. So you have that overall choice to make. And then every time you look at something, there is another choice. Sometimes you just have to knock on wood, close your eyes and point, because it's a judgment call and whatever you do, someone is going to be desperately unhappy."

Further complicating the process is the fact that some English and Latinate phrases have no corollary.

"We're blessed and damned in English, because it's really the most flexible language in the world," Sallis says. "We can put words wherever we want to. Whereas Russian has one word for something, and French may have two, we have twenty. So there are even more choices. There are things when I was translating *Saint Glinglin* ... I think I would probably make different choices now. But at the time I made what I thought was the best choice. And there are mistakes in there, of course. There are always going to be."

Longfellow, I observe, attempted several different translations of Dante's *Inferno.* Would Sallis attempt to recast his translation?

"If someone would pay me," he says. "I would like to fix it, but the French government actually paid for that translation and I don't think they're going to pay for a retranslation. However, I am talking with a small publisher in L.A. called TamTam Books, which is publishing Boris Vian novels. They published *I Spit On Your Grave, L'écume des jours.* They just published *Autumn In Peking* in the first English language translation ever. I would really like to do a novel of his called *L'herbe rouge,* which is a very short science fiction novel that I've been wanting to translate for a long time. If things work right and if *Autumn In Peking* gets the attention it deserves, and if the French government will come through with a grant, I will translate *L'herbe rouge* into English. I hope that works out, but it has to be enough money to cover my time and I figure I can do it in a month. It's a really short book and I know it really well."

Sallis is also a powerful essayist. His 2000 collection, *Gently into the Land of the Meateaters,* encompasses the writing life, lost children, broken marriages and remembered patients. But as some themes or seemingly autobiographical incidents recur, there is a sense they don't quite always seem to square with previous presentations. I try to get at these seeming inconsistencies by raising a caution Sallis makes in his biography of Chester Himes: "You warn," I say, "that Himes' own descriptions and accounts of his past are not particularly trustworthy."

Sitting under an insufficient table umbrella in the Arizona sun, Sallis says, "Oh boy …"

"I wonder," I press on, "are your essays more than nonfiction? Do you, well …"

He smiles. "Do I make up stuff?"

"Well, spin it … or enhance it," I say. Now I'm the one who is uncomfortable. "I wonder how autobiographical they are."

"They are very autobiographical," Sallis says. "I don't make up anything in them, but I do pick and choose. I take the fictioneer's approach in that I take the facts, but I can just take the facts that I want or need at that particular time. The only thing I have as a writer is what's inside my head, and my experiences. That's all any of us have, and I use those however I can when I'm writing to make something strong. I never started an essay thinking, 'I'm going to write about where I live,' or something. I would just start writing and I would bring out the autobiographical stuff.

"In the fiction, I treat the autobiographical elements quite differently," Sallis says. "There's the story of mine called 'I Saw Robert Johnson,' which I mentioned earlier. Everything in that story that's real, is real. That's where I was living, that's what I did every morning. But none of the rest of that story is real. I used the autobiographical part because it has the textures of real life, which helps convince the reader. Because you have to get the trust of the reader and you have to evoke your authority to the reader, or you don't have a reader. So it does that, but it also has the added benefit to me as a writer of giving a certain emotional valence to the story that it would not have if I just made the stuff up. There were moments in my life that were very confusing to me and sometimes writing an essay about it just really helped me to sort the whole thing out. I don't make any secrets about my past and if anybody asks me a straightforward question, I will give a straightforward answer. It's been a very ... *interesting* life."

Over the years, Sallis has talked about various books in progress, or works projected to be written. One of these is a novel called *Bottomfeeders*. It has been described as a comic novel about a cop killer. I inquire about the status of that novel.

"I've got about one hundred and fifty pages," he says. "I keep thinking I'll get back to it and I just haven't yet. I think I will, someday. But I don't know when."

Another oft-talked-about project is a first-person novel about Gilles de Rais, an infamous French pedophile/serial killer and captain under Joan of Arc.

"Again, I don't know if I'm ever going to do it," Sallis says. "I started researching and it scared me because I realized all the research I would have to do. I don't know what people eat, I don't know how they dress, I don't know where they live. And Joan of Arc is such a fascinating character and our perception of Joan of Arc ... I mean, this girl was wacky. And that doesn't come through in all the stories. And she was also totally incompetent, which doesn't come through in the stories, either. But of course she was incompetent: she was thirteen years old. And the Joan of Arc story would be part of this story. But I don't know if I'll ever do it as a novel. But I will certainly do it as a short story or a long poem or something at some point. Because I am so fascinated by him. And by her. It would start with him in prison, obviously, and then go back." Sallis smiles. "I have a page written, so obviously I'm serious about it."

Of the various literary mediums he has worked in, James Sallis says his favorite is the short story. Several other crime authors have expressed a similar love for the format. Unfortunately, the short story market in America has virtually collapsed.

"My sadness," he says, "if I have a regret or a concern as a writer, is that there is no market for short stories now, which really breaks my heart. I always say that I would have written nothing but short stories all my life if that had been possible. Now, when I write a novel, I let myself write two or three short stories as a reward. I really, really love the form. I love reading them and

I love writing them. But at my age, I have to be so careful about my income that I can't take the time out to write the stories when I want to. And I have dozens of them I'd love to write."

The outlets for short fiction he says, have winnowed down to essentially the two magazines: *Alfred Hitchcock* and *Ellery Queen,* which pay pennies per word.

"And if you don't place there, what do you do with it?" Sallis asks. "It's quite different from when I first started writing and there were fourteen science fiction magazines. A lot of my stories now, I don't even bother to send out. I just put them in collections. There are several stories in *A City Equal to My Desire* like that. Or sometimes I'll put them on the net … put them on my Web site. But it's not worth the time and effort to send them out and publish them in some obscure literary magazine."

With so much material out there now, I ask Sallis if he ever sees echoes of his own works in those of others. I point to some passages involving Lew Griffin's answering machine and unsettling moments of silent tape Lew Griffin is convinced have come from his missing son calling but not speaking. In Dennis Lehane's *Mystic River,* I point out, one of the characters has an estranged wife who calls on the phone but never speaks to him.

"I don't know if Dennis would agree," Sallis says. "And as far as I know, Dennis hasn't read my books. He's read my poetry, because Jim Hall introduced him to my poetry when he was a student, but I don't think he's even read a novel of mine. I take the Damon Knight approach: He said that we're all magpies as writers and we just steal what we need and use it. And that's perfectly legitimate. I steal like crazy. I read Ken Bruen because I can steal from him. I steal blithely from anyone. That's what literature does; that's what music does. You always build on what's before you. And in genre writing, even more transparently do you build on what's before you … what's around you."

Genre fiction is often dismissed by critics and "literary" writers as a ghetto of narrow choices and formulaic limitations. Sallis has always dismissed such thoughts. He is noted for remarking that literature isn't an "imposing sideboard with discrete drawers labeled poetry, mystery, serious novel, science fiction, but a long buffet table laid out with all manner of fine, diverse foods. You can go back and forth, take whatever you want or need."

As a novelist, Sallis found his voice in so-called genre writing.

"People are writing much more interesting crime fiction," he asserts. "I'm part of that, like George Pelecanos ... we started writing at kind of the same time as far as crime fiction goes, and I feel great affinity to George and what he's doing. But I feel a great affinity to Danny Woodrell, who started before me and published those early Houston/Shreveport novels. I think they're great and I love what he's doing now.

"There's just so much freedom," Sallis continues. "That freedom kind of started in the late '70s or early '80s when you had a lot of writers coming in who probably would have been that term we were talking about—'literary' writers—except they decided they would like to be read. A lot of them were activists. I'm thinking about people like James Crumley, Greenleaf ... Roger Simon. People like that who came into the field either from activism or from literary novels. Constantine is a perfect example—a literary novelist who became a crime novelist because he wanted to be read. Jean Redmann, a fine, fine New Orleans novelist. She told me one day—I said, 'Why are you writing crime fiction?'—she said, 'Because I'd like my books to be read, not just to be sent to libraries.' So there was a lot going on. Then women came in and started the female P.I. thing ... the minorities started coming in. They just made what was already a really, really viable and volatile melting pot more so, and turned up the heat."

It's almost become commonplace for contemporary crime writers to assert their notion that the crime novel is America's most potent literary form for delivering social commentary. But Sallis was perhaps the first to explicitly make the observation.

"It's so much more reflective of our cities, and what goes on in the cities, and what the cities do to us—how we try to cope with the cities," he says. "I always say it's not by accident that the American detective story eventuated at the same time that our population moved from a rural to an urban population. There's good reason for that. The detective story is our urban fiction and it still is and it probably will be for some time. Someone like Dennis with *Mystic River* is a good example."

We leave the coffee shop and walk some distance to my still unfamiliar rental car. The Texas plates I've counted on to help me identify the rental aren't much help, since Texas doesn't require tags on the backs *and fronts* of cars. I push the automatic door lock button on the key fob several times and we follow the faint clicks to the car. It's a strange moment, listening for clicking noises with a writer who has written so many novels and apocalyptic short stories filled with bugs and insect imagery.

Driving back to his home, we resume an earlier conversation about Sallis' writing instruction.

I tell Sallis of a recent interview I conducted with crime writer Victor Gischler, who until very recently also taught creative writing. Gischler expressed dismay to find that his students had tremendous storytelling urges, but no real experience or interest in reading. Gischler said that when he made an allusion to a book, or a situation from a book, he was too often met with blank faces. So he would try to recontextualize his examples by saying something like, "This is similar to what happened in *Jaws*..." I ask Sallis if he has had similar experiences.

"It depends on what level you're teaching," he says. "That can make a big difference. I teach at different levels. At Otis, I'm teaching a graduate writing program. And yes, there are a lot of would-be writers who don't read. One of the things that I do, as I mentioned when we were driving over, I read to them. And I threaten to bring them cookies and milk when I read to them, because they'll say, 'We know that story.' And I say, 'No you don't, as you'll find out.' There are a handful of stories I like. Updike's 'A&P,' Hemingway's 'Hills Like White Elephants,' and typically an O'Hara story called 'What Can I Say?' The stories that have so many barbs, just under the surface. I'm trying to get them to read as a writer reads. And let's talk about how this story came about and how it's put together. And how else you could have written it if you were John O'Hara, or Hemingway, or John Updike. So if they haven't read, they're going to get read to, and we're going to talk about the stories. Because, I'm not there to give them a cookbook about how to write. First of all, I don't know how to write; I just figure it out every time I do it. But I'm trying to make them sensitive to how a story comes into the world and how you shepherd it through the world once it is in the world to try and make it survive. So a lot of what I do is reading. In my novel class we read a novel each semester and we talk about it."

It's a varied menu laid out before Sallis' students … offerings drawn from that metaphorical buffet table Sallis has remarked on: "We read *The Man Who Fell to Earth* first semester. We read *The Stranger* second semester. We're now trying to decide what we're going to read the third semester. I'll take in chapters from Faulkner novels. This semester, I have read from Walter Tevis. I've read from Theodore Sturgeon multiple times. I've read from Faulkner, from Thomas McGuane. I've read from Updike … some WS Merwin. I just bring in different things that demonstrate whatever I'm talking about."

Sallis is also partial to a short story by Ted Chang called "Story of Your Life" "It's a wonderful science fiction story that's about living in a sort of a continuum rather than isolated incidents," as he desribes the story. "I read that to them to show them what you can do. I read the beginning of "Panama" to show what you can do with first-person narrator. Whatever we're discussing … if it's point of view, I try to bring in different things. If I'm talking about point of view, I bring in Sturgeon's 'Sell Me Your Blood' because it's written partly in second person. I bring in *How Like A God* by Rex Stout because it's written wholly in second person. As I'm reading, I'm illustrating something we're talking about, some technique. But I'm also just trying to get them to hear different things and to realize that there is no difference between the excellence of a Theodore Sturgeon story like 'The Man Who Lost the Sea' and the excellence of 'Hills Like White Elephants.' They're both excellent and one is not better than the other." Sallis laughs. "Actually, the Sturgeon is better, to my taste. But, as you know, I'm very anti-cannon. I'm very adamant that the best writers can be genre writers as easily as they can be 'literary' writers. And I always apologize for that because I don't really know what a 'literary writer' or 'literary novel' is. It's like Armstrong talking about jazz: 'I know what it is when I point to it.' I can't really define it."

PART II

KEN BRUEN

"December is a rough month ...
If you're on your own, it mocks you at every turn.
You open an old book and find a list of friends
you once sent cards to. Now, they're all dead or disappeared.
The television is crammed with toys for children
you never had, and boy, is it ever too late.
The radio is playing ballads
that once held significance or even hope."
—KEN BRUEN, *The Magdalen Martyrs*

The Thirty-Year Overnight Sensation

When we met in Arizona in March 2005, Ken Bruen was still living in a big, old family house in Galway, Ireland.

"It's a really old house, built by the Blakes, one of the twelve tribes of Galway," he says. "I love that fact. My name is 'Bruen' and we are also one of the twelve tribes. There's a nice kind of symmetry to it. On the outside, it looks *so* dark. It sits on its own grounds, right in the middle of Galway, which you don't find anymore."

The house has since been put up for sale.

Bruen's daughter, Grace, is now in her teens. Grace figures in many of Bruen's stories shared at signings. He does so at her urging: "Won't you mention me, Dad?" Her father assures Grace that he will. But that vow is not enough for her: "Mention me *a lot*." And he does.

The Irish myth rests heavily on the romance of the Irish storytelling tradition. But young Ken Bruen was oddly tight-lipped:

"I didn't speak until I was seven years of age, which is a real crime for an Irish child because *everybody* talks. In our family, I had two brothers and a sister, and, of course, my mum and dad. And they never shut it, morning, noon and night. And I never spoke. They used to say things like, 'If we had money, we'd get him assist. There's something seriously wrong with him.' All I did was read books. In our family there was no tradition of books, never any books in the house. I was talking to my editor about it. He comes from a background of books. I was saying, 'Wow, that must be just amazing to have books in the house when you're a child.' Then, what was worse, I wanted to study English. I had an opportunity to go to Trinity. Back then, Catholics weren't allowed in. Can you believe that? You had to go to the Archbishop of Dublin, who was not a nice man, and ask him. I went and I asked him and he said, 'No you can't. It would be a very bad influence for you.'"

A Bruen "book review" appeared in his native Ireland a few days after Bruen hit the road for his 2005 book tour. The piece doesn't really function as a review since the writer never shares her opinion about the quality of Bruen's books. She ends it with a quote given by Bruen to another interviewer: "What I most like is my overnight success after more than thirty years writing."

It's been a long, steep climb. Bruen's father was overtly skeptical of his son's desire to write ... and apparently of many other pursuits that his son undertook. "I believed I could never impress him," Bruen wrote in an essay entitled, "I Never Sang for My Father." When Bruen earned his Ph.D. in metaphysics, his father told him, "If you think you'll be called *Doctor* in this house, you can kiss my arse." When his father died, Bruen found copies of his own books by his father's bed—clippings and reviews interleaved throughout the volumes.

Ken Bruen wrote several novels that remained infuriatingly impossible to find until their republication as a single volume by Busted Flush Press in 2006, under the title *A Fifth of Bruen*. These early books, Bruen said, were released and "promptly sank from sight. All the years I spent writing in the dark and in the wilderness and going nowhere. As Derek Raymond said, 'I had that down escalator *completely* to myself.' There was no sign of it going anywhere else."

The Guards changed everything. "I got to meet Ed McBain," Bruen said. "I got to drink bourbon with James Crumley—all these legends I read about for so many years. I'm a complete groupie and a fan, and to sit down and talk with them has been marvelous. All the great work they have done ... Of all the real talents that I now know, they are incredibly humble. You compliment someone like, say, Jim Sallis, and they quickly change the subject."

And there's the travel that growing success has required: "I've been to America nine times in two years." He'll likely be back before year's end for the Bouchercon crime fiction convention.

Despite his strong identification with Ireland, and his long family ties with Galway, Ken Bruen is an avowed Americaphile. In the face of substantial pressure, particularly in the wake of the Iraq War, he has resisted urgings to weigh-in politically. In that resistance, he stands with countryman James Joyce; with the eight-hundred-pound American gorilla Hemingway; with Joseph Campbell: writers and scholars who steadfastly maintained that politics should never pollute fiction. Politicians come and go, but books endure, and they can date, *badly*—particularly when packed with the fleeting if fiery politics of their day.

The Irish author has talked, more than once, about possibly finding a home in New York City or Savannah.

I conducted Ken Bruen's first North American interview. He was in New York City at the time, not too long after the September Eleven terrorist attacks. Many years before, Bruen had served as a guard at the Twin Towers. He had just returned from a viewing of Ground Zero when we first spoke by phone.

A strange confluence of circumstances contributed to that colloquy. At the time, I was contributing some mystery author interviews to the Australian genre magazine *Crime Factory*. During my months-long tenure as a contributor, the editor and founder of *Crime Factory*, David Honeybone, recommended a single author to me. It came in an e-mail that was tinged with an air of urgency: "Find whatever you can by Ken Bruen and read it. He's the real thing."

I searched high and low in local bookstores and found nothing. I went to Amazon UK, ordered some Bruen books. In my reading life, there have so far been four crime authors who have claimed me from page one: James Ellroy, Daniel Woodrell, James Sallis and Ken Bruen, in that chronological order.

A few months after I read my first Bruen books, St. Martin's released *The Guards* in the U.S., the first of the Jack Taylor novels. I received another e-mail from David Honeybone: "Bruen is going to be in New York next week. Try to talk to him."

It took considerable effort. My requests for an interview surprised some people at St. Martin's: Bruen wasn't officially touring then—he was returning from an event in Australia and would be stopping off briefly at his New York publisher's office to sign some books for select booksellers before heading back to Ireland. Bruen's American editor, Ben Sevier, facilitated the interview. As I spoke with Bruen by phone for about forty-five minutes, he was signing promotional copies of his novel.

The Guards was Bruen's breakthrough book. It was picked up by several countries and taken into translation. It was nominated for a flurry of awards and eventually won the Shamus. *The Killing of the Tinkers*, a sequel, was released in the U.S. in January 2004 and secured his status as a rising light among American crime fiction fans.

March 2005 found Bruen touring America to promote *The Magdalen Martyrs*.

In *The Killing of the Tinkers*, ex-Irish cop Jack Taylor made a pact with the devil to protect a young woman.

There was some not-so-subtle, stomach-tightening reciprocity implicit in Jack's deal with über-thug Bill Cassell—and no prospect that the agreement comprised anything remotely resembling a fair exchange of trade.

"You'll get a call asking for a favor," Bill warned Jack. "It's not negotiable."

In *The Magdalen Martyrs*, a mortally ill Cassell calls in Taylor's marker. The third Jack Taylor book is also a dark ride through recently revealed Irish-Catholic history—and a strange meditation on motherhood.

The Magdalen laundries, relatively recently brought to light, quickly became the subject of documentaries, films and nonfiction books. The laundries were a sometimes last stop for unwed Irish teens during the 1950s. The girls were placed in the laundries—often presided over by purportedly sadistic nuns—by parents, or the church.

Cassell, dying of liver cancer, directs Taylor to find a particular nun whom he claims showed rare kindness to his mother while she was confined in the hellish laundries.

Jack expected so much worse in terms of possible "favors" he might be asked to perform for Cassell that he is infinitely relieved by the thug's request.

But he is also infinitely miserable.

Taylor has fought alcohol and cocaine addiction. This time out, Taylor has weaned himself from alcohol, cocaine and cigarettes. But sobriety isn't working for Jack—he's never felt worse. "Clean living," Taylor laments, "is killing me."

Jack is considering suicide until an acquaintance beats him to the punch, bequeathing Taylor substantial cash and guilt for not recognizing the suicidal signs he rues others are missing in his own words and behavior.

His friend's death edges always-addictive Jack over into pharmaceutical drug abuse and resulting conversations with apparently imagined priests and alcoholics.

As is often the case, Jack is also working a second case—investigating the possible murder of a rich man by his younger, wilder, substance-abusing wife. The supposed black widow's son-in-law is Jack's client.

Further complicating his life is the fact that Taylor is being stalked by a faceless, sociopathic enforcer, notable for his penchant for pungent, Juicy Fruit gum: "He comes up behind you, and you think you've been ambushed by an air freshener," Jack is memorably warned.

The follow-up to *Magdalen Martyrs* is *The Dramatist*, released in 2004 by Brandon. This is the book that devastates the Bruen faithful. In *The Dramatist*, Taylor is clean, sober and off cigarettes. Now a self-described "coffee snob," Taylor is making visits to his invalid mother and to church. The latter comes at some cost: "Till recently, I'd owned a leather coat," Jack laments. "It got nicked at mass. If I see a priest wearing it, I will truly throw my hat in."

Taylor is again working two cases. The first is a series of murders staged to appear as accidents—but volumes of John Millington Synge keep cropping up next to the seemingly random corpses. He also runs afoul of the legendary "Pikemen," a clandestine band of Irish vigilantes.

A clean and sober Taylor—a man whom in dissipation has always been a danger to his friends—proves *infinitely* more destructive to those around him. The senseless and wrenching death of a recurring character brings *The Dramatist* to a crushing conclusion. The novel's chilling final image of Taylor could serve as a dictionary illustration for noir.

The fifth Taylor book is *Priest*. This book deals with the Catholic Church's sexual abuse scandals and appeared in 2006 in the UK. "It was really painful to write," Bruen says. "I believe it cost me the most. I thought, 'I'll never be finished with this book. I'm sorry I started it.' It was just tearing me asunder. I had it actually finished, then I thought, 'It needs another hundred pages.' So I did another hundred pages and Transworld bought it."

Bruen is currently composing *Cross*, which the so-called father of "Hiberian noir" believes will likely be the last of the Jack Taylor novels.

He has also recently completed a final draft of what could be the first installment in a new series—the infamous *American Skin*.

But first, Ken Bruen has to survive his first American tour.

My wife, Debbie, takes the call around one p.m. that Ken Bruen has checked in and has asked that we call him. We meet Bruen in the lobby. He is wearing black trainers, jeans, a white T-shirt, gray vest and black leather jacket. His sunglasses are worthy of Bono. Bruen looks more like the advance man for a rock band than Ireland's first noir novelist. Man's got to go for effect, though: readers meeting him for the first time are always surprised to find this professorial guy with manners and charm—they expect some tattooed, wired headcase.

In repose, there is in Bruen a passing resemblance to Jason Robards. But his smile is infectious. His voice is soft; his words carefully chosen. His wedding band is a gold Claddagh ring. He's wearing a blue twine bracelet on his right wrist, a silver and gold watch on his left. He opens his arms. Admission: I've hugged two men in my life, my father and Ken Bruen (later, New Jersey crime writer Charlie Stella will prove to be the third).

Bruen's Arizona "handler," Pierre O'Rourke, suggests lunch. We eat out on a patio hard by an underpass that dives under a mall. It's a little like dining in a parking garage. Rumors have collected around Ken Bruen—fed by the blarney-prone bloggers and fans. Liquor comes up in their posts, *a lot*. The unimaginative among them have made the spirits most associated with Bruen, Jameson. But the Irish whiskey is not a first choice for Bruen. Give him a longneck, and he'll drag that sucker out. The poor souls who buy the stories of legendary drinking more often than not end up exceeding their own capacity for booze and embarrass themselves—murder brain cells and abuse their livers to no good end before the man they have dubbed "The Pope of Galway Bay."

And it's all a little distasteful—makes one wonder if the "fanboys" and "-girls" are really getting the gist of the Jack Taylor books.

In *Moth*, James Sallis's Lew Griffin remarks, "I remembered O'Carolan asking for Irish whiskey on his deathbed, saying it would be a terrible thing if two such old friends should part without a farewell kiss."

Jack Taylor would subscribe to the sentiment; Ken Bruen would not.

Bruen's stated intention is to deglamorize drinking. He knows more than most what the insulting myth of the drunken Irishman has cost his country and its people. He also lost a brother to alcoholism.

"I got a call from the Australian police saying they had found a body in the Outback and the only identification on the body was three book reviews of mine," he remembered. "I said, 'Could you describe the body?' It was my older brother who had died a homeless, vagrant alcoholic in the Outback.

"So, people say, 'Do you know of what you write?' And I tell them, 'Believe you me, I do.' This was a guy who had huge success. Owned four houses and all the rest of it. Then, gradually, alcoholism took over and he died of cirrhosis of the liver. He was only fifty-two. Getting his body home through the bureau of foreign affairs, it had to be a sealed casket.

"My mother was still alive at the time and we just had to lie to her and say he died really peacefully from a heart attack. We couldn't possibly tell her. But, in Ireland, there isn't a family that hasn't been touched in some way or another by alcoholism. So, one of the things I set out deliberately to do in the books, then and now, was I wanted to take the glamour out of booze. In Ireland, it's a hugely social thing. Everything revolves around the pub. We have this whole culture of 'alcohol is wonderful.' I mean, I take a beer myself, and I love it and I think beer and having a night out is terrific, but there is the darker side—alcoholism. It's destroyed so much of our country and people don't want to hear about that. I figure, at least, people can never accuse me of glamorizing alcohol. As I say, that's going to be my epitaph: 'He put people off drink—what a thing for an Irishman.'"

More dumbass myths: Bruen is often portrayed as some kind of Celtic Noir Nostferatu—allegedly never seen in sun, never seen eating. But we'll sit out there in the blazing "Valley of the Sun" for the better part of an hour, talking. We'll share a couple of meals together.

If Bruen had been wearing an Average White Band T-shirt, and if I'd snapped a picture of him eating his hamburger, well, crime writer Charlie Stella—who knows how absurd all these Bruen myths are—would ostensibly owe me a car for meeting a tongue-in-cheek challenge he set on his Web site.

And speaking of T-shirts, hell, someone's made some up: Black with green letters. Bruen's picture is spread across the front with a slogan: "The Martyrs Tour 2005 … Signing books 'til the Jameson is gone."

Lunch is a blur and some smalltalk—"a couple of hardboiled guys sitting around exchanging photos of our kids," as Bruen will later describe it.

Paradise Lost

We return to our hotel for our scheduled interview prior to Bruen's reading. We head to the hotel bar/patio for our first face-to-face interview.

The two of us share a love for the music of L.A.-born troubadour Tom Russell. ("A huge, massive talent who is not a household name," Bruen rues. "Can a musician change your life? Tom Russell changed mine.") There's a line in a song that Russell co-wrote with Dave Alvin: "I'm sitting here drinking in the last bar on earth."

We're nowhere near anywhere *that* remote or apocalyptic, but we are sitting in a bar that's having *its* last days on earth.

This place called Paradise Valley is a realtor's wet dream. It's a drop-jaw seller's market and appreciation rates are reaching science fiction levels.

The Radisson Resort complex where we are staying touts its view of Camelback Mountain. The Radisson isn't that old and still exudes a kind of careworn/posh aura. But in less than a week, it is scheduled for demolition to make way for a condo complex. Soon Paradise Valley will be crammed with condos; its already clogged roads will be made utterly undriveable by the resulting influx of new skin cancer candidates.

But, for now, unemployment looms for the hotel workers: consequently, most of the help staff is sulky. Food stocks are being allowed to run out and the menu options in the hotel bar are sparse. Example: they offer two kinds of club sandwiches, but can only make one today—something about cheese and mustard precludes "Club Sandwich v.2." There is no longer beer offered on tap and the bottled stuff available isn't the second, or the third, or even the *fourth* choice. Eventually we just stop asking for options and say, "Tell us what we can have."

We grab a couple of bottom-shelf longnecks and drift out onto the patio, where, eventually, we'll be menaced by a monster insect—some flying something that's big and black and buzzing and could be a refugee from a James Sallis short story. "Look at the size of that motherfucker," Bruen marvels. "They *do* grow 'em big out here." I'll feint a swing at the thing with the leatherette folder our bar bill has been tucked into; turns out the carapaces of this species of bug could be harvested for Humvee armor.

"The road it gives, and the road it takes away," Tom Russell sings in another of his songs. As he kicks back for the first time in several hours, Bruen stares off at the vacant pool and shares some war stories from the road.

There are always … *complications.* The latest: Bruen's favorite shirts have gone missing. The logistics of keeping clothes clean when you're traveling light and touring long have finally undone Bruen. He recently sent some shirts down for cleaning one night at a hotel. The laundress elected to starch his shirts, too. But there wasn't time for that. He was, Bruen rues, *refused* return of his own garments before his scheduled departure. Presumably, his shirts will catch up with him somewhere down the road.

Bruen also shares a story about his Boston appearance that didn't go quite to plan in terms of promotion:

"Everybody says 'You have to go to Kate's Mystery Bookstore—it's essential for every writer. Everybody loves Kate and she has made so many people … this, that and the other. She is so excited about you coming. You were going to come last year and then you were gonna come Christmas, but now, you're coming.' So I said 'That's great, looking forward to it.' We go out there and the escort says, 'We're about ten minutes early. Do you wanna have a coffee or something?' I said, 'Does Robert Parker live around here?' She says, 'Yeah, just down there.' I said, 'Could I see his house?' She said, 'Well, okay.' I'm just interested, you know? I mean, I've been reading this guy for *so* long, I want to see where he lives, right?

"So we drive down by his house. A very ordinary place. If someone didn't say to you, 'That's Robert Parker's house,' you would think this is just a nice little house in suburbia. She said, 'What do you think?' I said, 'It's about the size of my garage.' She said, '*Oh* … ' She thought I was *serious*. So I just let her run with it, because if I have to explain it, what's the point, you know? So, anyway, just before we get out of the car, she says, 'There's something I forgot to tell you.' I said, 'Okay.' She said, 'You know this event has been being planned since last October.' I said, 'Yeah.' She said, 'Well, Kate sent out e-mails to everybody for *May 18* instead of March 18.' I look at my watch: it's two minutes before we go in. I said, 'You're telling me now?' She said, 'Yeah, because there won't be anyone there.' Well, there was. A couple of friends of mine who have nothing to do with mystery writing—I just told them I was going to be there."

Bruen smiles. "Luckily I didn't say I was going to be drawing huge crowds because they would have very quickly sussed me out.

"We were just about to walk up the porch and she said, 'There's one more thing.' I thought, 'Now what?' She said, 'Kate fell today. She's hurt her ankle, and she'll be receiving you on a divan.' So I said, 'That's okay, I can do divans.' Again, it went right by her. She said, 'Well, you don't have to kneel down or anything.' I said, 'Oh, don't I? *Okay*.' I said, 'I'll tell you what: if I make any mistakes, you cue me in, will you?' She said, 'I will!' So anyway, there were about ten people there and I talked for a little while. I didn't do any Grace or family stories. It just wasn't that kind a vibe, you know? So I read from the book. When I finished reading I said, 'Does anyone have any questions?' Kate of all people said, 'Did you write poetry?' I said, 'Yeah, I used to.' She said, 'Any chance of us seeing it soon?' And I said, 'No.' She said, 'As a favor to me, because you've been in my shop, would you consider it?' I said, 'Yeah, I'll consider it.' So that was my first night in Boston."

Boston was an early stop on Bruen's tour schedule. Now he is in the homestretch. He's road-weary and beat to the wide. He's been away from home for weeks and really just wants to get back to Ireland.

Though he loves America, and he's racking up über frequent flyer miles, Bruen's not really seeing much other than airports, hotel rooms, bookstores and the surface roads that connect them.

"The astonishing thing is, you get back to the hotels—and the hotels are fabulous—but you're so knackered," he says. "No matter how luxurious it is, you get home at ten p.m. and I'm so dizzy, I can hardly see. I have time to have a hot bath, go to bed, set the clock for five a.m. and then go to the airport at six. Then, wherever I arrive, it's off again."

Friends surprise him, turning up along the way, which helps, he claims. A couple of fellow crime writers recently turned up as a "surprise" at one of his Midwest signings.

And everywhere he goes, there are those who come to his readings with the single-minded mission to seek Bruen's help in bolstering their own writing careers.

"The one thing I registered at every single bookstore: the number of writers who are starting out," he says. They all try to foist their manuscripts off on him. "I have to say, 'I'd love to. If I had the time, I would.' But I certainly can't read manuscripts— I can't carry them on the road. They say, 'We'll send them to you.' I have a great out on that now: 'I'm judging the Shamuses. I have so much to read, I couldn't possibly get to your manuscript, and if it's as good as you're telling me, you ought to get it out right away instead of letting it hang around in there.'"

Judging the Shamuses has also been an eye-opener for Bruen.

"The number of books that arrive from all these publishers," he laments, "I didn't think there were *so many*. It's for best P.I. novel. And I'm actually presenting the Shamus in the category that I won last year. So that will be fun. Anyway, the idea is that you whittle it down to five. There are three judges, and we all give our number of points to them, and then, if there is a tie, majority rules, etc. etc. We're nearly there. Very close to being there. But boy, I've read some strange novels—from private eyes on skis in Hawaii to … " Bruen's voice trails off. He shrugs. Unsaid: *I've read some really bad books.*

"Three things astonish me about many of them," Bruen says. "One is that any writer thought that this book was good enough to send to a publisher. Secondly, when a great writer like James Sallis doesn't have a huge publishing deal, that these kinds of books have been published by the likes of Putnam and Simon & Schuster. And, thirdly, that the publishers would think that they are worthy of *any* award apart from being put up against a wall and being shot. I mean, are they kidding? They are very flashy, hardcover books and obviously a lot of money went into design and everything for this absolute piece of crap. Now *there's* a mystery.

"One day, I had about twenty-five of these, and the ones that just amused me to even just look at the dust jackets I put on one pile, and then the ones that I thought 'just maybe there's something going on here' I put in a second pile. Then the ones I was kind of currently reading I had here. A friend came into the study one morning to bring me a cup of tea and she just picked up the pile that 'amused' me if, I can put it that way. She lifted this one up. She's laughing out loud and she said, 'Are they serious?' She was just reading the blurb. I said, 'Just read some more.' She said, 'Oh, come on, this is a joke, isn't it?' I said, 'No, this is a *contender*.'

"She looked at the book—and she now knows the big players just from hearing me talk about them—and she said 'Simon & Schuster? Aren't they big?' I said, 'Yeah, very big.' She said, 'Can I go American for a moment?' I said, 'Please do.' She said, 'What were they thinkin?'"

It's all another wrinkle in his new life as Bruen, to use a publishing buzz-term, "breaks" as an author.

It's been two years since our first interview together. "A lot of water under the bridge," as Bruen puts it. "When you and I did that interview two years ago, I had no idea then—I mean, *The Guards* was just out—just where the journey was going to go. One of the great things is meeting some people along the way. Like Charlie Stella. Sunday, I was in San Francisco and I had a great talk with Eddie Muller. I said, 'I reckon *Cheapskates* is Charlie's best book. His other books are terrific, but this is a huge leap. And that short story he did in the *Mississippi Review* that we were all in ['Father Diodorus'], well, he took a lot of flak over it. I thought that was a brilliant, brilliant story."

Bruen has one more appearance in Texas after his signing later this evening in Scottsdale: It's going to be "noir night" at Murder by the Book in Houston—a crew of writer friends ... the "boyos" as Bruen calls them. Scottsdale is the mellow calm before the Texas storm. As his first American tour is winding down, I ask Bruen about the prospects for another when St. Martin's releases the fourth Jack Taylor novel, *The Dramatist*, presumably in about a year.

"I would," Bruen says. "But I would only tour if—do you hear me? *If* ... I'm already laying down conditions. It's already gone to me head!"

"You've gone Diva," I say.

He smiles, sips his beer. "Exactly. I'll only do it if there are peeled oranges in my room."

The waitress interrupts. She's too tanned, too blonde ... missing many of Bruen's subtler attempts at mild humor. But she's chipper in a way most aren't, despite her pending unemployment. She leaves and Bruen resumes, laying out his vision for how author tours should be conducted: "I think you should do a day," he says. "Just *go* for it. Three or four interviews. Do the signings. And then have the next day off. Because I really think then that everyone benefits. Because the way they do it now, every day is murder. By the end of the tour, it's not fair to everybody who has shown up to see you. Because there is no way in the world that they're going to get your best shot."

The waitress returns. "I assume the bottles are okay," she says. She's not from Arizona—too strong a southern accent—maybe from Alabama, or Georgia. Bruen nods: "They'll do. We're macho guys." She leaves, smiling in affable confusion.

"One of the upsides of doing the tour—literally a whistle-stop tour of America, and you know better than anyone else, I'm so pro-American—is that I just love to hear all the different accents," Bruen resumes. "At least when I wake up in the morning, I know I'm gonna hear that accent they do in Boulder, or wherever. Funnily enough, you know, I've completely finished writing *American Skin*. I'm wondering, if I was to have another look at it, how it would play now, after the last ten or twelve days? I wonder would it change? It's bound to. Bound to have an effect."

I've been in Arizona a couple of days now, and gotten around a bit—gotten out into the desert. That's more like the terrain that figures in much of the American Southwest-set portions of *American Skin*. But Ken Bruen hasn't seen any of that country this trip: again, the run-and-gun pace of the tour precludes sightseeing.

But the writer in him is always observing, absorbing atmosphere. He's been watching the various forms that Homeland Security assumes from airport to airport. Those screenings are written about in some detail in *American Skin* as Bruen's hero, Blake, returns to New York. Bruen has seen one significant security flap so far.

"It was in Minneapolis," Bruen says. "I was flying out and this guy completely lost it at the counter. I saw just how effectively they deal with that. He was a big guy. It took two or three to, let's say, *restrain* him. But the panic among people who were about to get on the plane—I realized just how close to the surface the paranoia is, and with good reason."

Two years have also restructured the terrain for authors in terms of the Internet and how it affects publicity and access to fans. "When we talked two years ago," Bruen said, "isn't it strange that blogging was only in its infancy? Everyone was using e-mail of course, but blogging ... it hadn't really started yet."

He may wish that it still were in its early stages. The Internet has benefited Bruen in some ways, but it has also exacted a price. It is, in the words of Kris Kristofferson, a favorite Bruen songwriter, "a blessing" *and* "a curse."

Bruen is a frequent subject across many blogs. Somehow, his wife and daughter even became fair game for some. In a rare instance, they both would post some items on a blog run by Bruen's friend Ray Banks, an up-and-coming crime novelist. "Sometimes it's for better, a lot of times for worse," Bruen says of much of the other bloggers' attention.

He has recently launched his own Web site that includes a discussion board. He sees the potential value of having an official site and rallying fan interest through that site.

But he's also been sniped at by anonymous or semi-anonymous readers elsewhere on the Web—often by lesser "authors" and mean-spirited, would-be critics. And, as a result of some truly bizarre bureaucratic snafus, he's been falsely declared dead twice in the past year. "We're very superstitious in Ireland," Bruen will tell fans assembled at his reading later that evening. "We believe everything happens in threes. And I'm getting on a lot of airplanes. I cannot tell you how paranoid I've been getting on airplanes ever since. So if you hear anything happened to me on the rest of the journey, don't believe it. Check it out first."

Some fans even presumed to write short stories "inspired" by the false reports of Bruen's death. Always gracious, Bruen greeted these "stories" with an air of humor that masked some real unease—his inherent politeness perhaps confused for permission or, in some cases, as encouragement.

Apart from the concerns for himself, Bruen also has qualms about the effect that the Web can have on the careers of aspiring writers. There is a fear that young fiction writers are dissipating their energy blogging to an audience composed largely of other bloggers.

"To quote Emily Dickinson—is it Emily Dickinson?—'Blogging is all I know of heaven and hell,'" Bruen says. "And I really mean that. I think two things go on in America that is unlike anyplace else in the world in terms of selling books: One is word-of-mouth, and the other is booksellers 'hand-selling.' They can make or break an author. I think blogging, in some ways, is almost taking over from that mythical word-of-mouth. Because if you take someone like Sarah Weinman, she's the central point for all the bloggers. Everyone links everywhere else. Everyone I spoke to about it, on the road, so to speak, they all said they refer to her first, and then go to wherever else.

"During Edgar Week, Jason Starr said to me, 'Sarah Weinman is calling you the It Boy.' I said, 'She's calling me the fucking *what*? And what's more, who is she?' He said 'It's all over her blog.' And I just wasn't that familiar. I knew the concept, but it wouldn't have been something I would ever have looked up. So I said, 'Do a lot of people read this?' He said, 'They're starting to.' Boy, talk about prophetic words. So, being called the 'It Boy,' well, there isn't a person in the world that isn't going to sneak a peek to see what exactly that means and why. So I checked her out.

"In actual fact, apart from that piece on me, I found it very interesting because she was talking about publishing deals, all sorts of stuff that you would have to wait to hear from *Publisher's Weekly*. And lots of it you would never hear. She was talking about book deals, and then there were the comments and all sorts of people joining in. What I also liked was down the right hand side, she had two or three books that she had touted, almost like pick of the week. I thought, 'Boy, if that takes off, that could really make a writer.'"

That's the tolerable side of the Web equation.

"The down side, for me anyway, is that there is no control," Bruen said. "People can just say anything they like, about anyone, and make a name for themselves by taking a shot at somebody. They can go as personal as they like. There're no parameters. It's a free-for-all. I think it was you, actually, who said that if you were to add up all the names of those who actively comment on these key sites, it's about thirty or forty—*if that*. The same people feeding off each other and often saying, 'you're the best, you're the best, you're the best.' I think that can be a very bad thing, because there is no real critical analysis going on there. It's just an echo chamber. But blogging is definitely taking over from word-of-mouth."

• • • • •

2005 is a watershed year for Bruen. As he wearily tours the U.S., he has the hardcover of *The Magdalen Martyrs* to sign. There is also St. Martin's trade paperback release of *The Killing of the Tinkers*. His first two novels, *Rilke on Black* and *Her Last Call to Louis MacNeice* have been rejacketed and rereleased by Serpent Tail. An exceptionally snarling short story, "White Irish," appears in the Akaschic anthology *The Cocaine Chronicles*, and two other short stories, "Murder By the Book" and "The Dead Room," have been released in limited edition collectibles by Busted Flush Press and ASAP, respectively. August will bring St. Martin's release of

Bruen's novel *Vixen*, the latest Inspector Brant book. Bruen also concluded editing of an anthology for Akashic, *Dublin Noir*.

And half a world away, Jack Taylor is getting a new home. Brandon, Bruen's Irish publisher, abruptly dropped the series. "My Irish publisher had decided that he had gone as far with the Jack Taylor series as he thought he could go," Bruen said. "He didn't really see there was much point in carryin' on. We parted on good terms and he said, 'I wish you the best of luck.'

"My new agent put *Priest* out there, and the American rights were of course sold to St. Martin's. All other world rights were up for grabs. She knew I was keen that Jack Taylor always come out in Ireland first. It seems right to me. It's a big deal to me. I would like that people in Galway get to see the book before anybody else does. I do this even though the Irish press will generally slaughter me, but they are gradually starting to say that Jack Taylor is something special. They're finally comin' around to say that maybe crime writing is not such a bad thing, particularly because all these young kids are writing it now. There is such a volume of it, they are having to take it seriously."

Bruen has since signed with Transworld.

"It's a big difference for me," he said. "The Irish publisher had done a terrific job with *The Guards* and the first four books. I particularly loved the covers. The covers were just brilliant. If you turn the cover of the [Brandon] *Magdalen Martyrs*, there is actually the silhouette of a gun there. It is so clever. The guy doesn't even bother to tell anyone: if you just happen to see it, great. I love that kind of thing. I was sitting in my study, where this huge double window is, and the light hit off the cover and I thought, 'There is a silhouette of a gun on that.' It's a shadow, but it's also the silhouette of a gun. I thought, 'What an artist.'"

Bruen also has a new agent, Marianne Gunn O'Connor. "She's very famous in Ireland, because she represents the prime minister's daughter," Bruen says. "The prime minister's daughter wrote a twenty-page synopsis of a 'Chick-Lit' book called *P.S., I Love You*. A guy dies and leaves his wife a letter for every day of the year. At the end of each letter is 'P.S., I Love You.' She sold this book, by a twenty-year-old on twenty pages and she got an advance of $2 million. I'm a little bit cynical, anyway. I think the fact that she was the prime minister's daughter didn't hurt. But then Marianne, my agent, says, in the forty countries the book went to number one in, they never heard of her. So, she's a pretty good agent."

O'Conner now has Bruen because of *American Skin*. His past agent was, he says, "a great guy." They were, Bruen says, "great friends." But they saw "different directions" for Bruen's career, particularly regarding *American Skin*.

The book has been discussed in numerous interviews. An early draft of the opening passages of *American Skin* was released via the *Mississippi Review* in January 2005 as part of a themed issue entitled "High Pulp." The buzz is that *Skin* is a shade of noir too dark for some audiences.

Bruen smiles and shakes his head: "This book has become the bane of my life. I'm sorry I ever mentioned it. I originally set out to write it as an Irish guy trying to pass himself off as American, which goes against the whole world opinion at the moment, because of all the anti-American feeling and that kind of thing. The crucial thing is that at the very moment when he needs to be Irish, he finally passes for American. All his other attempts, people say, 'Geez, I love your Irish accent. That brogue and etc.' At the *one* crucial moment he *needs* to be Irish, he passes for American."

The title of *American Skin* derives from the controversial Bruce Springsteen song "41 Shots," which alienated the "Boss" from the NYPD.

A key character in *Skin* is an "über-psycho" named Dade who is obsessed with Tammy Wynette. "He almost hijacked the book," Bruen says. "A force of nature." The opening chapter, by design, was intended to be as dark as anything Bruen has written. "I wanted to lay down, up front, the ground rules for this novel," Bruen said.

American Skin, has, I say, already achieved legendary status among the crime fiction cognoscenti, without ever having been read by more than a handful.

"It's almost like the Truman Capote book, *Unanswered Prayers*," Bruen says. "'Does the book exist?'"

The final draft, which Bruen sent to me for background a few days before our interview, expands relationships between several key characters and benefits from the closely examined arc of two distinctly different love affairs. That opening is still brutal stuff, though, particularly for any parent. And the language and texture of the writing is very different from Bruen's other books. He has found a new voice.

I acknowledge the buzz being reaped by *American Skin* is something many writers would kill to have. On the other hand, I ask, "At some point, does the intrinsic weight of that buzz become an actual threat to the book?"

"It does," Bruen says. "Can any book live up to the hype? When the book finally comes out, there's bound to be a bunch of people who say, 'What's the big deal? That's not that dark.'"

A number of changes were proposed for the final draft of *American Skin*, but Bruen steadfastly refused, dismissing a number of top-selling authors in the process who were held up as examples to be emulated. "I'm delighted with the position I'm in," Bruen says. "But to reach a wider audience, if I had to do that, it would not be worth it. Because I would not be able to write."

"You would gain the world and lose your soul?" I say.

Bruen smiles. His wife, he said, put it more succinctly. "She said, 'Ken, at this stage in your career, they cannot give you enough money to sit down every day and write *shite*, because it would kill you.' And that is the truth."

Bruen says that when his contracts with "big publishers" have ended, he will return to the independents. It's not the first time I've heard him say it. I say, "You still intend that?"

He nods. "More strongly than ever. To have the freedom to write the way you really want to write … I hate to say it, but money can't buy it." Bruen pauses. "There's a writer you and I respect, hugely, and he's on his second novel and it looks like he's about to be picked up by a big publisher. He sent me his second novel. It's brilliant. There's a character almost like Dade [from *American Skin*], but even crazier. And very, very funny. They want him to lose that character. In other words, he loses the book. He said to me, 'What should I do?' I said, 'I can't tell you.' Because

I *can't*. I said, 'All I can say is, it looks like you're at a crossroads. Do you want to write the way you want to write, or do you want to write what will bring you a lot of success, according to *them*?' But the big sellers are the ones that write according to formula."

Some critics have seized on the stylistic flourishes in the Jack Taylor books, particularly. These include epigraphs lifted from other books, as well as references to and descriptions of the works of other authors whom Taylor—and by extension, presumably Bruen—reveres. Several times in the Taylor series, bookish Jack's library is lost, usually to violence. Beloved booksellers help him reconstruct his collection, and Taylor's readers get an education in the process.

Bruen explains: "The other night, in a Q&A after the reading, someone asked me, 'Why is there so much music in your books?' I said, 'It's because I love music.' They said, 'Well, a lot of the people I've never heard of.' I said, 'That's one of the reasons why I mention them. I do it in the same way that I mention a lot of mystery writers who would not be mainstream. I do it because I like them and I know they're not mainstream.'

"The number of people who have never read John Straley is astonishing to me," Bruen continues. "He was a poet for a long time and his writing really shows it. There's a very funny writer in Canada I never hear mentioned called Lawrence Gough. I think it may be because his name is so like Lawrence Block. He is just black, black humor. And outside of Canada, I think it's almost impossible to get his books."

We talk a bit more about Bruen's life now in contrast to where he was two or three years ago. "The last two years have been phenomenal. *The Guards* took off so well. Then *The Killing of the Tinkers*. I didn't know that if your book gets talked about, for good or bad, you get asked to do all sorts of short stories. But the one short story collection that I really wanted to be included in was the one for Bruce Springsteen, based on his song "Meeting Across the River." I didn't make the cut. I really enjoyed writing the story and that song of Bruce's is the *perfect* crime or noir short. I was delighted with the short story I wrote. When I heard I didn't make the cut I was disappointed. It wasn't so much because

I thought I'm not good enough. But I *deserved* to be in there: I've been supporting the Boss for *thirty* years. I've paid my dues. Jesus!"

The big black bug has finally fled for parts unknown. We talk about James Sallis for a while. One of the great appeals of Arizona for Bruen is the prospect of perhaps actually meeting Sallis. "When I come back in my next life," Bruen has said, "I want to come back as James Sallis."

Bruen's Jack Taylor is also a Sallis enthusiast. "Won't it be great if Jim Sallis comes out?" Bruen says as we walk back to our respective rooms.

Bruen and Sallis

We ride over to the bookstore with Bruen … meet Barbara Peters, "proprietress" of the wonderful Poisoned Pen Bookstore and Poisoned Pen Press.

We also meet the legendary independent publisher Dennis McMillan. Based on descriptions from various authors over the years, I have this image of McMillan in mind. But that image misses the mark. Spotting Dennis in the crowd during his reading, Ken Bruen will describe Dennis as a kind of latter day, "crime fiction version of Truman Capote."

"Wrong sexual orientation," McMillan will bark back from where he is sitting. Tonight Dennis wears a chocolate (horse hair?) hat with a wide brim. He's wearing a long poncho and green pants. He drives a red Humvee.

James Sallis is nowhere in sight.

The Poisoned Pen's Patrick Millikin is one of the quiet engines of the crime fiction world. He's an important opinion-shaper and his recommendations are closely followed by discerning readers.

In 1997, Millikin wrote an article on George Pelecanos for *Firsts: The Book Collector's Magazine*. I'm still kicking myself for not following Patrick's recommendation to buy a copy of *Nick's Trip* when it was still relatively affordable.

Millikin is currently enrolled in a class on the novel being taught by James Sallis at an Arizona college. Patrick says he thinks Sallis has a musical gig planned tonight. We ask Patrick if he knows where Sallis is playing. Bruen: "We'll go there and find him. It will be great." But Patrick is having difficulty tracking Sallis down. The prospects for a hoped-for Bruen/Sallis summit are dimming.

Bruen is introduced to his fans. He tells his stories about his wife and daughter. He talks about his father and their vexed relationship regarding Bruen's efforts at writing ... his earning of a degree in metaphysics. He speaks of his own brother's loss to alcoholism and his aims with the Jack Taylor books to examine addiction and the state of modern Ireland. He finishes to great applause and begins signing piles of books.

Quietly, through a side door, James Sallis slips in. Tonight's musical gig, he explains, was very informal, at a private residence, "and nothing much was happening there."

Sallis waits patiently, talking with us, joking with Dennis McMillan while Ken Bruen chats with fans and signs books. Sallis admires some of the Hard Case Crime paperbacks stacked on a display table. "Now there is a cover," Sallis says, lifting one of the Hard Case titles and pointing to its evocative, pulp-style illustration. Bruen signs his last book, rises, and spots Sallis. They embrace. The arrival of Lew Griffin's creator has clearly delighted the creator of Jack Taylor.

They walk together, talking, as Patrick leads us through the backstreets of Scottsdale to a Mexican restaurant we'll close down, gathered around a table, swapping food and stories and literary gossip as the lights go off around us and the wait staff loiters with intent, looking increasingly perplexed.

Bruen and Sallis talk a good bit about Sallis' *Cypress Grove*, a favorite of Bruen's. Bruen tells Sallis he particularly admires the way in which Sallis handled the many flashbacks in *Cypress Grove*. "I think," Bruen says, "those were actually my favorite part of the novel." Sallis smiles and says he likes those parts best, too, and, as Bruen predicted, promptly changes the subject. They lean close throughout the dinner, discussing their art ... talking about various writers one or the other or both have encountered.

A couple of pictures are taken of them talking. It's an important moment: like those shots of Pancho Villa and Emiliano Zapata, maybe, when they met for the one and only time there in Mexico City, on the other side of that border we're not so far from tonight; like the snapshots of Hemingway and Fitzgerald motoring together across France that should have been taken, but were not.

Bruen shares some of his war stories from the tour. He talks of the punishing pace. Sallis agrees and says he no longer will do those sorts of book tours for just those reasons.

At some point, Sallis realizes the hour. He should, he says, call his wife. He asks, "Does anyone have a phone?" Four cell phones are simultaneously whipped out and offered to him. He takes Patrick Millikin's cell phone. Sallis' brow furrows: "Does anyone have my number?" I hand him my business card on which I've scrawled his home phone number for reference regarding the interview conducted with Sallis the previous day.

Ken Bruen smiles, says, "I live for the day when I can go anywhere, say 'Anyone got a phone, anyone got my number?' and be given both."

Good-byes are said in the parking lot of the Poisoned Pen Bookshop. We ride back to the hotel with Bruen. We stop in that soon-to-vanish hotel bar because it seems like something we should do.

But it's exhaustion all the way around. We sit in frequent silence like characters in Sallis' *Cypress Grove*. David Letterman, whom Bruen purportedly dislikes, is on the television. We have early flights out tomorrow. And Texas, with all those other crime writers, looks to be a long night-into-next-day for Bruen.

We hug again, say our good-byes.

· · · · ·

My wife and I have two young daughters, and air travel, particularly now, is a roll of the dice.

So we're traveling home on separate planes. This is being done at my insistence—morbid sort that I am.

Southwest Airlines has some screwball policy whereby seats are made available as you find them. So an Arizona woman sits down next to me. It's a three-and-a-half-hour flight back to my state and my city. The stranger in the seat next to me is going there to visit family, she tells me.

Okay, enough with the small talk, I think.

I twist away from her in my cramped seat and start rereading a copy of Bruen's *The Guards*. Forty-five minutes in, the silence is broken again and the Arizona woman starts talking. I get her whole life story. She's a Bruen character, if there ever was one. She tells me she used to be a model. You can see the ghost of that model in her face. "This was," she says, unnecessarily, "a few pounds ago."

She makes no bones about it: she has a drinking problem.

No news there: the burst capillaries in her cheeks and nose telegraph their own sad story.

The relatives she's going to visit are problem drinkers, too. Her doctor has proscribed some pills to discourage her drinking.

Jesus … I just want to read Ken Bruen's book. *Again.*

My neighbor the ex-model signals a flight attendant. She orders a "Jack and Coke."

Uh oh. I know about Antabuse from reading James Ellroy and Ken Bruen.

I say, "Maybe with the pills, you shouldn't have that."

She smiles, says, "Haven't started taking them yet. I plan to be drunk when I land. *Then* I'll take the pills." It's her plan, and she sticks to it. As she drinks, she becomes increasingly effusive and loud. I get her whole story—her attraction to older men; her stunning successes in the mad market of Arizona real estate. But what she really wants to do is be a "vocal talent." Her Bart Simpson is dead-on. But three drinks in, Bart begins to slur.

The other passengers look over at me—it's writ large on their faces: "You poor poor bastard." There, but for the grace of their gods, went I.

She finally notices the book on my lap as we're coming in for our final approach. "Good book?"

I say, "Yeah."

She says, "Have I heard of him?"

"You should have." I give her *The Guards*.

APPENDIX
Select Bibilographies

Ken Bruen

Funeral: Tales of Irish Morbidities (Dorrance Publishing Co., 1992).

Shades of Grace (Images Booksellers, 1993).

Martyrs (Minerva Press, 1994).

Sherry: and Other Stories (Adelphi Press, 1994).

Time of Serena-May and Upon the Third Cross: A Collection of Short Stories (Adelphi Press, 1995).

Rilke on Black (London, New York: Serpent's Tail, 1997).

Her Last Call to Louis Macneice (London, New York: Serpent's Tail, 1997).

The Hackman Blues (Great Britain: Do-Not Press, 1997).

A White Arrest (Great Britain: Do-Not Press, 1998).

Taming the Alien (Great Britain: Do-Not Press, 2000).

The McDead (Great Britain: Do-Not Press, 2000).

London Boulevard (Great Britain: Do-Not Press, 2001).

The Guards (Ireland: Brandon, 2001; Ireland: Brandon, New York: St. Martin's Minotaur, 2003).

The Killing of the Tinkers (Ireland: Brandon, 2002; New York: St. Martin's Minotaur, 2004).

Blitz: or Brant Hits the Blues (Great Britain: Do-Not Press, 2002; New York: St. Martin's Minotaur, 2004).

The White Trilogy Omnibus (Boston, Massachusetts: Kate's Mystery Books, 2003).

The Magdalen Martyrs (Ireland: Brandon, 2003; New York: St. Martin's Minotaur, 2005).

Vixen (Great Britain: Do-Not Press, 2003; New York: St. Martin's Minotaur, 2005).

The Dramatist (Ireland: Brandon, 2004; New York: St. Martin's Minotaur, 2006).

Dispatching Baudelaire (Ireland: Sitric Books, 2004).

The Dead Room (Clarkston, Michigan/Mission Viejo, California: ASAP, 2005).

Murder by the Book (Houston, Texas: Busted Flush Press, 2005).

Priest (London: Bantam Press, 2006; Scorpion Press, limited edition, 2006).

Dublin Noir, editor (New York: Akashic, 2006; Ireland: Brandon, 2006).

Caliber (New York: St. Martin's Minotaur, 2006).

American Skin (Boston: Kate's Mystery Books/Justin Charles & Co., 2006).

Cross (London: Bantam Press, 2007; Scorpion Press, limited edition, 2006).

Ammunition (New York: St. Martin's Mintotaur, 2007).

Sanctuary (Ireland: Transworld, 2008).

Once Were Cops (New York: St. Martin's Minotaur, 2008).

Stephen J. Cannell
STANDALONE THRILLERS

The Plan (New York: William Morrow & Co., Inc., 1995).

Final Victim (New York: William Morrow & Co., Inc., 1996).

King Con (New York: William Morrow & Co., Inc., 1997).

Riding the Snake (New York: William Morrow & Co., Inc., 1998).

The Devil's Workshop (New York: William Morrow & Co., Inc., 1999).

Runaway Heart (New York: St. Martin's Press, 2003).

SHANE SCULLY NOVELS
The Tin Collectors (New York: St. Martin's Press, 2001).

The Viking Funeral (New York: St. Martin's Press, 2002).

Hollywood Tough (New York: St. Martin's Press, 2003).

Vertical Coffin (New York: St. Martin's Press, 2004).

Cold Hit (New York: St. Martin's Press, 2005).

White Sister (New York: St. Martin's Press, 2006).

Three Shirt Deal (New York: St. Martin's Press, 2008).

At First Sight (Vanguard Press, 2008).

Lee Child
Killing Floor (New York: G.P. Putnam's Sons, 1997).

Die Trying (New York: G.P. Putnam's Sons, 1998).

Tripwire (New York: G.P. Putnam's Sons, 1999).

Running Blind (New York: G.P. Putnam's Sons, 2000).

Echo Burning (New York: G.P. Putnam's Sons, 2001).

Without Fail (New York: G.P. Putnam's Sons, 2002).

Persuader (New York: Delacorte Press, 2003).

The Enemy (New York: Delacorte Press, 2004).

One Shot (New York: Delacorte Press, 2005).

The Hard Way (New York: Delacorte Press, 2006).

Bad Luck and Trouble (New York: Delacorte Press, 2007).

Nothing to Lose (New York: Delacorte Press, 2008).

Max Allan Collins
The Baby Blue Rip-Off (New York: Walker & Co., 1982).

No Cure for Death (New York: Walker & Co., 1983).

True Detective (New York: St. Martin's Press, 1983).

Kill Your Darlings (New York: Walker & Co., 1984).

True Crime (New York: St. Martin's Press, 1984).

A Shroud for Aquarius (New York: Walker & Co., 1985).

Midnight Haul (Vermont: A Foul Play Press Book, 1986).

Nice Weekend for a Murder (New York: Walker & Co., 1986).

The Million Dollar Wound (New York: St. Martin's Press, 1986).

Spree (New York: TOR Books, 1987).

Primary Target (Vermont: A Foul Play Press Book, 1987).

The Dark City (New York: Bantam, 1987).

Butcher's Dozen (New York: Bantam, 1988).

Neon Mirage (New York: St. Martin's Press, 1988).

Bullet Proof (New York: Bantam, 1989).

Dying in the Post-War World (Vermont: A Foul Play Press Book, 1991).

Stolen Away (New York: Bantam, 1991).

Murder by the Numbers (New York: St. Martin's Press, 1993).

Carnal Hours (New York: Dutton, 1994).

Blood and Thunder (New York: Dutton, 1995).

Damned in Paradise (New York: Dutton, 1996).

Flying Blind: A Novel about Amelia Earhart (New York: Dutton, 1998).

Majic Man: A Nathan Heller Novel (New York: Dutton, 1999).

Angel in Black (New York: New American Library, 2001).

Kisses of Death (Norfolk, Virginia: Crippen and Landru Publishers, 2001).

Chicago Confidential (New York: New American Library, 2002).

Road to Purgatory (New York: William Morrow, 2004).

Road to Paradise (New York: William Morrow, 2005).

Black Hats [Patrick Culhane, pseud.]. (New York: William Morrow, 2007).

James Crumley

One to Count Cadence (New York: Random House, 1969).

The Wrong Case (New York: Random House, 1975).

The Last Good Kiss (New York: Random House, 1978).

Dancing Bear (New York: Random House, 1983).

The Muddy Fork (Northridge, California: Lord John Press, 1984).

Whores (Missoula, Montana: Dennis McMillan, 1988).

The Mexican Tree Duck (New York: Mysterious Press, 1993).

Bordersnakes (New York: Mysterious Press, 1996).

The Final Country (New York: Mysterious Press, 2001).

The Right Madness (New York: Viking, 2005).

Pete Dexter

God's Pocket (New York: Random House, 1983).

Deadwood (New York: Random House, 1986).

Paris Trout (New York: Random House, 1988).

Brotherly Love (New York: Random House, 1991).

The Paperboy (New York: Random House, 1995).

Train (New York: Doubleday, 2003).

Paper Trails (Ecco, 2007).

James Ellroy

Brown's Requiem (New York: Avon, 1981).

Clandestine (New York: Avon, 1982).

Blood on the Moon (New York: Mysterious Press, 1984).

Because the Night (New York: Mysterious Press, 1984).

Suicide Hill (New York: Mysterious Press, 1986).

Silent Terror (Killer on the Road) (New York: Avon, 1986).

The Black Dahlia (New York: Mysterious Press, 1987).

The Big Nowhere (New York: Mysterious Press, 1988).

L.A. Confidential (New York: Mysterious Press, 1990).

Murder and Mayhem. Introduction. (New York: New American Library, 1992).

White Jazz (New York: Alfred A. Knopf, 1992).

Fallen Angels. Preface by James Ellroy. Also contains the Ellroy short story "Since I Don't Have You" and its teleplay for the Showtime cable network. (New York: Grove Press, 1993).

Hollywood Nocturnes (New York: Otto Penzler Books, 1994).

American Tabloid (New York: Alfred A. Knopf, 1995).

My Dark Places (New York: Alfred A. Knopf, 1996).

L.A. Noir (New York: Mysterious Press, 1998).

Crime Wave (New York: Vintage Crime, 1999).

The Cold Six Thousand (New York: Alfred A. Knopf, 2001).

Destination: Morgue! (New York: Vintage, 2004).

Kinky Friedman

Greenwich Killing Time (New York: Beach Tree Books, 1986).

A Case of Lone Star (New York: Beach Tree Books, 1987).

When the Cat's Away (New York: Beach Tree Books, 1988).

Frequent Flyer (New York: William Morrow & Co., 1989).

Musical Chairs (New York: William Morrow & Co., 1991).

Elvis, Jesus & Coca-Cola (New York: Simon & Schuster, 1993).

Armadillos & Old Lace (New York: Simon & Schuster, 1994).

God Bless John Wayne (New York: Simon & Schuster, 1995).

The Love Song of J. Edgar Hoover (New York: Simon & Schuster, 1996).

Road Kill (New York: Simon & Schuster, 1997).

Blast From the Past (New York: Simon & Schuster, 1998).

Spanking Watson (New York: Simon & Schuster, 1999).

The Mile High Club (New York: Simon & Schuster, 2000).

Steppin' on a Rainbow (New York: Simon & Schuster, 2001).

Meanwhile Back at the Ranch (New York: Simon & Schuster, 2002).

Kill Two Birds & Get Stoned (New York: Harper Collins, 2003).

The Prisoner of Vandam Street (New York: Simon & Schuster, 2004).

Ten Little New Yorkers (New York: Simon & Schuster, 2005).

Craig Holden
The River Sorrow (New York: Delacorte Press, 1994).

The Last Sanctuary (New York: Delacorte Press, 1996).

Four Corners of Night (New York: Delacorte Press, 1999).

The Jazz Bird (New York: Simon & Schuster, 2002).

The Narcissist's Daughter (New York: Simon & Schuster, 2005).

Matala: A Novel (New York: Simon & Schuster, 2007).

Elmore Leonard
The Bounty Hunters (Boston: Houghton, Mifflin, 1953).

The Law at Randado (Boston: Houghton, Mifflin, 1954).

Escape from Five Shadows (Boston: Houghton, Mifflin, 1956).

Last Stand at Saber River (New York: Dell, 1959).

Hombre (New York: Ballantine, 1961).

The Big Bounce (New York: Fawcett, 1969).

The Moonshine War (Garden City, New York: Doubleday, 1969).

Valdez is Coming (New York: Fawcett, 1970).

Forty Lashes Less One (New York: Bantam, 1972).

Mr. Majestyk (New York: Dell, 1974).

Fifty-Two Pickup (New York: Delacorte Press, 1974).

Swag (New York: Delacorte Press, 1976).

Unknown Man No. 89 (New York: Delacorte Press, 1977).

The Hunted (New York: Dell, 1977).

The Switch (New York: Bantam, 1978).

Gunsights (New York: Bantam, 1979).

City Primeval (New York: Arbor House, 1980).

Gold Coast (New York: Bantam, 1980).

Split Images (New York: Arbor House, 1981).

Cat Chaser (New York: Avon, 1982).

Stick (New York: Arbor House, 1983).

LaBrava (New York: Arbor House, 1983).

Glitz (New York: Arbor House, 1985).

Bandits (New York: Arbor House, 1987).

Touch (New York: Arbor House, 1987).

Freaky Deaky (New York: Arbor House, 1988).

Killshot (New York: Arbor House, 1989).

Get Shorty (New York: Delacorte Press, 1990).

Maximum Bob (New York: Delacorte Press, 1991).

Rum Punch (New York: Delacorte Press, 1992).

Pronto (New York: Delacorte Press, 1993).

Riding the Rap (New York: Delacorte Press, 1995).

Out of Sight (New York: Delacorte Press, 1996).

Cuba Libre (New York: Delacorte Press, 1998).

Be Cool (New York: Delacorte Press, 1999).

Pagan Babies (New York: Delacorte Press, 2000).

Tishomingo Blues (New York: William Morrow, 2002).

Mr. Paradise (New York: William Morrow, 2004).

The Hot Kid (New York: William Morrow, 2005).

Up in Honey's Room (New York: William Morrow, 2007).

Elmore Leonard's 10 Rules of Writing (New York: William Morrow, 2007).

Road Dogs (New York: William Morrow, forthcoming).

Alistair Macleod

No Great Mischief (Toronto: McClelland & Stewart Inc., 1999).

Island: The Collected Stories (Toronto: McClelland & Stewart Inc., 2000).

Tom Russell

BIBLIOGRAPHY

And Then I Wrote: The Songwriter Speaks (Vancouver, B.C.: Arsenal Press, 1995).

Tough Company (Sacramento, California: Mystery Island Publications, 2005).

DISCOGRAPHY

The Early Years, 1975-79, Dark Angel, DACD2 (CD).

Road to Bayamon, 1989, Philo, 1116 (CD)

Cowboy Real, 1991, Philo, 1146 (CD).

Hurricane Season, 1991, Philo, 1141 (CD).

Poor Man's Dream, 1992, Philo, 1139 (CD).

Box of Visions, 1993, Philo, 1158 (CD).

The Rose of the San Joaquin, 1995, Hightone Records, 8066 (CD).

The Long Way Around, 1997, Hightone Records, 8081 (CD).

Song of the West, 1997, HMG Hightone Records, 2501 (CD).

The Man from God Knows Where, 1999, Hightone Records, 8099 (CD).

Heart on a Sleeve, 2000, Edsel Records, 641 (CD).

Borderland 2001, Hightone Records, 8132 (CD).

Museum of Memories, 1972-2002, Dark Angel, DACD3 (CD).

Modert Art, 2003, Hightone Records, 8154 (CD).

Indians Cowboys Horses Dogs, 2004, Hightone Records, 8165 (CD).

Hotwalker, 2005, Hightone Records, 8177 (CD).

Raw Vision, 2005, Philo, 11671248-2 (CD).

Love and Fear, 2006, Hightone Records, 8190 (CD).

Lost Angels of Lyon, 2007, Frontera Records (CD).

Wounded Heart of America, 2007, Hightone Records, 8196 (CD).

Tom Russell Anthology: Veteran's Day, 2008, Shout Factory/Hightone Records, 8263363-10998 (CD).

James Sallis

A Few Last Words (New York: McMillan, 1970).

The Guitar Players: One Instrument and Its Masters in American Music (New York: William Morrow, 1982; Lincoln, Nebraska, and London: Bison Books/University of Nebraska Press, 1994, rev. ed.).

Jazz Guitars: An Anthology, editor (New York: William Morrow, 1984).

The Long-Legged Fly (New York: Carroll & Graf Publishers, 1992; Harpenden: No Exit Press, 1996).

Moth (New York: Carroll & Graf Publishers, 1993; Harpenden: No Exit Press, 1996; New York: Walker & Co, 2003).

Saint Glinglin, by Raymond Queneau, trans. by James Sallis. (Dalkey Archive Press, 1993; trade paperback 2000).

Difficult Lives: Jim Thompson – David Goodis – Chester Himes (New York: Gryphon Books, 1993; rev. ed., 2000).

Black Hornet (New York: Carroll & Graf Publishers, 1994; Harpenden: No Exit Press, 1997; New York: Walker & Co, 2003).

Limits of the Sensible World (Austin, Texas: Host Publications, 1994).

Renderings (Seattle, Washington: Black Heron Press, 1995).

Ash of Stars: On the Writings of Samuel R. Delany, editor (Jackson, Mississippi: University Press of Mississippi, 1996).

The Guitar in Jazz, editor (Lincoln, Nebraska: University of Nebraska Press, 1996).

Death Will Have Your Eyes (New York: St. Martin's Press, 1997; Harpenden: No Exit Press, 1997).

Eye of the Cricket (New York: Walker & Co, 1997 & 2000; Harpenden: No Exit Press, 1998).

Bluebottle (New York: Walker & Co, 1999; Harpenden: No Exit Press, 1999).

Gently into the Land of the Meateaters (Seattle, Washington: Black Heron Press, 2000).

Time's Hammers: Collected Stories (Edgbaston, Birmingham: Toxic, 2000).

Sorrow's Kitchen (East Lansing: Michigan State University Press, 2000).

Chester Himes: A Life (Edinburgh: Payback Press, 2000; New York: Walker & Co, 2001).

Ghost of a Flea (New York: Walker & Co, 2001 & 2000; Harpenden: No Exit Press, 2001).

Cypress Grove (New York: Walker & Co, 2003; Harpenden: No Exit Press, 2003).

My Tongue in Other Cheeks: A Selection of Translations (Obscure Publications, 2003).

A City Equal to My Desire (PointBlank Press, 2004).

Drive (Arizona: Poisoned Pen Press, 2005).

Cripple Creek (New York: Walker & Co, 2006).

Potato Tree (Austin, TX: Host Publications, 2007).

Salt River (New York: Walker & Co, 2008).

Andrew Vachss

Flood (New York: Donald I. Fine, Inc., 1985).

Strega (New York: Alfred A. Knopf, 1987).

Blue Belle (New York, Alfred A. Knopf, 1988).

Hard Candy (New York: Alfred A. Knopf, 1989).

Blossom (New York: Alfred A. Knopf, 1990).

Sacrifice (New York: Alfred A. Knopf, 1991).

Shella (New York: Alfred A. Knopf, 1993).

Down in the Zero (New York: Alfred A. Knopf, 1994).

Footsteps of the Hawk (New York: Alfred A. Knopf, 1995).

Batman: The Ultimate Evil (New York: Warner Books, 1995).

False Allegations (New York: Alfred A. Knopf, 1996).

Safe House (New York: Alfred A. Knopf, 1998).

Choice of Evil (New York: Alfred A. Knopf, 1999).

Dead and Gone (New York: Alfred A. Knopf, 2000).

Pain Management (New York: Alfred A. Knopf, 2001).

Only Child (New York: Alfred A. Knopf, 2002).

The Getaway Man (New York: Vintage Books, 2003).

Two Trains Running (New York: Pantheon Books, 2005).

Mask Market (New York: Pantheon Books, 2006).

Terminal (New York: Pantheon Books, 2007).

Another Life (New York: Pantheon Books, 2008).

Randy Wayne White

Sanibel Flats (New York: St. Martin's, 1990).

The Heat Islands (New York: St. Martin's, 1992).

The Man Who Invented Florida (New York: St. Martin's, 1993).

Captiva (New York: G.P. Putnam's Sons, 1996).

North of Havana (New York: G.P. Putnam's Sons, 1997).

The Mangrove Coast (New York: G.P. Putnam's Sons, 1998).

Ten Thousand Islands (New York: G.P. Putnam's Sons, 2000).

Shark River (New York: G.P. Putnam's Sons, 2001).

Twelve Mile Limit (New York: G.P. Putnam's Sons, 2002).

Everglades (New York: G.P. Putnam's Sons, 2003).

Tampa Burn (New York: G.P. Putnam's Sons, 2004).

Dead of Night (New York: G.P. Putnam's Sons, 2005).

Dark Light (New York: G.P. Putnam's Sons, 2006).

Hunter's Moon (New York: G.P. Putnam's Sons, 2007).

Black Widow (New York: G.P. Putnam's Sons, 2008).

Daniel Woodrell

Under the Bright Lights (New York: Henry Holt & Company, 1986).

Woe to Live On (New York: Henry Holt & Company, 1987).

Muscle for the Wing (New York: Henry Holt & Company, 1988).

The Ones You Do (New York: Henry Holt & Company, 1992).

Give Us A Kiss (New York: Henry Holt & Company, 1996).

Tomato Red (New York: Henry Holt & Company, 1998).

The Death of Sweet Mister (New York: G.P. Putnam's Sons, 2001).

Winter's Bone (New York: Little, Brown & Company, 2006).

ACKNOWLEDGMENTS

Special thanks to all the authors who took the time to talk about their lives and works, but particularly to Ken Bruen and James Sallis. In my mind, the state of Arizona will always be associated with these two men.

A special nod to the staff of Poisoned Pen Bookstore in Scottsdale Arizona, particularly Patrick Millikin, who was instrumental in bringing Bruen and Sallis together.

Grateful thanks to my wife, Debbie, who took that trip to the desert with me, and to our daughters Madeleine and Yeats who have actually made the acquaintance of several of the men interviewed in this collection.

I'm grateful to my agent, Svetlana Pironko, and to Ben LeRoy of Bleak House Books and to Moisson Rouge for taking their first sorties into nonfiction with this book.

Lastly, I salute my editor, Alison Janssen, who did such a splendid job with my first two novels, *Head Games* and *Toros & Torsos,* and now *Rogue Males.* Thanks for having my back, sharing the mojitos and *always* caring about the words and the characters. I cherish your friendship and counsel.

Although this book is dedicated to James Crumley, more needs to be said. Anyone who's read my first three novels (or seizes on the running thread through this collection of interviews) will quickly detect what an influence Hemingway has had on my writing.

In a very real sense, James Crumley is the crime fiction equivalent of Hemingway for me. The hour or so I spent on the phone with him remains a favorite memory and his books remain great companions. It pains me beyond words we've lost him. He kindly contributed a wonderful blurb for my first novel. I wish to hell he could have held this book in his hands.

ABOUT THE AUTHOR

Edgar®-finalist Craig McDonald is an award-winning journalist, editor and fiction writer.

His debut novel, *Head Games,* was selected as a 2008 Edgar® nominee for Best First Novel by an American Author. It was also nominated for Anthony and Gumshoe awards. *Toros & Torsos,* McDonald's second novel, appeared in autumn 2008 and made several "year's best" lists.

His other nonfiction books include *Art in the Blood,* a collection of interviews with twenty major crime authors that appeared in 2006.

McDonald was also a contributor to the NYT's nonfiction best-seller, *Secrets of the Code.* He recently won national awards for his profiles of crime novelists James Crumley, Daniel Woodrell and James Sallis.

He is a member of the Mystery Writers of America, and the International Association of Crime Writers.